I0054781

Salesforce Data Architect Certification Guide

Comprehensive coverage of the Salesforce Data Architect exam content to help you pass on the first attempt

Aaron Allport

<packt>

BIRMINGHAM—MUMBAI

Salesforce Data Architect Certification Guide

Copyright © 2022 Packt Publishing

All rights reserved. No part of this book may be reproduced, stored in a retrieval system, or transmitted in any form or by any means, without the prior written permission of the publisher, except in the case of brief quotations embedded in critical articles or reviews.

Every effort has been made in the preparation of this book to ensure the accuracy of the information presented. However, the information contained in this book is sold without warranty, either express or implied. Neither the author, nor Packt Publishing or its dealers and distributors, will be held liable for any damages caused or alleged to have been caused directly or indirectly by this book.

Packt Publishing has endeavored to provide trademark information about all of the companies and products mentioned in this book by the appropriate use of capitals. However, Packt Publishing cannot guarantee the accuracy of this information.

Publishing Product Manager: Ali Abidi

Senior Editor: David Sugarman

Content Development Editor: Nathanya Dias

Technical Editor: Devanshi Ayare

Copy Editor: Safis Editing

Project Coordinator: Farheen Fathima

Proofreader: Safis Editing

Indexer: Tejal Daruwale Soni

Production Designer: Joshua Misquitta

Marketing Coordinator: Shifa Ansari

First published: November 2022

Production reference: 1281022

Published by Packt Publishing Ltd.

Livery Place

35 Livery Street

Birmingham

B3 2PB, UK.

ISBN 978-1-80181-355-6

www.packt.com

Contributors

About the author

Aaron Allport is a Salesforce architect and has worked with CRM systems and integrations for his entire professional career. Aaron specializes in Salesforce technical architecture and integration, helping his clients ensure they get the most from their technology investment. Aaron has spoken at Dreamforce, written about everything from DevOps to data architecture online, and can regularly be found at the Salesforce London developer meetup.

To my mother, Deborah – you taught me that anything is possible.

To Steph, Isla, Noah, and Theo. You're my world. This book wouldn't be possible without your love, encouragement, and support.

About the reviewer

Rajvardhan Oak is a cyber security researcher who is passionate about making the internet a safer place for everyone. His research interests are cyber security, privacy, and their intersection with machine learning. He currently works as an applied scientist at Microsoft. As part of the ad fraud detection team, his work involves analyzing network traffic and building models to filter click fraud. He is also pursuing a Ph.D. at the University of California Davis, where his research examines the underground ecosystems of reputation manipulation via fraudulent reviews. He also has extensive experience in programming and a strong command over data governance, privacy-preserving analytics, and threat modeling, as well as other security areas.

Table of Contents

5

Data Governance   73

6

Understanding Large Data Volumes   85

Section 2: Salesforce Data Architect Design

8

12

Territory Management   157

Section 3: Applying What We've Learned – Practice Questions and Revision Aids

13

Practice Exam Questions   167

14

Cheat Sheets   193

15

Further Resources   203

16

How to Take the Exam   211

17

Answers to Practice Questions   219

Index   223

Other Books You May Enjoy   232

Preface

Salesforce skills, and particularly those of Salesforce architects, continue to grow in demand as the Salesforce ecosystem continues to grow all over the globe. This book focuses on one topic area of the Salesforce architect curriculum, namely data architecture. The Salesforce Certified Data Architect exam may seem a little daunting when reading the exam outline for the first time (I certainly thought so). But it needn't be. I was lucky to be able to pass the exam the first time, and that was possible by gathering information and going through the Salesforce documentation over several months. This book is the book I wish I'd had when studying for the exam, because it specifically covers the material necessary for the theory side of the exam.

We'll start by going through each of the areas covered in the exam outline in turn, from data modeling, master data management, Salesforce data management, data governance and large data volumes to data migration. Understanding these is pivotal to getting the theory tested in the exam covered. Moreover, the theory can be directly applied to the solutions you build and maintain in your role as a Salesforce architect.

We then turn our attention to applying concepts through additional topics that, while not always directly called out in the syllabus, will round out your knowledge of applying Salesforce data principles. These include a deeper dive into accounts and contacts, APIs and Apex, tuning performance, backup and restore, and territory management. Each of these topics will explain how the data model, sharing, and therefore any solutions built with these topics in mind are affected.

Lastly, we'll look at practice questions (with answers) and some revision aides. By the end of this book, you'll have covered the topics required to pass the Salesforce Certified Data Architect exam and also be able to implement Salesforce data design best practices in your day-to-day role as a Salesforce architect.

Who this book is for

This book is for both aspiring Salesforce architects and those already familiar with Salesforce data architecture who want to pass the Salesforce Certified Data Architect exam and have a reference guide to revisit the material as part of the day-to-day job. Working Salesforce Platform knowledge is assumed, and an understanding of Salesforce architectural concepts would be beneficial.

What this book covers

Chapter 1, *Introducing the Salesforce Data Architect Journey*, introduces the credential, by providing a high-level overview of the topic areas and exam curriculum, as well as outlining the rest of the book.

Chapter 2, *Data Modeling and Database Design*, covers how the Salesforce data model is architected, the design decisions behind that, and how the model affects sharing and security.

Chapter 3, *Master Data Management*, introduces the subject of **Master Data Management** (**MDM**), and how to effectively design and implement an MDM strategy on the Salesforce Platform.

Chapter 4, *Salesforce Data Management*, covers Salesforce license types, object access, and how to govern the data on the platform when architecting performant solutions that combine data from one or more Salesforce instances.

Chapter 5, *Data Governance*, covers the concepts behind building compliant solutions and how the Salesforce Platform can underpin an enterprise data governance strategy.

Chapter 6, *Understanding Large Data Volumes*, delves into considerations that apply to larger/massive amounts of data (referred to as *large data volumes*) and how performance on the platform is affected, as well as techniques for mitigating such scenarios.

Chapter 7, *Data Migration*, looks at getting data in and out of the platform in a planned and optimal way.

Chapter 8, *Accounts and Contacts*, covers the account/contact model, including person accounts and contacts to multiple accounts, account skew, and the implications this has on the performance of queries and reports.

Chapter 9, *Data APIs and Apex*, gets into the various Salesforce Platform APIs, Apex operations (including database, batch, and asynchronous), and how to deploy them effectively when designing data operations.

Chapter 10, Tuning Performance, looks at the various methods available to tune performance when designing scalable applications on the Salesforce Platform.

Chapter 11, Backup and Restore, outlines the methods available to get data out of and back into the Salesforce Platform, focussing on data backup and restore.

Chapter 12, Territory Management, introduces Salesforce Territory Management and how it pertains to the data model and usage design on the Salesforce Platform.

Chapter 13, Practice Exam Questions, presents exam-like questions to further put into practice the theory you will have learned and bolster your understanding of the topic areas of the exam curriculum.

Chapter 14, Cheat Sheets, introduces handy reference *cheat sheets* that provide a quick reference guide for aiding revision or for the day-to-day job.

Chapter 15, Further Resources, highlights links to other information that can enhance your understanding of the material we cover in this book.

Chapter 16, How to Take the Exam, describes what you will need to do to take the exam.

Chapter 17, Answers to Practice Questions, provides the answers to the questions provided in *Chapter 13, Practice Exam Questions*.

To get the most out of this book

You will need to be familiar with general Salesforce terminology and have a working knowledge of Salesforce in order to fully grasp the concepts covered in this book. All topics covered assume basic familiarity with the theory behind the Salesforce multitenant architecture.

Software/hardware covered in the book	Operating system requirements
Salesforce	Windows, macOS, or Linux with a web browser

We cover how to sign up for and obtain a Salesforce Developer Edition instance, which can be used for all topics, examples, and scenarios covered in this book.

Download the color images

We also provide a PDF file that has color images of the screenshots and diagrams used in this book. You can download it here: `https://packt.link/YQqWX`.

Conventions used

There are a number of text conventions used throughout this book.

`Code in text`: Indicates code words in text, database table names, folder names, filenames, file extensions, pathnames, dummy URLs, user input, and Twitter handles. Here is an example: "The `start` method is used to define the query."

A block of code is set as follows:

```
public class dmlStatementTest {
    public void testStatement() {
        List<Account> accounts;
        accounts.add(new Account(Name='Packt UK'));
        accounts.add(new Account(Name='Packt India'));

        insert accounts;
    }
}
```

Bold: Indicates a new term, an important word, or words that you see onscreen. For instance, words in menus or dialog boxes appear in **bold**. Here is an example: "Users will need the **View Encrypted Data** profile permission enabled within their profile or via an assigned permission set to read encrypted field values."

> **Tips or Important notes**
> Appear like this.

Get in touch

Feedback from our readers is always welcome.

General feedback: If you have questions about any aspect of this book, email us at customercare@packtpub.com and mention the book title in the subject of your message.

Errata: Although we have taken every care to ensure the accuracy of our content, mistakes do happen. If you have found a mistake in this book, we would be grateful if you would report this to us. Please visit www.packtpub.com/support/errata and fill in the form.

Piracy: If you come across any illegal copies of our works in any form on the internet, we would be grateful if you would provide us with the location address or website name. Please contact us at copyright@packt.com with a link to the material.

If you are interested in becoming an author: If there is a topic that you have expertise in and you are interested in either writing or contributing to a book, please visit authors.packtpub.com.

Share your thoughts

Once you've read *Salesforce Data Architect Certification Guide*, we'd love to hear your thoughts! Scan the QR code below to go straight to the Amazon review page for this book and share your feedback.

https://packt.link/r/1-801-81355-8

Your review is important to us and the tech community and will help us make sure we're delivering excellent quality content.

Download a free PDF copy of this book

Thanks for purchasing this book!

Do you like to read on the go but are unable to carry your print books everywhere?

Is your eBook purchase not compatible with the device of your choice?

Don't worry, now with every Packt book you get a DRM-free PDF version of that book at no cost.

Read anywhere, any place, on any device. Search, copy, and paste code from your favorite technical books directly into your application.

The perks don't stop there, you can get exclusive access to discounts, newsletters, and great free content in your inbox daily

Follow these simple steps to get the benefits:

1. Scan the QR code or visit the link below:

https://packt.link/free-ebook/9781801813556

2. Submit your proof of purchase
3. That's it! We'll send your free PDF and other benefits to your email directly

Section 1: Salesforce Data Architect Theory

By the end of this section of the book, you will have covered all the theory necessary to pass the exam. Each topic will have been covered in sufficient depth so that you will be able to answer questions as required when attempting the credential. You will also be able to come back to this part of the book time and time again after having passed the exam as the topics outlined will become a handy reference in your day-to-day job as a Salesforce Data Architect.

This section comprises the following chapters:

- *Chapter 1, Introducing the Salesforce Data Architect Journey*
- *Chapter 2, Data Modeling and Database Design*
- *Chapter 3, Master Data Management*
- *Chapter 4, Salesforce Data Management*
- *Chapter 5, Data Governance*
- *Chapter 6, Understanding Large Data Volumes*
- *Chapter 7, Data Migration*

1
Introducing the Salesforce Data Architect Journey

The Salesforce Certified Data Architect credential is an important part of every Salesforce Architect's certification journey. It forms a constituent part of the Application Architect domain of the Certified Technical Architect credential, but it can stand alone, given the varying complexities and knowledge required to pass the exam. As architects, we're entrusted to build scalable foundations that our users can execute effectively upon, and data is the life-blood of a business. Understanding the relationship, quirks, and considerations of data and the Salesforce platform is crucial for designing applications that give users value. Passing this credential demonstrates advanced knowledge of these concepts. This book will arm you with the theory and skills necessary to pass the exam.

In this chapter, we'll learn about the Salesforce Certified Data Architect credential by covering the various curriculum areas and why they are important to understand to not just pass the exam, but also excel in this aspect of the day-to-day role of a Salesforce Architect.

Next, we'll get an overview of the learning journey covered in this book.

By the end of this chapter, you'll be able to understand the topic areas that constitute the credential, know what a Salesforce Data Architect is, and understand how the learning journey throughout this book is structured.

In this chapter, we'll cover the following topics:

- What is the Data Architecture and Management credential?
- Introducing the exam
- Profile of a Salesforce Data Architect
- Introducing the learning journey

What is the Data Architecture and Management credential?

The **Salesforce Certified Data Architect credential** is one of several introduced by Salesforce to initially address three main challenges:

- As Salesforce implementations increase in size and complexity, there is an increasing need for good data management, including best practices in data architecture and management in Salesforce. Data is the life-blood for many businesses, and the architecture of Salesforce as the platform to hold that data is important.

- There was a huge gap in the knowledge required between the Certified Technical Architect credential and the other credentials available. The only prerequisite for CTA in the past was that you had to hold the Salesforce Certified Administrator certification and answer a multiple-choice *pre-exam*!

- Not everyone wants to necessarily be a full-blown Salesforce Certified Technical Architect. Instead, they may want to focus on one or more specific technical domains or aspects of the Salesforce platform.

Simply put, this credential puts the focus on the data architecture aspects of the Salesforce platform. Candidates who pass this credential will have had to learn about the wide range of theory, techniques, and considerations that constitute the credential syllabus, which is based on the real-world knowledge that's required of a Data Architect on the Salesforce Customer 360 platform. By learning everything that's required to pass the Salesforce Certified Data Architect credential, candidates will have a toolkit of knowledge and understanding to draw from, improving their ability to deliver solutions while considering the data aspects of the Salesforce platform.

Introducing the exam

The exam format consists of 60 multiple-choice questions, and candidates are given 105 minutes to complete the exam. The passing score that's required at the time of writing is 58%, and there are no written prerequisites for the exam (although, as you will discover quite quickly, it is extremely challenging to dive straight into this exam without the required learning and foundational knowledge of the Salesforce platform). Those unfamiliar with the Salesforce platform will struggle with many of the concepts introduced in this book, so it would be more practical to have experience in the platform at a sufficient capacity to understand how the data model works, what standard objects are available, and so on. This would typically equate to a few years of working with the platform, but this is subjective based on previous experience.

Breaking down the question count, testing time, and passing score required, we can deduce the following:

- We have 1 minute and 45 seconds to answer each question.
- We require 35 correct answers to pass the exam.

The exam is taken virtually, either at a test center or online, both using Webassessor. The mechanics of this will be covered toward the end of this book.

> **Preparing for Success**
>
> As you most likely already know, resources are available online such as Trailhead (`https://trailhead.salesforce.com`) – specifically, the Data Architect and Management Trailmix (`https://trailhead.salesforce.com/en/users/strailhead/trailmixes/architect-data-architecture-and-management`) – and blogs that cover the theory around a specific topic. To bolster your learning journey, I'd like to introduce some habits that you can employ to boost your potential for success.

Playground environments

Salesforce provides free **Developer Edition** orgs (sometimes referred to as **DE** orgs) that have many of the paid-for features of the core Salesforce platform (so this won't include Marketing Cloud or Tableau, for example). These allow candidates to try out many of the concepts explained in this book in a real Salesforce environment to explore what the real implications of a particular concept or feature are. For example, it is entirely possible to create an external object that interacts with an external data source so that we can see what the usability and other limitations are when interacting with off-platform data in this way. I would fully encourage you to have at least one DE org in your learning toolkit. You can sign up for a DE org at `https://developer.salesforce.com/signup`.

Documenting designs and design decisions

Another habit to aid in the learning process and beyond is to start documenting the following:

- Artifacts
- Design decisions

While it may not be an end goal for everyone, the **Certified Technical Architect (CTA)** review board exam requires candidates to produce several artifacts. These include a data model, system integration landscape, actors/licenses, role hierarchy, and so on.

One of the most crucial artifacts to produce is the data model because it conveys how information is linked together, where objects are used, the expected data volumes, data owners, org-wide default sharing, and where **Large Data Volumes (LDVs)** may be a concern, which means that mitigations will need to be planned for. You should become comfortable with producing this artifact as you assess your requirements and produce solutions. Having the correct data model will ensure that you have a solid sharing and visibility strategy, reporting strategy, and integration strategy. It's little wonder that this is considered a core artifact of the CTA review board, given how crucial it is to effectively design a technical solution on the Salesforce Customer 360 platform.

Let's look at an example data model diagram. As we can quickly ascertain from this relatively simplistic example, a lot of information can be explained quite easily that you can understand using the key provided (which any good diagram will contain):

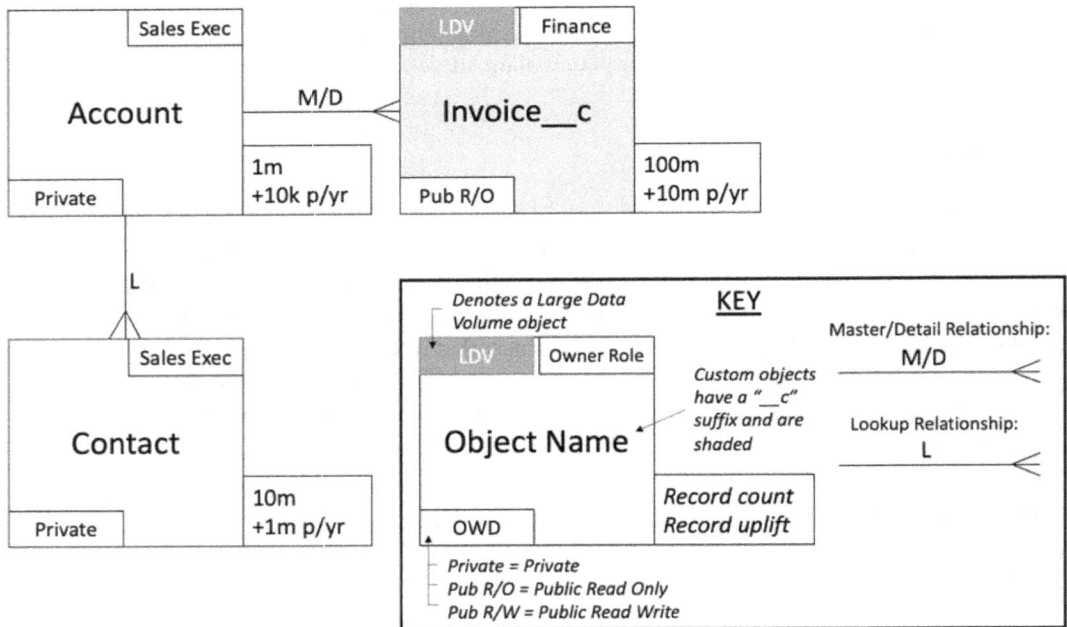

Figure 1.1 – Data model example

Design decisions are an important factor in any Salesforce solution. Salesforce comes with its own unique set of features and limitations that need to be considered and worked with, so getting into the habit of documenting such decisions and linking those back to individual requirements will prove very useful when you're answering questions on the implications of, say, a specific feature's requirements and its impacts on a solution. There's no prescribed format for this as such – I've seen examples of in-line annotations for a requirements document (which is the preferred method for some CTA candidates when they're taking the review board exam), and I've also seen Excel spreadsheets with line items for each requirement with *functional considerations* and *technical considerations* columns where such items are documented.

Other Salesforce credentials in the Application Architect domain

As you'll know, there are several Salesforce certifications for each of the CTA domains. Looking at the Application Architect domain specifically, the following credentials comprise it:

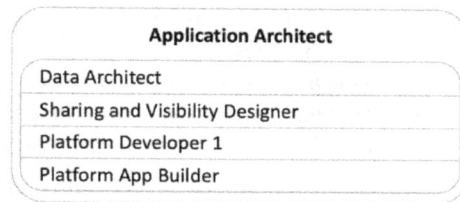

Application Architect
Data Architect
Sharing and Visibility Designer
Platform Developer 1
Platform App Builder

Figure 1.2 – The Application Architect domain

You may already have some or all the other credentials in the Application Architect domain. For those of you who may not, I strongly encourage you to gain your Platform App Builder and Platform Developer 1 credentials as you go through your journey as a Salesforce Data Architect. Both of these exams contain foundational questions related to data on the platform and can act as another *enabler* for success with the Salesforce Certified Data Architect credential.

The Sharing and Visibility Designer credential will have some overlap with the Data Architect credential as data and sharing on the Salesforce platform are relatively intertwined. When you complete this credential, I suggest moving on to the Sharing and Visibility Designer credential because some of the concepts that will be introduced in this book are pertinent to that credential. You can see how the Application Architect credentials relate and why it is useful to gain the foundational learning that's introduced in the Platform Developer 1 and Platform App Builder credentials if you have not already done so (although these are not strict prerequisites to taking the Data Architect exam). The Application Architect domain credential is automatically awarded upon completing the constituent exams, as per the preceding diagram.

Now that we know about the credential and what the exam looks like (including some tips and habits to help bolster learning), let's break down the Salesforce Data Architect job profile.

Profile of a Salesforce Data Architect

According to the **Salesforce Certified Data Architect Exam Guide** (located at `https://trailhead.salesforce.com/help?article=Salesforce-Certified-Data-Architecture-and-Management-Designer-Exam-Guide`), a Salesforce Data Architect is someone who does the following:

> *… assesses the architecture environment and requirements and designs sound, scalable, and performant solutions on the Customer 360 Platform as it pertains to enterprise data management. The candidate is knowledgeable about information architecture frameworks covering major building blocks, such as data sourcing, integration/movement, persistence, master data management, metadata management and semantic reconciliation, data governance, security, and delivery.*

> *The candidate also has experience assessing customers requirements in regards to data quality needs and creating solutions to ensure high-quality data (for example, no duplicates, correct data) and can also recommend organizational changes to ensure proper data stewardship. The candidate has experience communicating solutions and design trade-offs to business stakeholders.*

Let's break this definition down a little.

The first paragraph of that definition contained a lot of terms, but ultimately, it describes someone who can understand the requirements and applies data architecture principles and experience when formulating a solution or design. To me, this is part-and-parcel of our day job: understanding requirements and designing solutions. There is also mention of performance, data management, security, scalability, and governance. The second paragraph focuses on data quality and stewardship. All these aspects are covered in this book.

When we turn our attention to what the profile of a Data Architect is, a lot of parallels can be drawn to the humble Salesforce administrator, consultant, or architect – we listen to what our stakeholders want and design solutions that address those requirements, all while being mindful of the considerations and trade-offs that may present themselves along the way.

A Data Architect applies their knowledge of the data architecture of the Salesforce Customer 360 platform, including its features and their impact on the system when producing designs or solutions, such as the following:

- Sharing and security impacts based on the relationship choice between objects
- Large data volume considerations and mitigations
- Knowing what type of object to use where (standard, custom, big, or external)
- Indexing
- Performance

- Data stewardship and governance

- Loading and extracting data from the platform, and the methods available to affect the performance of these

With the definition of the profile of a Salesforce Data Architect broken down a little, we can turn our attention to the learning journey that will be outlined in this book.

Introducing the learning journey

Throughout this book, the certification learning journey will be broken down into the theory and the designer parts of the exam. The theory will align closely with the curriculum that's described in the exam guide, with the *designer* section dedicated to learning about the practical concepts referenced in the theory – for example, learning about Person Accounts and how they affect the data model and sharing thereof.

The learning journey starts with the theoretical concepts behind the exam:

- Data Modeling and Database Design:

  - Understanding how the Salesforce data model is architected, the design decisions behind that, and how the model affects sharing and security.

  - Understanding the different types of objects and how these fit into the data model design strategy.

  - Understanding data skew, which will provide you with an understanding of this concept in Salesforce.

- Master Data Management:

  - Understanding how to effectively design and implement a **Master Data Management** (MDM) strategy on the Salesforce platform.

  - Being able to articulate the concept of a *golden record*, preserve data traceability across multiple data sources, and understand how this affects the context that business rules run in.

- Salesforce Data Management:

  - How Salesforce license types affect the data model and the sharing options available to work with. Understanding these, as well as how to govern the data on the platform, is crucial to designing scalable, performant solutions that combine data from one or more Salesforce instances.

- Data Governance:

  - Being able to safeguard data on the Salesforce platform is a key part of the Salesforce Data Architect's role. This chapter covers the concepts behind building compliant solutions and how the Salesforce platform can underpin an enterprise data governance strategy.

- Large Data Volumes:

  - Whilst the Salesforce platform can cope with large amounts of data, some considerations apply to larger/massive amounts of data (referred to as *large data volumes*) and how the performance on the platform is affected.

  - This chapter covers LDV considerations and mitigations, as well as scalable data model design and data archiving strategies.

- Data Migration:

  - How do you get good quality data into the Salesforce platform?

  - How do you ensure loading large amounts of data is smooth, reliable, repeatable, and timely?

  - How do you effectively export data from the Salesforce platform?

Next, we'll look at the designer concepts that apply practical knowledge and practices to hone the theory:

- Accounts and Contacts:

  - We will cover the Account/Contact model, including Person Accounts and Contacts to Multiple Accounts, account skew, and the implications this has on the performance of queries and reports.

- Data APIs and Apex:

  - We will understand the various Lightning Platform APIs and Apex operations (including database, batch, and asynchronous), and how to deploy them effectively when designing data operations on the Salesforce Customer 360 Platform.

- Tuning Performance:

  - We will learn about the various methods that are available for tuning performance when designing Salesforce applications on the Salesforce Customer 360 Platform.

- Backup and Restore:

  - We will understand the methods that are available for getting data out of and back into the Salesforce platform while focusing on data backup and restore. This is useful when you're designing ETL and other solutions as part of an overall Salesforce IT estate.

- Territory Management:

    - We will understand territory management and how it pertains to the data model and its usage design on the Salesforce Lightning Platform.

Lastly, there is a section of this book that's dedicated to exam success that focuses on the following:

- Practice questions and answers

- Cheatsheets

- Introduction to further reading on some of the concepts and topics mentioned in this book

- An overview of Webassessor, including how to sign up for and take the exam

Summary

In this chapter, we learned about why the Salesforce Certified Data Architect credential exists, the exam format, and the profile of a Salesforce Data Architect to truly understand why the concepts behind this exam are useful in your day job. Lastly, we covered this book's learning journey to set the tone for the rest of this book.

In *Chapter 2, Data Modeling and Database Design*, we will begin our learning journey by revisiting the Salesforce data model, how different objects affect it, as well as touching on concepts such as data skew and ownership skew. We'll cover how to effectively describe the Salesforce data model while considering sharing, record counts, and performance as appropriate.

Practice questions

Answer the following question to test your knowledge of this chapter:

1. What is the Salesforce Certified Data Architect credential?

2. Why does the credential exist?

3. What is the typical profile of a Salesforce Data Architect?

Further reading

Read the official Salesforce exam guide: `https://trailhead.salesforce.com/help?article=Salesforce-Certified-Data-Architecture-and-Management-Designer-Exam-Guide`.

2
Data Modeling and Database Design

In this chapter, we'll begin our journey into the theory behind the credential syllabus, starting with Data Modelling and Database Design. You will learn how a Salesforce data model is architected, the design decisions behind it, and how a data model you may create in your job as a Salesforce Data Architect affects sharing and security. We'll go over the Salesforce sharing model so that you have an overview of what is available when considering options around data access.

Next, we'll look at the different types of objects (such as standard, custom, big, and external), and how they fit into a data model design strategy. While we're there, we'll cover the different relationship types so that you can understand when to apply them.

Turning to performance, we'll cover data skew to provide you with an understanding of this concept in Salesforce. We'll then cover diagramming techniques so that you can begin to effectively design and represent Salesforce data models.

In this chapter, we'll be covering the following topics:

- The Salesforce data model
- Understanding Salesforce sharing and security
- Exploring standard, custom, external, and big objects
- Overcoming data skew
- Bringing it all together with data modeling

The Salesforce data model

Salesforce abstracts the underlying data structure in its database for a given customer org by providing a faux RDBMS view of the objects within it. For example, take the diagram you find when viewing the Sales Cloud ERM at `https://architect.salesforce.com/diagrams/template-gallery/sales-cloud-overview-data-model`:

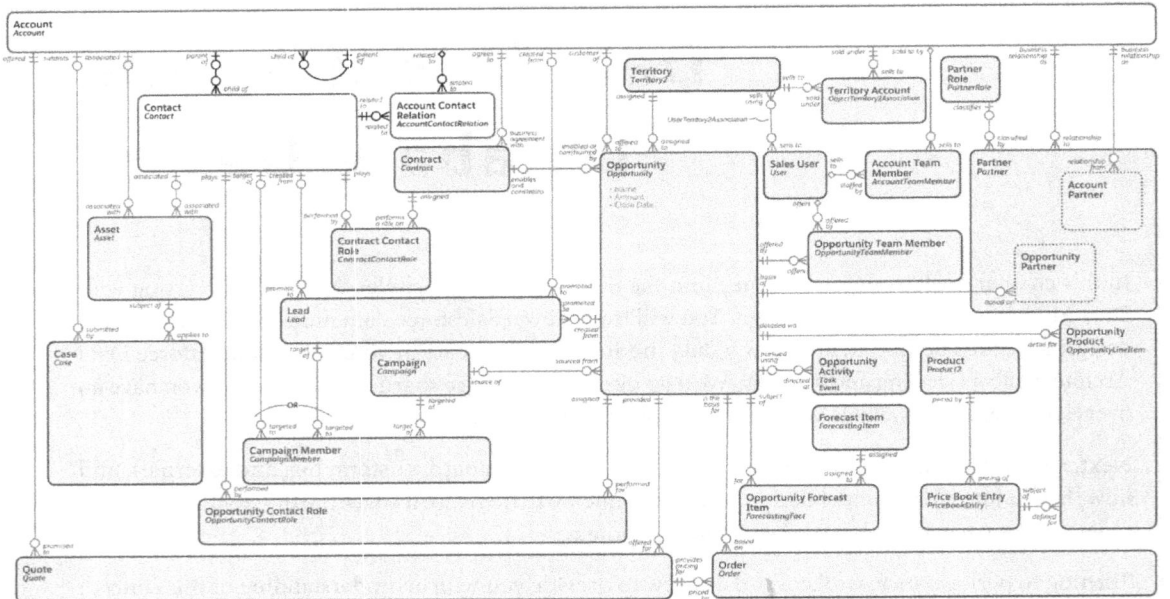

Figure 2.1 – The Salesforce Sales Cloud data model

As we can see, a contact record will have an `AccountId` represented as a lookup (which would be a foreign key in RDBMS terminology). Take this example for Account and Contact from Schema Builder for a brand-new Developer Edition org:

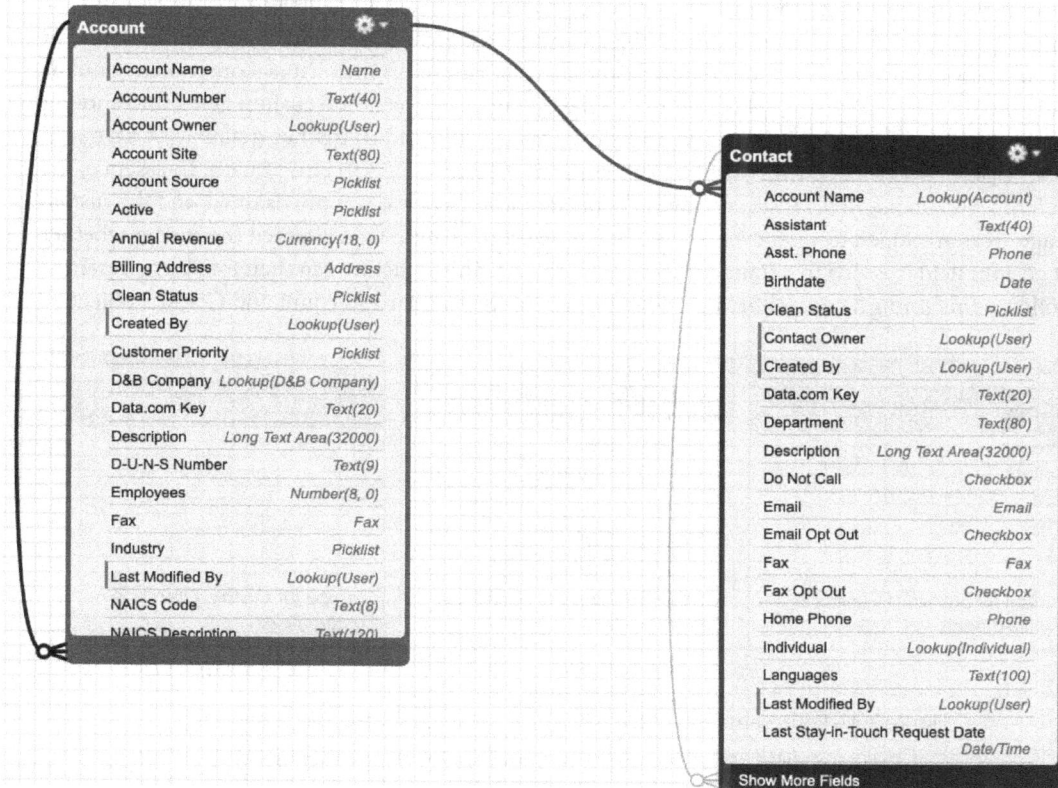

Figure 2.2 – Account and Contact represented in Schema Builder in a brand-new Developer Edition org

See for Yourself

Feel free to sign up for a (completely free) Developer Edition Salesforce org at `https://developer.salesforce.com/signup` in order to follow along with the examples in this book, including exploring Schema Builder.

Salesforce would have you think that Account and Contact exist as two separate database tables (and indeed there would be a separate table for each standard or custom object in the schema). Indeed, it is perfectly normal to think about the objects in this way in your day-to-day work as a Salesforce Data Architect.

The truth is, however, that Salesforce has a few large, underlying database tables (one for objects, one for fields, one for data that maps to those objects and fields, pivot tables, and so on) that provide for a virtual data structure for each org that is materialized at runtime. One virtual storage area contains standard objects and standard fields, another contains standard objects and custom fields, and another contains custom objects and their custom fields. This is explained in further detail at `https://developer.salesforce.com/wiki/multi_tenant_architecture`. In essence, the *standard object/standard fields* storage area is populated when a new org is provisioned, and the *custom* storage areas are added to whenever a new custom object or custom field is added (no matter whether that custom field is added to a standard or custom object). This structure can therefore be represented as follows, imagining a custom field is added to each of the standard Account and Contact objects:

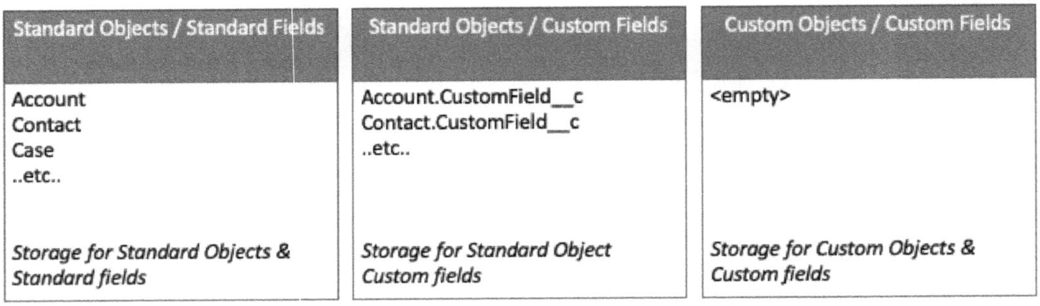

Standard Objects / Standard Fields	Standard Objects / Custom Fields	Custom Objects / Custom Fields
Account Contact Case ..etc..	Account.CustomField__c Contact.CustomField__c ..etc..	\<empty\>
Storage for Standard Objects & Standard fields	*Storage for Standard Object Custom fields*	*Storage for Custom Objects & Custom fields*

Figure 2.3 – Representation of the Salesforce database (object data only) with
a custom field added to the Account and Contact standard objects

Let's now add a custom object to see how the virtual storage is affected and what that change looks like in Schema Builder:

Standard Objects / Standard Fields	Standard Objects / Custom Fields	Custom Objects / Custom Fields
Account Contact Case ..etc..	Account.CustomField__c Contact.CustomField__c ..etc..	CustomObject CustomObject.CustomField__c
Storage for Standard Objects & Standard fields	*Storage for Standard Object Custom fields*	*Storage for Custom Objects & Custom fields*

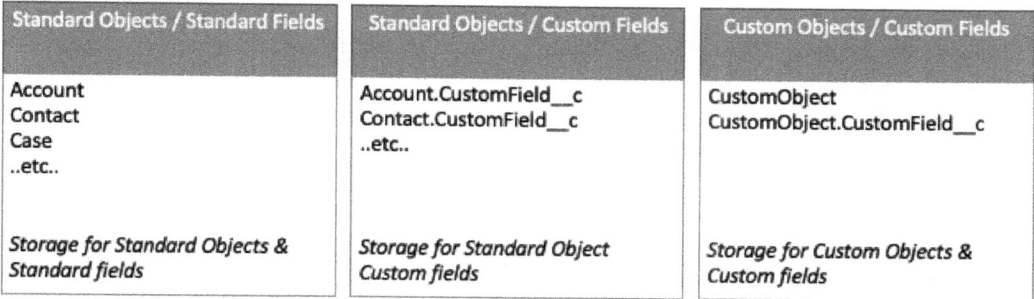

Figure 2.4 – Representation of the Salesforce database (object data only) with a custom object added to the org and a custom field added to that new custom object

Figure 2.5 includes both the custom object and the custom field in the schema:

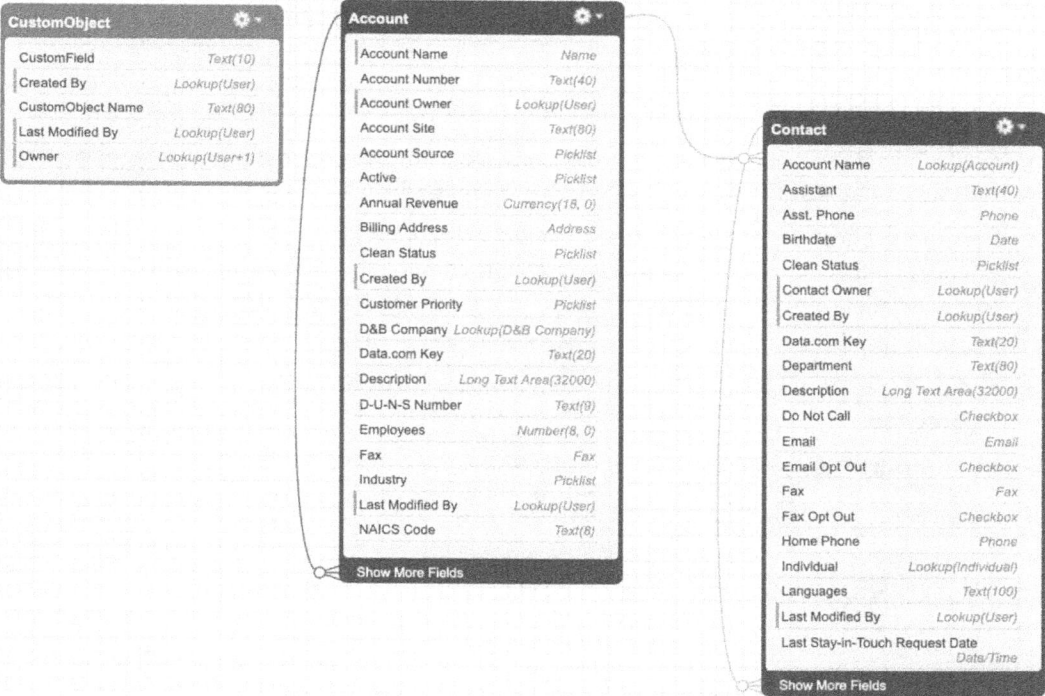

Figure 2.5 – Schema Builder with the representation of the newly added custom object and custom field

Armed with the knowledge of how the underlying Salesforce data model is represented (which is important for performance tuning and the like, covered later in this book), we can now turn our attention to what standard objects are available in Salesforce. These objects have been created to address common use cases (such as accounts to represent companies and contacts to represent people), and therefore should be used as much as possible. This not only reduces reinventing the wheel, but also Salesforce has extended the standard functionality to account for specific use cases, such as account teams. Account teams extend the sharing model for accounts to allow bespoke sharing among a team of folks that will collaboratively work on an account. Similar functionality is available for cases and opportunities (called **case teams** and **opportunity teams**, respectively). This teams functionality is an example of a standard feature supported in the Salesforce data model that isn't extended to custom objects.

A full and exhaustive listing of the available objects in Salesforce and their fields is provided by the API documentation (available at `https://developer.salesforce.com/docs/atlas.en-us.api.meta/api/sforce_api_objects_list.htm`), but some of the most commonly used objects are as follows:

- **Account** – Represents a company or institution that you may do business with.
- **Contact** – Represents a person (who is normally associated with one or sometimes many accounts).
- **Lead** – Represents a prospect or unqualified sale. Leads are typically used in a presales scenario, with the goal of converting the lead into an account, contact, and optionally, an opportunity.
- **Person Account** – A *grouping* account/contact object (mainly to allow opportunities to be associated to individual buyers instead of accounts/companies). This is essentially the account/contact relationship changed from a lookup to *Controlled By Parent*. This has effects on sharing and data visibility.
- **Case** – Represents a tracked issue or work item requiring attention. It's typically used by support staff.
- **Opportunity** – Represents a business deal.
- **Opportunity Line Item** – An item that forms part of the opportunity and is used to drive its value.

> **Standard Object Data Model Diagrams**
>
> The Salesforce standard data models are available at `https://developer.salesforce.com/docs/atlas.en-us.api.meta/api/data_model.htm` (remember, they show the logical representation of the objects and their relationships, not the physical database structure).

Now we are aware of the standard objects, and the three tables that facilitate standard objects/standard fields, standard objects/custom fields, and custom objects/custom fields, we can now turn our attention to understanding how data queries work, paying attention to performance across these tables.

When issuing a form of query to the Salesforce database for data, such as **Salesforce Object Query Language** (**SOQL**) or a REST API call, that request is turned into system-generated SQL for the underlying database. It is not possible to tune the SQL that is generated but being mindful of how our data queries will affect the generation of the SQL provides us with something that we can affect to a certain extent. It is within these parameters that we can optimize our data queries.

For example, consider this SOQL query for the first 10 account record names as they would appear in an alphabetically sorted list:

```
SELECT Name FROM Account ORDER BY Name ASC LIMIT 10
```

Given that we're querying a standard field from a standard object, Salesforce will only need to retrieve data from the standard objects/standard fields table for `Account`.

When adding a custom field into the mix (which we'll assume is unimaginatively called `CustomField` for the purposes of this explanation), we're then asking the underlying database query to have a JOIN in order to allow data from the Standard Object/Custom Fields table to be retrieved. Therefore, a query as simple as this will cause data to be retrieved from more than one underlying database table:

```
SELECT Name, CustomField__c FROM Account ORDER BY Name ASC
LIMIT 10;
```

Now consider a third scenario. We are going to query a custom object (called `CustomObj__c`) that has a lookup to an account (called `Account__c`), and also place the name of the account and the custom account field from the last example in the results:

```
SELECT Name, Account__c.Name, Account__c.CustomField__c FROM
CustomObj__c ORDER BY Name ASC LIMIT 10;
```

We've now queried the Custom Object/Custom Fields, Standard Object/Custom Fields, and Standard Object/Standard Fields tables, all for the retrieval of 10 rows worth of data from 3 fields!

It is therefore best practice to design our data access queries to avoid joins as much as possible, therefore ensuring we get the best performance possible. Given the way in which the underlying Salesforce data is structured, having a well-structured data model (avoiding joins as much as possible) means reporting, dashboards, and list views will perform well.

Chapter 6, Understanding Large Data Volumes, describes the issues that can arise with large amounts of data (particularly with performance) and how to mitigate them.

With the Salesforce data model now introduced, let's turn our attention to sharing and security, which affect how data is accessed.

Understanding Salesforce sharing and security

Any data access in Salesforce is determined by a layered security model. With each layer, data access is gradually opened up. Therefore, it is imperative that at the lowest level the sharing and security requirements are well understood in order to configure the security settings as appropriate. The layers of the Salesforce security model can be visualized as follows:

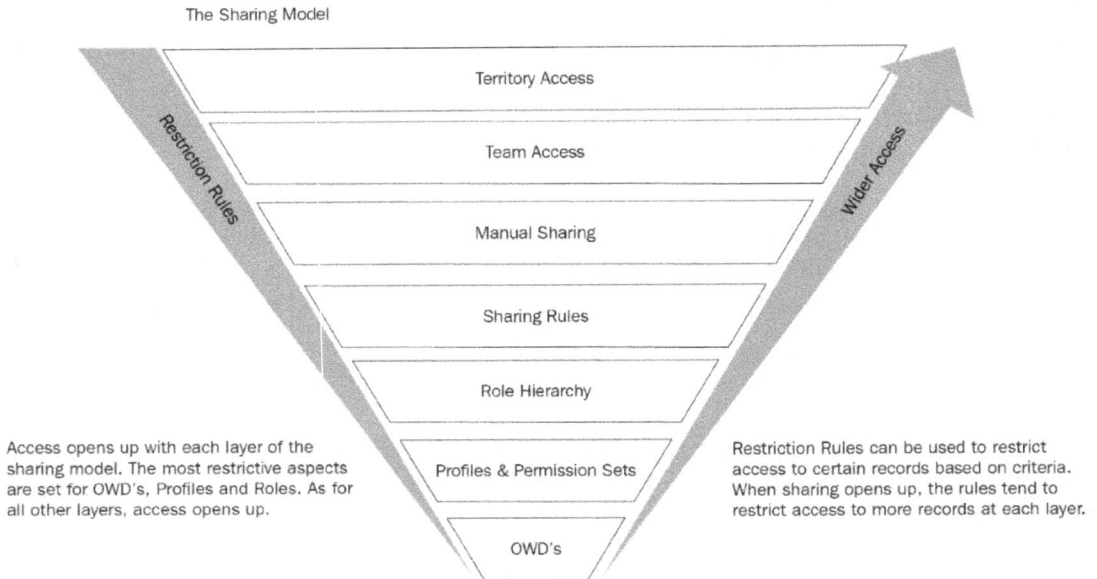

The Sharing Model

Restriction Rules

Wider Access

Territory Access

Team Access

Manual Sharing

Sharing Rules

Role Hierarchy

Profiles & Permission Sets

OWD's

Access opens up with each layer of the sharing model. The most restrictive aspects are set for OWD's, Profiles and Roles. As for all other layers, access opens up.

Restriction Rules can be used to restrict access to certain records based on criteria. When sharing opens up, the rules tend to restrict access to more records at each layer.

Figure 2.6 – A visual representation of the layers of the Salesforce security model

The layers that make up the security model, how they are configured, and their impacts are explained in this section.

Organization-Wide Defaults

The access that users have to each other's records by default is specified in the **Organization-Wide Defaults** (**OWDs**) for a Salesforce instance. Essentially, OWDs lock data access down to the most restrictive level, and then the other sharing and data access tools (explained in the following sections) are used to gradually open up data access to your users. For example, setting a read-only account OWD will mean that users cannot edit accounts by default. If users require the ability to only edit accounts they own, grant edit and read access at the object level through the use of a profile or permission set, leaving the OWD set to read-only for accounts. There are separate OWDs for internal and external (through a Salesforce Community or otherwise) users. The premise of access is the same, but the external OWDs facilitate *locking down* to a more restrictive data access model by default. For example, you may opt for all regular (sometimes referred to as *internal*) Salesforce users having read-only access to all accounts by default, with external users accessing Salesforce through a community having an OWD of private for account records so that those external users can only see account records they own. The values available to be set for OWDs are explained in the following subsections.

OWD values

There are several options available when setting OWDs in your Salesforce instance, and they all have an impact on how data access works for a given object or associated records/objects.

Private

Only the record owner, or those users higher than the record owner's role in the role hierarchy can view, edit, and report on records of this object.

Public Read-Only

All users can see records of this object type, but only the record owner and those folks higher than the record owner's role in the role hierarchy can view, edit, and report on records of this object.

Public Read/Write

All users can view, edit, and report on data held in records of this object.

Public Read/Write/Transfer

Only applicable to case and lead objects, all users can view, edit, transfer, and report on data held in lead or case records where this option is set.

Public Full Access

This is only applicable to the campaign object. All users can view, edit, delete, transfer, and report on data held in campaign records if this option is set.

Controlled by Parent

Users can perform actions on related records (such as edit or delete) based on access to the parent record. For example, if a custom object called *Invoice* has Account as its parent object, and Invoice's OWD is set to Controlled by Parent, then a users access to Account automatically means they have access to the invoice record associated with the account record. If the user has edit permissions on an account, then they will automatically have edit access to the associated invoice record.

> ### It Is Imperative That OWDs Are Correct
>
> OWDs were until recently the *only way* to restrict user access to a record. Changing an OWD will have an impact throughout the Salesforce Org (not least on the time it will take to perform sharing re-calculations), resulting in users potentially being able to see more data than they should do. Therefore, it is crucial that a users data access is thoroughly understood before implementing OWDs. Since the release of Winter '22, a feature called restriction rules facilitates restricting access to certain records to a select group of users. This is explained in further detail in the *Restriction rules* section. Restriction rules are used to restrict users and are not a substitute for a well-designed OWD strategy.

Profiles and permission sets

Specifying the object-level security access is the main function of profiles (although additional settings are present, such as login hours, IP ranges, and the like, that aren't in the scope of this exam). By specifying Create, Read, Edit, and Delete access to specific objects, users access to those objects can be further opened up beyond the OWDs already set in the organization. Field-level security is also set in profiles and permission sets, so it is here where Read or Edit access to specific fields is done.

Every user must have a profile assigned to them. Permission sets can be used to grant further selective access to objects and other features through organization settings available in the permission set. Managed packages typically use permission sets to allow assigned users access to the functionality offered by the managed package.

> ### A Quick Word on View All and Modify All
>
> **View All** and **Modify All** essentially allow users to be given blanket Read or Edit access across the organization for a given object. They effectively ignore sharing rules for a specific object. Therefore, if users are assigned a profile or permission set with **View All** set for accounts, they will have read access to every account. Similarly, **Modify All** against accounts gives edit access to any account in the organization. **View All Data** and **Modify All Data** permissions are set at the organization level, and sharing is effectively ignored to grant read or edit access to all objects and records in the organization to users that have this permission.

Role Hierarchy

Much like the structure of an organization, the role hierarchy is used to determine data access for groups of users and ensures that managers always have the same level of data access as their employees (regardless of the OWDs in place for that object). Each level of the role hierarchy should align with a level of data access needed by a particular group of users. Role hierarchies therefore deviate slightly from an organization chart as the system administrator will typically sit in a role toward the top of the hierarchy. Depending on the licensing in place for your Salesforce org, external users may have roles assigned, and therefore they may be subordinates to one of the internal roles.

The role hierarchy provides a special provision for access to cases, contacts, and opportunities outside of the OWD setup. Roles determine a users access to cases, contacts, and opportunities, irrespective of which user is the owner of those records. For example, you can set the contact object access so that all users in a particular role have edit rights to all contact records associated with account records that they own, regardless of which users actually own the contact records.

> **Role Hierarchy Limits**
>
> Organizations are allowed 500 roles by default, which can be increased by Salesforce if required (but you should be questioning if this increase is required, or a more effective role hierarchy design will work better).

Just like when changing the OWD for a given object, changing a users role will incur a sharing recalculation, as Salesforce will need to re-evaluate to correct the users access to data, as necessary. Also, just because you have two people in the same role, access to each other's data is not guaranteed (as this would depend on the rest of the sharing setup of the organization). Sharing rules can be used in this instance.

> **Role Hierarchy Best Practices**
>
> Keep to the following best practices when designing your role hierarchy: no more than 10 levels of branches, no more than 25,000 internal roles, and no more than 100,000 external roles.

The role hierarchy is a foundational aspect of the entire Salesforce sharing model, and therefore taking the time to get it right is crucial. No one wants a soup of sharing rules for users having correct data access because the role hierarchy isn't designed properly!

Sharing rules

Sharing rules exist to provide exceptions to the OWD and role hierarchy, opening up users record access based on conditions. Sharing rules fall into two categories:

- **Owner-based sharing rules**: These allow records to be shared with other users based on the owner of the record, such as peers within the same role.

- **Criteria-based sharing rules**: These allow records to be shared with other users based on the criteria of the record (a value of a field, for example). Record ownership is not a consideration, as that scenario is covered by owner-based sharing rules.

Manual sharing

In bespoke sharing scenarios not covered by the mechanisms we've covered already, manual sharing exists to provide a facility to manually share a record, granting read and edit permissions, with users who don't have access to the record. Manual sharing, as the name implies, is a user-driven process that involves clicks in the Salesforce user interface to grant record access to other users. It is possible to create manual shares programmatically (for more information, see the dedicated subsection on *Programmatic sharing*).

Sharing a record with another user creates a share record in the Salesforce database. Programmatic solutions will need to manage record shares for share reasons other than *manual share*. Programmatic shares with a *manual share* row cause can be maintained using the **Share** button on the record, much like the out-of-the-box share button functionality.

> **When Manual Shares Cease to Work**
>
> If a record owner of a shared record changes, then the manual share is removed. If the sharing doesn't open up access beyond what is set in the OWD for that object, the share isn't created in the first place. Both of these statements are also true in programmatic scenarios.

Team access

Accounts, opportunities, and cases have a *teams* record-sharing concept, whereby groups of users can work collaboratively on accounts, opportunities, or cases. The record owner, someone higher in the role hierarchy (who therefore inherits the same level of record access), or administrators can add people to a team to work collaboratively on a record or modify the access level (say, from read-only to read/write).

Teams are generally used to give specific users in Salesforce an elevated level of access to a record so that they can work collaboratively on an account, opportunity, or case. For example, if a user already has write access to a particular account record, adding them as read/write in the account team for that record has no effect.

Creating a team against an account, opportunity, or case record creates a team record and an associated share record in the Salesforce database. Programmatic solutions will have to maintain both of these records. See the dedicated subsection for more information on programmatic sharing.

> **What About Multiple Teams Accessing One Record?**
>
> If multiple teams are required to access a particular record, then territory management or programmatic sharing may be more suitable. There is only one team per account, opportunity, or case, and therefore the concept of multiple teams against a single record is not supported.

Territory hierarchy access

It is possible to create a hierarchy to represent your organization's sales territories. This essentially facilitates automatic account assignment based on criteria to denote it belonging to a particular branch of the territory model. *Chapter 12, Territory Management*, covers territory management in further detail.

Programmatic sharing

Using what used to be known as Apex managed sharing, programmatic sharing allows the use of code to build sharing settings when data access requirements cannot be fulfilled using any of the means described in the preceding sections. Code-based sharing solutions can be quite fancy and sophisticated, but equally require careful management, and therefore it is important to understand how programmatic sharing works before embarking on a code-based sharing solution.

Each object in Salesforce has an associated share object. This has two naming conventions (one for standard objects and another for custom objects). For standard objects, the associated share object is named `objectShare`, such as `AccountShare`, `CaseShare`, and so on. For custom objects, the associated share objects are named using a format similar to `object__Share`. In the example of a custom object called `MyObject__c`, the associated share object is called `MyObject__Share`.

Objects that are on the detail side of a master-detail relationship don't have an associated share object because access to the object on the Master side of the relationship grants implicit access to the object on the detail side. Custom objects that have a Public Read/Write OWD also do not have an associated share object.

When programmatically sharing a record using code, the associated share object requires an entry with a *row cause* to essentially store the reason the sharing has taken place. Sharing a record with a user through the Salesforce UI creates an entry in the associated share object with a row cause of *manual share*. Programmatic sharing can create entries with using the *manual share* row cause, but custom row cause values can be used. The values in a share object entry are as follows:

- `ParentID`: ID of the record being shared. This value cannot be changed once the row is created.

- `RowCause`: As explained in the previous paragraph, this is the reason why the record is being shared. This can be *manual sharing* to simulate the **Share** button in the Salesforce UI being pressed, or a custom reason can be used. Custom sharing reasons need to be created in the Salesforce UI before they can be used. Objects have an Apex sharing reasons related list in the Management Settings of the object in Salesforce Setup.

- `UserOrGroupId`: The Salesforce ID of the user or group that the record is being shared with.

- objectAccessLevel: The level of access being granted as part of the share. The name of the property is the share object name of which the record is being shared followed by AccessLevel. For example, CaseShareAccessLevel. Values can be edit, or read, or edit or read-only access, respectively.

> **A Note on Records Shared Programmatically with Manual Share Row Causes**
>
> When records that are shared with row causes of *manual share* (both programmatically and through the UI) change owner, any manual share row cause records are removed from the associated share object. Custom row shares are persisted when a shared records owner changes.

Restriction rules

Generally available as of the Winter '22 release, restriction rules can be used to control the records a specific user group is allowed to see. As per the documentation for creating a restriction rule (https://help.salesforce.com/s/articleView?id=sf.security_restriction_rule_create.htm&type=5), *When a restriction rule is applied to a user, the data that the user has access to via org-wide defaults, sharing rules, and other sharing mechanisms is filtered by the record criteria that you specify.*

At the time of writing, restriction rules are available for the following objects:

- Custom objects
- Contracts
- Events
- Tasks
- Time sheets
- Time sheet entries

Up to two restriction rules can be created per supported object in the Enterprise and Developer editions, and up to five restriction rules per supported object in the Performance and Unlimited editions.

Now that we have an understanding of sharing and security on the Salesforce platform and how it affects data access, we can now look at each Salesforce object type.

Exploring standard, custom, external, and big objects

Salesforce objects can broadly fit into one of four types. While you will no doubt have worked with the standard and custom object functionality available on the platform, it is necessary to understand how they work at a lower level to truly understand what it means to issue SOQL queries against those object types and how it affects performance. Secondly, you may not have worked with external objects and big objects before. These are different when it comes to data storage and access (external object data isn't stored on the platform and is accessed on-demand through an external data source. Big object data ensures consistent performance but data lives in a separate location to standard/custom objects within the Salesforce platform).

---

sObjects

An **sObject** is the generic form of any Salesforce Object. The standard Salesforce objects and the custom objects you create are concrete types of sObjects (they all inherit common properties and behavior). Another way to think of an sObject is that it abstracts the actual representation of any Salesforce object, much like objects in the **Java** programming language all inherit from the *Object* base class.

Standard objects

Depending on your license type, Salesforce provides access to many standard objects that are designed to fulfill many business use cases with minimal customization.

These objects and their fields, in an out-of-the-box state, will all be held in the standard objects/standard fields underlying database table. From an object access perspective, additional Salesforce licenses such as *Service Cloud* will essentially grant access to the underlying Service Cloud standard objects such as milestone and entitlement and their out-of-the-box fields.

Standard objects and standard fields don't have a special suffix and therefore are represented as `Account` (in the example of a standard object name) and `Name` (in the example of a standard field name) when issuing SOQL queries. Here's an example:

```
SELECT Name FROM Account
```

Without any customization, querying for standard object data is very fast. This is because there is only one database table being queried for. As soon as a single custom field is added to a standard object, that field is created in the Custom Objects/Custom Fields table, and therefore any queries for that field will essentially cause a JOIN query issued to the underlying Salesforce database, as we now require results from both tables.

Custom objects

Custom objects and their custom fields are all created in the Custom Objects/Custom Fields table in the underlying Salesforce database. Custom object data resides within the Salesforce database, and both custom objects and custom fields have a __c suffix. In the example of a SOQL query issued for data held in a custom field called `MyField` in an object called `MyObject`, the syntax would look as follows:

```
SELECT MyField__c FROM MyObject__c
```

Queries on data held purely within these objects will be relatively quick, but any data on parent objects (especially where that object is a standard object) will incur a small performance penalty as the results will require the use of a JOIN in the underlying SQL query issued to the Salesforce database.

External objects

While the data for both standard and custom objects is held on-platform within the Salesforce database, external object data is held off-platform in an external data source, typically within another application. The idea behind external objects is that data is held off-platform, but end users interact with it as if it were on-platform. Salesforce uses web service callouts to access external data in real time. External data is available to users in real time through Salesforce, and the external object will always return the most up-to-date data from the external data source.

External objects require an external data source definition in the Salesforce instance, which is then used to determine how to access the external system.

External objects are denoted in Salesforce with a ___x suffix in the object name. For example, invoice data from SAP for an order within Salesforce will have the name Invoice___x. External objects support indirect and external lookups to link the data with your Salesforce records.

External objects are supported in Salesforce API version 32 and later and are available with Salesforce Connect and Files Connect.

Big objects

Big objects are used to store and manage huge amounts of data (up to 1 million records out of the box, but this can be scaled up at an additional cost to tens of millions or even billions of records). Big objects provide consistent performance. In my experience, big objects tend to lend themselves to auditing and archiving use cases, but anything that requires consistent performance when working with hundreds of millions or billions of records is what big objects are designed for.

Big objects work using a distributed database and are not transactional in nature. Therefore, sharing isn't supported on big objects other than object and field permissions. Additionally, this means that automation from workflow, to flow, to triggers is not supported on big objects.

Idempotence

When the same record representation (that is, exactly the same set of data for a record) is inserted multiple times to a big object, only a single record is created. This is so that writes to the big object can remain idempotent. Inserting the same record representation into an **sObject** (whether standard or custom) will result in multiple entries.

Object relationship types

Salesforce objects are linked together through relationships in one of several ways. These relationship can affect sharing and data access. The various relationship types are explained here.

Master/detail relationship

A Master/detail relationship closely links two objects together, so much so that certain behavior of the child record is affected. This includes sharing, where access to the Master (or parent) record gives access to the detail (or child) record. Master/detail relationships also support roll-up summaries.

When Master records are deleted, all child records are deleted. However, un-deleting a Master record restores all child records. When a detail record is deleted, it is moved to the recycle bin. If a detail record is deleted and subsequently the Master record is deleted, the detail record cannot be restored as it no longer has a Master record to associate to.

Many-to-many

Lookup and master-detail relationship types are both one-to-many (where many records can be linked to one other record, for example an account having multiple contacts). Many-to-many relationships (for example, linking a case to more than one custom bug record, and multiple custom bug records to the same case) are represented using two master/detail relationships connected via a junction object (a custom object with two master-detail relationships). Many-to-many relationships can only therefore be used to connect one object to a different object. In our cases and bugs example, we have the standard case object with a master-detail relationship to our `BugCaseAssociation` junction object, and a custom bug object with a master-detail relationship to our `BugCaseAssociation` junction object. This can be represented pictorially:

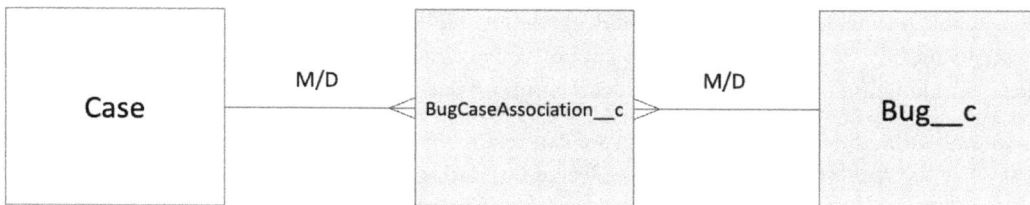

Figure 2.7 – Representing a many-to-many relationship with two master-detail relationships

With master/detail and many-to-many relationships now covered, let's look at the other relationship types.

Lookup relationship

A lookup relationship links two objects together, except that sharing is not affected (and therefore the child object can have separate sharing, unlike that of master-detail relationships where sharing is affected), and roll-up summaries aren't supported. Lookup relationships support linking two objects together, but that can include looking up to records of the same object type (think account hierarchies where an account record can have a parent account record to represent the hierarchy of a company group structure). An object with a lookup relationship to itself is called a **self-relationship**. The user object should instead use a hierarchy relationship (see the *Hierarchical* section) when looking up to itself.

External lookup

When linking external object records to a Salesforce standard or custom object, and the external object is the parent object, then an external lookup relationship is used. The standard external ID field on the parent external object is matched against the values of the child object's external lookup relationship field.

Indirect lookup

When linking external object records to a parent object whose data exists in Salesforce as either a standard or custom object, an indirect lookup relationship should be used to associate the records. When creating an indirect lookup, you specify which field in the parent object and which field on the external object to match against and therefore associate records. A custom, unique, external ID field is selected on the parent object to match against the child external object's indirect lookup field, which comes from the external data source.

Hierarchical

Only available on the user object, a hierarchical relationship is a special type of lookup to associate one user to another (where the record does not directly or indirectly refer to itself). Storing a users manager as a lookup to another user record is a common use-case for this functionality.

Now we know the different ways in which we can relate objects and their data to each other, let's look at what happens when performance is affected by relating too many records to a single ancestor record or user.

Custom hierarchy (parent/child) relationships

It is possible to create custom parent/child hierarchies by utilizing a custom `Sub` object that does a double lookup (of type lookup relationship) on the object you wish to create the parent/child relationship for. One lookup has a name format of `Parent`, the other `Sub`. For example, to create a parent/child opportunity relationship, create a custom object called `SubOpportunity` with a lookup called `ParentOpportunity` and another `SubOpportunity` that both look up to the opportunity object. This is explained in more detail at `https://help.salesforce.com/s/articleView?id=000326493&type=1`.

Overcoming data skew

Automatic scaling is an expected feature of the Salesforce platform, particularly as the count of records for a particular object increases. Customers will demand a consistent level of performance when tens of thousands of records of the same type are present within the system. There are a couple of performance degradations that happen in a couple of select use cases. These are as follows:

- A user owns more than 10,000 records of the same type (such as a user owning over 10,000 account records). This is known as **ownership skew**.

- A single account record has a large number of child records, such as 10,000 or more contact records with the same account as their `AccountId` lookup. This is known as **account skew**.

- Similar to account skew, when a large number of child records (10,000+) are associated with the same parent there can be performance problems. This is known as **lookup skew**.

We'll look at the causes for each of these and how they can be mitigated.

Ownership skew

When a single user or queue is the owner for more than 10,000 records of a particular type (such as contact), then performance issues due to ownership skew may arise. In Salesforce instances, it is very common to have a default user or queue that owns all otherwise unassigned or unused records. Changes to sharing settings or other sharing-related operations affect performance because re-calculating sharing based on a change of role for the owning user or another sharing-related calculation will result in a long-running Salesforce operation, locking the records while this operation takes place.

Ownership skew mitigation

To mitigate ownership skew, consider the following:

- Based on the data projections for large amounts of records that will result in a single owner (such as a default owner for lead records), consider having multiple owners for such ownership scenarios. Assignment rules are available for leads and cases (standard objects that tend to have high volumes), but other automation techniques are available to assign records based on the criteria of the record to an appropriate owner.

- If one user must be used, performance impacts can be reduced by not assigning the user to a role. This removes any role-based impacts from sharing calculations.

- If the owning user must have a role, then that role should exist at the top of the role hierarchy. The user therefore will not need to be moved around the hierarchy, reducing the impact of sharing calculations being a long-running process.

- Ensure any owning user is not a member of a public group that is used in the criteria for any sharing rules. If this is the case, changes to the record owner will trigger re-calculations of those sharing rules also, further slowing things down.

Account skew

Some standard Salesforce objects maintain a special data relationship to facilitate record access under private sharing models. This is especially true of accounts and opportunities (and, in fact, is how account and opportunity teams are facilitated with regard to sharing and access to select records).

Account skew is the result of an account record having a large number of child records. I've seen this manifest with some clients as a single account record called **Unassigned Accounts** that has many tens of thousands of child account records that may be old, unused, or otherwise unassigned accounts. This scenario causes issues with performance and record locking.

When updates are made to a child record, Salesforce will lock the parent account record (to maintain record integrity in the database). Therefore, updating a large number of child records under the same account record will potentially cause contention (where multiple processes or operations try to access the same thing at the same time) with trying to lock the parent record (which is done using a separate system thread).

When updates are made to the parent account record, such as changing the owner, then all sharing will have to be recalculated on all child records. This can trigger a chain reaction because sharing rules, role hierarchy calculations, and many other operations related to sharing will have to take place. This will lead to long-running processes and potentially record locking issues.

Account skew mitigation

To mitigate account skew, distribute child records across multiple parent account records. 10,000 is the magic number here. By distributing records across multiple accounts, we can avoid account skew and its performance impacts related to record locking and sharing operations.

Lookup skew

Similar in principle to account skew, lookup skew can happen when there are a large number of child records associated (via the lookup field on those child records) with a single parent record. While account skew is specific to the account object, lookup skew can affect multiple objects.

Lookup skew mitigation

Try the following to mitigate lookup skew:

- Remove unnecessary workflows, process builders, or flows from affected objects in order to reduce saving time when records for affected objects are created or saved.

- Distribute the skew across multiple records. For example, have separate parent object records for the lookups on the child records to reduce or even eliminate record locking and sharing recalculations.

- Use picklist values instead of lookups. This will mean that there won't be linking to actual parent records but reports on those picklist values can instead be used to query the associated data for a given parent record. This mitigation technique doesn't lend itself to large amounts of lookup values, and therefore should only be used when the number of picklist values is low.

Data skew summary

We've explored the three types of data skew in Salesforce and how to mitigate them. When designing an effective data management strategy within Salesforce, be mindful of data skew and how it can affect performance. By designing for data skew from the outset when building a data strategy, even the largest orgs can perform without degradation.

Now we understand the different types of data skew and their impact, let's combine what we've covered throughout this chapter.

Bringing it all together with data modeling

We've covered a lot in this chapter, but now it is time to put the theory into practice and produce something tangible in the form of a data model. Now we know the OWDs we can set, the relationships between objects we can influence, and the owners of records, we can bring them together to produce a data model.

Throughout this book, any data model diagrams will be drawn to the following format (essentially an expanded legend from the example diagram in *Chapter 1*, *Introducing the Salesforce Data Architect Journey*):

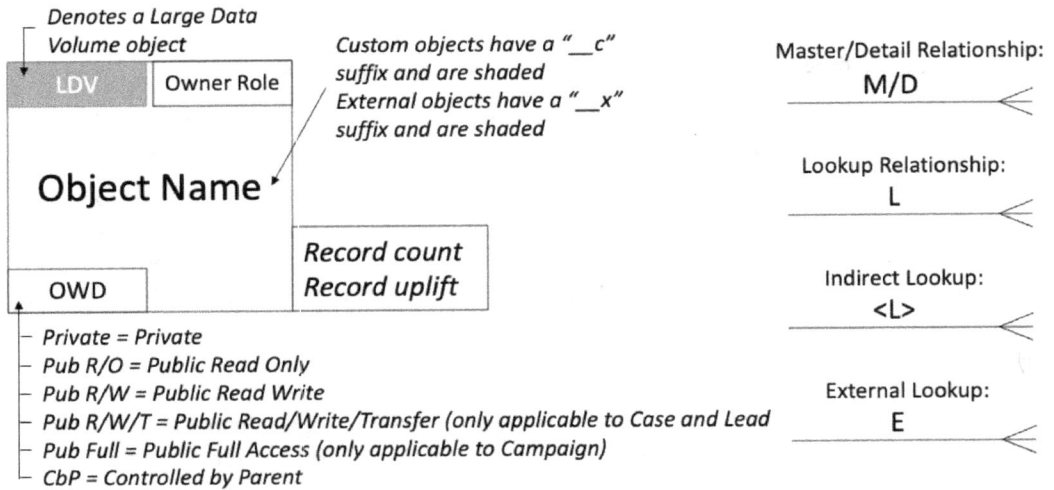

Figure 2.8 – The format for diagramming Salesforce objects used throughout this book

Now we've looked at the data modeling format, let's now look at a data modeling example.

Data modeling example and explanation

With our data modeling format now covered, let's take a look at an example data model to show how much information we can glean from a single artifact. Here's the example, which is similar to the one shared in *Chapter 1*, *Introducing the Salesforce Data Architect Journey*:

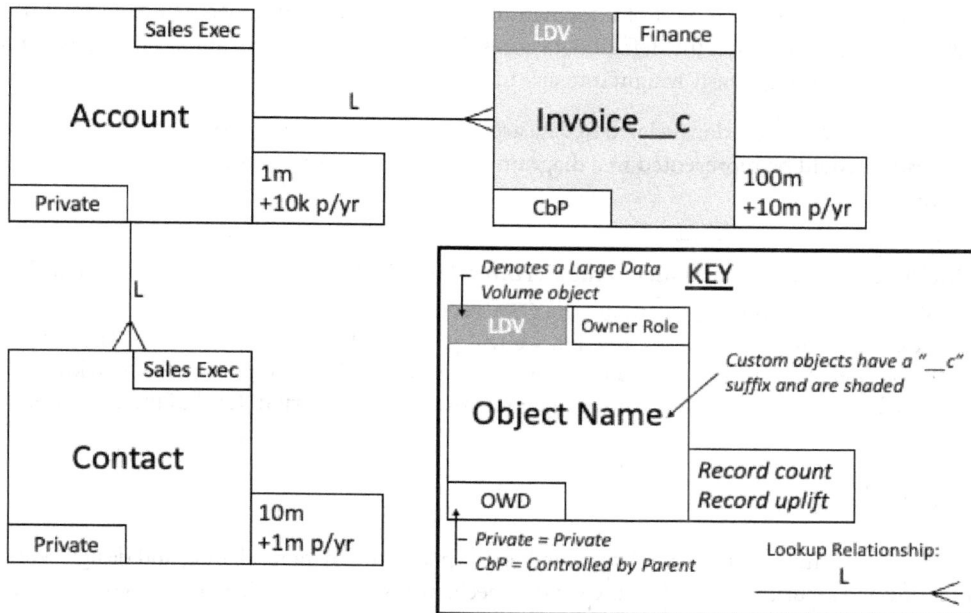

Figure 2.9 – Example data model

Let's look at the data model and see what we can determine from it:

- There is a private OWD model in play, so only record owners of Account and Contact and roles higher up in the role hierarchy will be able to view and edit records (unless records are shared using one of the other methods explained in this chapter, such as manual sharing).

- The *Sales Exec* role is designated the owner of accounts and contacts, with *Finance* the owner of the `Invoice__c` custom object. However, we can see that the OWD for `Invoice__c` is set to Controlled by Parent, so Sales Exec folks that own account records will be able to view and edit `Invoice__c` records as well.

- The `Invoice__c` object has been designated *LDV* given the amount of data, so we'll need to ensure that we consider data skew. In this instance, we have both account skew and ownership skew to think about, and therefore we should ensure that no account record is the parent of more than 10,000 `Invoice__c` records, and also no single person from the Finance department owns more than 10,000 `Invoice__c` records, otherwise performance issues (as explained in the *Overcoming data skew* section) may occur.

As I'm sure you'll agree, there is a lot of information packed into a seemingly small diagram, but it can quickly be determined what the default data access looks like and the sharing implications of the relationships, and we also get early insight into any LDV implications.

When answering practice questions related to data access and its effect on other objects, try to visualize how the question could be represented in a diagram where it makes sense to do so in order to get to the right answer.

> **The Importance of the Data Model in the Certified Technical Architect (CTA) review board**
>
> Those of you who are looking to pursue the **CTA** review board will be required to produce a data model that's similar in nature to what we will produce throughout this book. The data model is considered a core artifact of the review board, and as such it is important that you know how to quickly produce clear data model diagrams that convey the right level of information.

Summary

We've started our learning journey and begun with concepts around data modelling and design. We've covered sharing and security, delving into the various mechanisms available in Salesforce to control access to data. We've paid particular attention to how the OWDs and role hierarchy can have a profound impact on the data that your users can access. We've seen how OWDs affect data model design for solutions on the Salesforce platform, and why it is important to get these right based on a solid understanding of the impact of a particular OWD setting when building Salesforce solutions that address customer requirements.

We've also covered the different object types available on the platform, highlighting the differences between standard, custom, external, and big objects and the various use cases for each. Again, the use of certain object types (and in particular big objects and external objects) can affect the user experience with regard to data access.

We've covered relationships and their effect on Salesforce functionality and data access, and we've seen the different methods of objects and their data together on the Salesforce platform, highlighting how we relate data held in external data sources with that held within Salesforce.

We've also looked at performance around data with regard to data skew and the methods available to mitigate the impacts of a user owning more than 10,000 records or an account being the parent account for more than 10,000 child records.

With a solid grounding in the concepts highlighted in this chapter, you now understand why it is important to plan for the future from the outset of the design on your Salesforce data model to mitigate the risks associated with data skew and other factors that affect performance.

Lastly, we brought together the concepts when modeling data solutions and introduced a standard for data model diagrams.

In *Chapter 3, Master Data Management,* we'll dive into what **Master Data Management (MDM)** is and learn how to effectively design and implement an MDM strategy on the Salesforce platform. We'll look at the concept of a *golden record*, preserve data traceability across multiple data sources, and learn how this affects the context in which business rules run.

Practice questions

1. The *Public Read/Write/Transfer* OWD is applicable to which objects?

2. Performance issues related to an account record that has more than 10,000 child records is known as what?

3. What OWD is available for the campaign object that isn't available to others?

4. What type of Salesforce object is used to access data held in an external system in real time?

5. True or false: Big objects will store multiple commits of the same representation of a row of data.

6. What OWD causes the object to inherit the same data access permissions as the object it is associated with?

7. How is a many-to-many relationship created?

8. What type of relationship is only available on the user object?

9. What happens to the child records when a master record in a master-detail relationship gets deleted?

10. True or false: sharing the child object is affected when using a lookup relationship.

Answers

1. Lead and case.

2. Account skew.

3. Public Full Access.

4. External object.

5. False – Big objects only store a single row for multiple commits of the same representation of data.

6. Controlled by Parent.

7. Two master-detail relationships, one on each object, relating them to each other.

8. Hierarchical relationship.

9. Child records are also deleted.

10. False.

Further reading

- *Data Access in Salesforce*: https://developer.salesforce.com/docs/atlas.en-us.dat.meta/dat/dat_components.htm

- *Salesforce Standard Objects*: https://developer.salesforce.com/docs/atlas.en-us.api.meta/api/sforce_api_objects_list.htm

- *Salesforce Data Model Diagrams*: https://architect.salesforce.com/diagrams#template-gallery

- *Salesforce Object Relationships Overview*: https://help.salesforce.com/articleView?id=overview_of_custom_object_relationships.htm&type=0

- *Restriction Rules*: https://help.salesforce.com/s/articleView?id=release-notes.rn_forcecom_sharing_restriction_rules.htm&type=5&release=234

3
Master Data Management

Next up in our learning journey is **Master Data Management** (**MDM**). As part of the exam curriculum, you should be able to understand how to effectively design and implement an MDM strategy on the Salesforce platform, so we'll cover what MDM is and how to implement it.

In addition, you will be able to articulate the concept of a *golden record*, so we'll cover the background to this concept and some techniques for implementing it (because depending on the system landscape and what system is designated as the data master, the golden record may not necessarily be on the Salesforce platform).

We'll then turn our attention to preserving data traceability across multiple data sources and understanding how this affects the context in which business rules run.

In this chapter, we'll cover the following topics:

- Introducing MDM
- Implementing MDM
- The golden record
- Consolidating data attributes from multiple sources
- Preserving traceability and business rule context

Introducing MDM

MDM is the discipline of determining and maintaining a *single source of truth* for shared data across an enterprise. As you can probably imagine, maintaining multiple copies of the same information across an IT enterprise is inefficient and can lead to data inconsistencies. Unless people and technology are 100% aligned, maintaining multiple copies of the same data is virtually impossible. Siloed businesses (where each business division is effectively separated in terms of people and technology) suffer from data inconsistencies, and the quality and classification of data they hold is often flawed. These scenarios require bringing together the data held by different systems into a data master, or *single source of truth*.

A single source of truth can be visualized conceptually as follows:

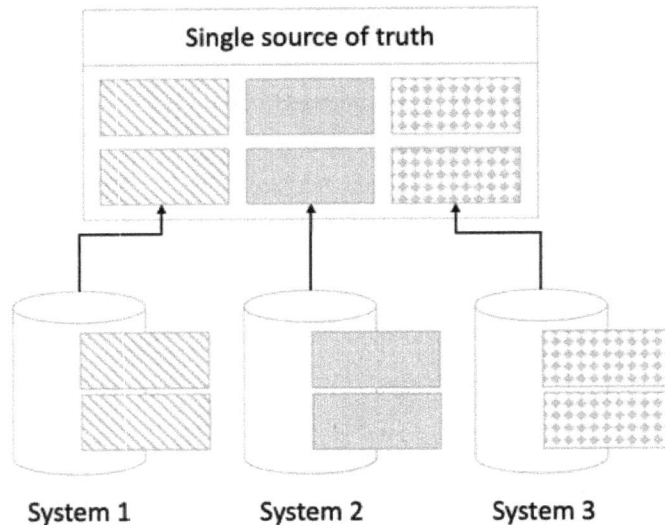

Figure 3.1 – Bringing data held in different systems to form a single source of truth

An example of inadequate MDM was realized by myself recently, and it involves my local car dealership. I enquired about, and ultimately purchased, a car from them, and as such, data about me and my purchased vehicle was on the sales team database. This is important to the dealership because they can send me reminders of when my car is due for a service and the like. Unfortunately for me, the dealership's marketing department doesn't have integration with the sales department, and as such, I continue to receive marketing emails from the dealership enticing me to purchase the car I already own.

This particular scenario happened because the car dealership departments have unconnected systems. I'm represented twice in the IT enterprise, as a prospect in one system and a qualified (and converted) sales lead in another. If the car dealership's different departments' data was centralized into a single source of truth, they could see that I had purchased a car, and perhaps turn their marketing efforts to upselling and cross-selling activities, such as deals on car accessories or a servicing package.

MDM should be an ongoing process, as part of a wider organizational data strategy. For example, when one organization acquires another organization, its data must be cleansed, de-duplicated, classified, and reconciled with that held by the acquiring organization. The benefits of consolidating data into a shared single source of truth ensure people in organizations are using the latest, cleansed, and correctly classified data. The single source of truth is often referred to as the *golden record*. We'll cover this concept in the section titled *The golden record*, later in this chapter.

Let's now cover some key terms used in MDM and their definitions.

Key terms

The following terms are used a lot in the field of MDM. When dealing with MDM situations as a Salesforce Data Architect, you may come across these.

Harmonizing data

Data harmonization is the practice of taking data from multiple sources and processing it (often through machine learning and automation) into a standard, accurate, and comprehensive format, meaning anyone interacting with the data can do so in the same way (utilizing a common data language). For example, calling a product a **Stock Keeping Unit** (**SKU**) instead of a *product code* internally and a *product* externally.

Consolidating data

As the name would suggest, **data consolidation** is the practice of bringing together and consolidating data from several data sources into a centrally managed *data master* or *hub*. It should be noted that this is slightly different from the golden record, as that refers to the surfacing of information, whereas data consolidation refers to the actual management of consolidated data (although it is perfectly acceptable to surface golden records from the MDM data hub).

Data survivorship

Data survivorship is concerned with what happens to data that is identified as a duplicate across the IT enterprise. Typically, data record survivorship can be categorized as follows:

- **A survival-of-the-fittest approach**: The record deemed most suitable is taken as the one to use.

- **Forming a golden record**: The suitably identified pieces of data (as determined by business rules on data quality) are brought together to form a single source of truth.

- **Context-aware survivorship**: Duplicate data records aren't actually altered, in that they aren't merged into other records, archived, or deleted. This is typically used in enterprises that need to form different views of data (think different golden records depending on the context in which data is being viewed or interacted with). As you would expect, this approach involves an extra layer of data management and, therefore, may have performance concerns associated with it.

Thresholds and weights

When matching data, weights are the values given to data records, and thresholds are what determine the action to be taken on those records. For example, a threshold may cause two records to automatically be linked, or flag two records for manual intervention. Weights are what calculate the matching score that feeds into the thresholds. For example, a matched email address, postcode, and surname would give a higher score than matching two records purely on a first name, as these may be common across the data set. Our high-weighted record match may feed into a threshold that automatically links the records together.

Canonical modeling

A canonical data model is a way of modeling data in its simplest form. Typically, this is used in a middleware scenario whereby data is modeled differently in source systems. A canonical data model can be used as a common format from which system-specific data models can be generated or fed into.

An example of a canonical data example would be for a customer master (Salesforce) and a new contact requiring creation in two different connected systems through a middleware layer. Because the two source systems represent contacts in different formats, the middleware would take the Salesforce contact and convert it into a canonical (or simplest) format, from which a transformation can be done to the system-specific format for each source system requiring interaction to create the contact. New connected systems can immediately take advantage of this modeling logic.

Hierarchy management

This is a relatively simple concept whereby the hierarchy of various data records and elements is represented. For example, you may break company geographies or markets into EMEA (Europe, Middle East, and Africa), then by country. You may have account hierarchies represented as group accounts, then regional accounts, followed by local office accounts.

Now that we know what MDM is from a theoretical standpoint, we can turn to the considerations for implementing MDM.

Implementing MDM

As part of the fundamental design of an MDM strategy, consideration should be given to the system landscape, budget, and technical capabilities within an organization for implementing MDM. Several models for implementation exist and can be broadly bucketed into the following categories:

- Source of record
- Central registry
- Consolidated golden record
- Coexistence of the golden record

These different implementation methods are explained here.

Source of record

A single system can be identified as the *source of record* or definitive source of information. All data operations are performed in that one system or application. This implementation model is extremely simple, and therefore doesn't lend itself well to organizations of siloed departments or where data federation is necessary. Take my experience of the car dealership. I'm represented twice in the IT enterprise, as a prospect in one system and a qualified (and converted) sales lead in another. This, therefore, is a case of two sources of record (known as data silos) existing in the IT enterprise in the car dealership. This scenario only lends itself to the most simple of IT enterprises, where everything is managed from one application. It may be the case that Salesforce is used for sales and service, with simple integration to a finance system for the issuance and processing of invoices. Salesforce is the system of record, as the finance system doesn't have any operations performed in it directly; it effectively acts on the instructions of Salesforce.

Central registry

A central registry links data from multiple systems together through the use of IDs and matched records (which can be cleansed and de-duplicated when identified). Master data changes are still made in the respective source system, with a *single source of truth* being created on demand by pulling together data from source systems in real time when needed. When it is difficult to determine an authoritative data source in an organization, this method may be suitable. There is a cost consideration as a system to be used as the central registry may not be available prior to implementing the MDM strategy, and additionally, there are processes associated with the population and maintenance of the registry over time.

Consolidated golden record

Master data, as identified from multiple sources, is combined to form a *golden record*, or single source of truth. Any updates to the golden record are applied to the original sources, typically using middleware. There is a cost consideration to this approach in the implementation of the middleware processes to facilitate data updates to the source systems. This is probably the most common implementation scenario when implementing Salesforce, as it typically is introduced to the IT enterprise to be the definitive source of truth. In order to get there, however, data must be taken from source systems. In short, if there is one system identified as a single view of a customer in an organization, and a number of downstream systems require updating when customer information is updated in Salesforce, this approach is most suitable.

Coexistence of the golden record

Similar to the consolidated golden record implementation method briefly explained previously, MDM changes can happen in both the golden record system and any source system for master data. While this approach can take longer to implement, data can be mastered in the *golden record* system or any of the master data source systems. As data is synchronized, the quality in any given system is consistent. Access to quality data is therefore improved, as users in a given company department may only use one system and not necessarily the *golden record* system. The same cost considerations for the implementation of processes using a middleware tool would apply here. This scenario is perhaps useful in scenarios where an organization may have specialist or legacy applications used by certain functions. Take an organization with a specialist system that is used for a critical function and is actively used by a select group of users as their only system given the nature of their job, yet they need to see the golden record of the customer. This scenario would therefore apply because the system may have updates applied to it that need to make their way back up to Salesforce. This *parallel* or coexistence of the golden record may be necessary for the scenarios where certain applications need to have the same quality golden record information as Salesforce.

Which implementation method is best?

Each implementation method has its own merits and may be suitable depending on a number of factors. As architects, it is our job to advise according to the goals and strategic initiatives of the organization, giving consideration to maintainability.

What has any of this got to do with Salesforce?

Now we know what MDM is, and the theory behind how to implement it, let's turn our attention to MDM and Salesforce. Typically, Salesforce is implemented to bring together data from a company's enterprise in order to break down information silos and provide a consistent view of the data across various business units or departments. Salesforce is therefore a de facto source of truth and immediately becomes the data master when implemented in such scenarios. Our single source of truth would therefore exist in Salesforce.

Salesforce almost always needs to communicate data changes with one or more systems. Therefore, implementing a middleware system is typically used to facilitate the communication and data field mapping between connected systems that constitute our golden record in Salesforce. As part of the Salesforce system design, the produced data dictionary for the objects and fields created in Salesforce can be passed to the middleware team in order to facilitate the data mapping in order to broker data updates between Salesforce and connected systems.

The initial data migration exercise to Salesforce should be used as the point in which the single source of truth for a given record is constructed from the source systems, cleansed, de-duplicated, and enriched as required or appropriate prior to loading into Salesforce and then turning on the integration for changes to only be enacted in connected source systems after the go-live date.

Now we know what MDM is, let's explore the concept of the *single source of truth* in more detail.

The golden record

As we now know, the **golden record**, or **single source of truth**, is essentially a data record where the definitive source of information is stored in order to orchestrate business operations. Users should be able to view a golden record to see the correct version of a piece of information. While the definitive source of information for users may well be the golden record, integration of associated systems may be responsible for the updates to that data, or pushing golden record data updates to those associated systems, as explained in the previous section.

Golden records may not necessarily contain every piece of information held across all systems in the enterprise but may instead contain the identifiers necessary for the retrieval of that information. As Salesforce architects, it is our job to determine where the line is between which information should be held inside and outside of Salesforce, depending on whether Salesforce is where the golden record resides. Some information should be inside Salesforce, where it makes sense to master it in there; other information, that needs to be surfaced in Salesforce but not necessarily to live on the Salesforce platform, should be pulled in as necessary upon viewing.

What data should reside in the golden record?

When designing the golden record, think about the users, what data they need access to, and when. Process-critical data should be brought into the Salesforce platform, but data that won't be frequently accessed or reported on can be shown on-demand from an external system when required.

For example, a customer record for a bank may exist as a Person Account in Salesforce, and associated with it will be the actual bank account records in a separate system. Depending on the system landscape and how those other systems are interacted with, the identifiers for those separate bank account records may be located in one of the following:

- Salesforce (either against the Person Account record, or a record associated with it)
- A middleware system, such as MuleSoft
- A separate system to be interrogated by the middleware, or Salesforce if no middleware exists

When determining where the golden record will reside as part of an MDM strategy, consider the following:

- What information needs to be represented on the golden record?
- What information needs to be physically located on the golden record, and what information can be referenced for on-demand retrieval?
- Where do all the golden record data sources reside?
- Are new integrations required?
- Do existing integrations need to be updated or capture additional attributes?
- What is the right data source for each field for the golden record?
- What rules need to be put in place for data updates to or from the golden record?

Remember the diagram in *Figure 3.1* from the *Introducing MDM* section? We're going to use that conceptual overview of a golden record as our requirement to be explored using several implementation techniques that follow. Look at that diagram in *Figure 3.1* again before moving on.

In our conceptual scenario, we want data from these three different systems to be brought together to form a golden record of our customers. Taking the golden record residency examples introduced at the start of this section, let's look at how those differences would be represented.

Salesforce holding the golden record associations

In scenarios where Salesforce is to be considered as the data master for customer information, connected system identifiers can be represented as either custom fields on a particular record, or as a custom object associated with the record.

For example, a contact record in Salesforce is the golden record for data relating to a person across a company's enterprise. In order to ensure associated records are correctly updated when data in Salesforce is updated (such as HR system data that shouldn't reside on Salesforce), a middleware platform (such as MuleSoft) will need to interrogate Salesforce to determine the associated systems and record identifiers in those systems that require updating when the contact record is updated. This essentially adds a round-trip into data update or retrieval operations, as IDs in Salesforce need to be queried to know which associated system records to affect.

The following diagram shows an example of how this may be sequenced when Salesforce holds the record associations:

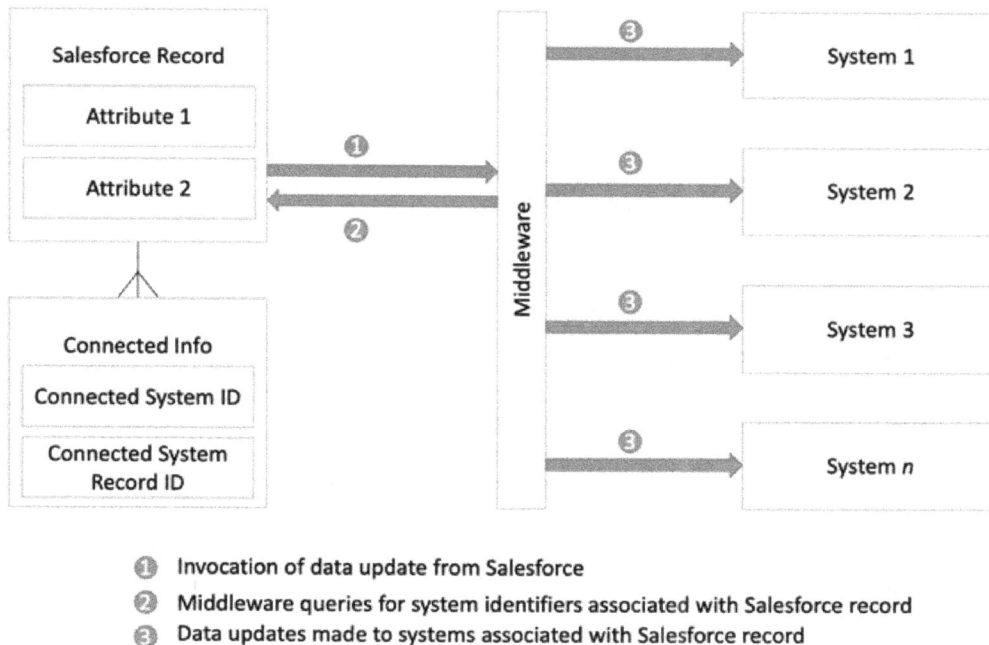

① Invocation of data update from Salesforce
② Middleware queries for system identifiers associated with Salesforce record
③ Data updates made to systems associated with Salesforce record

Figure 3.2 – Salesforce holding the golden record associations

In the next section, we'll take a look at the representation of a golden record when middleware holds the record associations.

Middleware holding the golden record associations

Taking our example from the previous section, if the middleware (such as MuleSoft) holds golden record associations, we can essentially have Salesforce only care about itself in terms of record integrity, with the onus being passed to the middleware to ensure that data operations to or from associated systems are correct. This does reduce the initial querying of Salesforce to determine those associated system IDs, but an additional process needs to be put in place to ensure that the middleware is updated appropriately if an associated system is added to, or removed from, the IT enterprise.

The following diagram shows an example of how this may be sequenced when middleware holds the record associations:

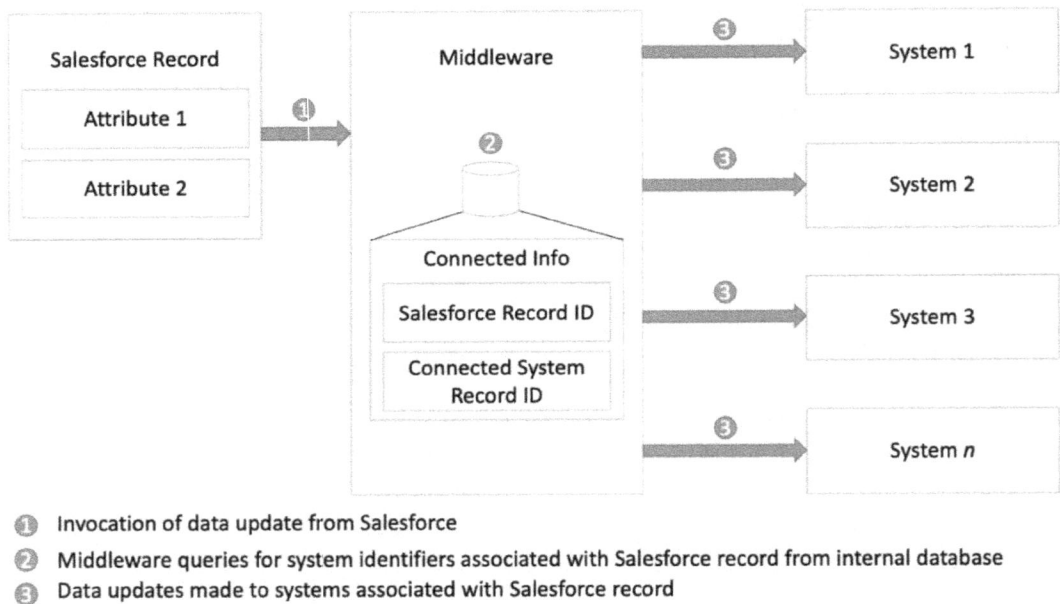

① Invocation of data update from Salesforce

② Middleware queries for system identifiers associated with Salesforce record from internal database

③ Data updates made to systems associated with Salesforce record

Figure 3.3 – Middleware holding the golden record associations

Next, let's look at the representation of a golden record when a separate system or external registry holds the record associations.

A separate system holding the golden record associations

Requiring a callout to another separate registry system or similar (typically orchestrated through the use of middleware, such as MuleSoft), the golden record doesn't necessarily know what records constitute it, and therefore, a registry of identifiers to piece together record information is used to then orchestrate the callouts to other separate systems. This action could be initiated by Salesforce calling the middleware to piece together a golden record using the Salesforce record ID, which is then referenced in the registry system to orchestrate a number of system callouts and process the returned data back to the user. Alternatively, middleware, or a batch-processing system, could orchestrate data updates into the golden record on a scheduled basis.

The following diagram shows an example of how data updates may be sequenced when a separate system holds the record associations:

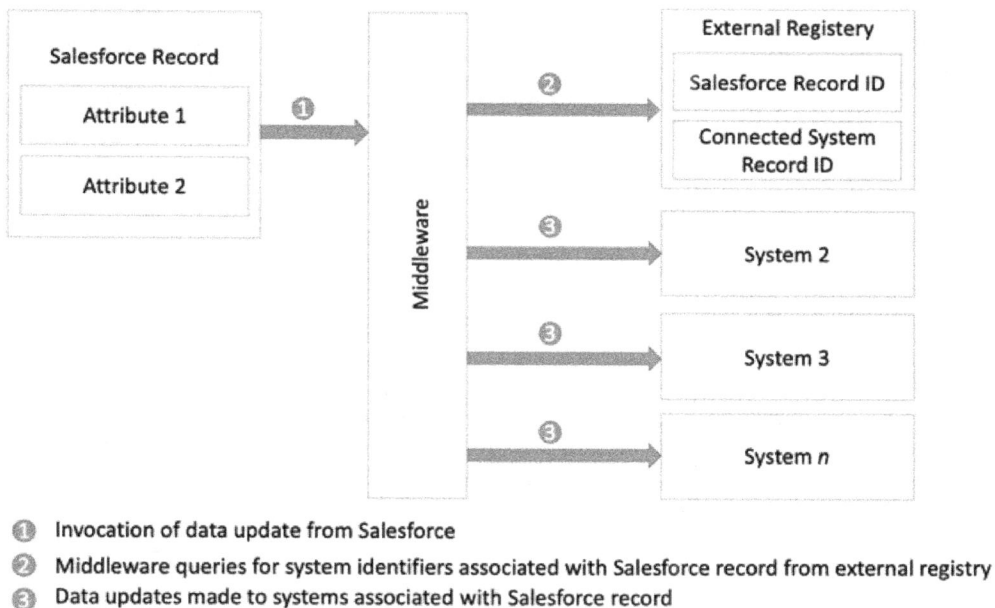

1. Invocation of data update from Salesforce
2. Middleware queries for system identifiers associated with Salesforce record from external registry
3. Data updates made to systems associated with Salesforce record

Figure 3.4 – Querying an external registry for the system identifiers associated with the Salesforce record

Of course, sometimes you may wish to use data that is kept outside of Salesforce.

Using Salesforce Connect to pull in data in real time for read-only purposes

In scenarios where data on a Salesforce record doesn't necessarily need to reside within Salesforce (pulled on-demand from one or more systems or data sources), Salesforce Connect can be used to effectively present data to a user as if it resides within Salesforce (having the same user interface and a degree of interactivity). Salesforce Connect uses the principle of **adapters** to bring in data from an external source. For example, there are adapters for OData 2.0, OData 4.0, and Cross-Org (Salesforce to Salesforce) available out of the box, and there is a framework for writing a custom adapter available in Apex.

If a middleware solution (such as MuleSoft) is not available (or indeed not desirable), then point-to-point integrations to external systems for the purpose of data access may be necessary, and that's a perfect use case for Salesforce Connect.

When using Salesforce Connect, external objects (as you'll remember from *Chapter 2, Data Modeling and Database Design*) are mapped to data tables in external systems. This data can be interrogated and used by users when performing operations in Salesforce such as search, associating data in external systems with data held within Salesforce (using either an external or indirect lookup relationship), or viewing a record feed.

By default, external data sources are read-only in Salesforce, but it is possible to make them writable. For example, imagine there was order data being viewed from SAP, associated with a custom account held in Salesforce. It is possible to enable the external data source as a writable external object, so that new orders could be created from Salesforce, writing back to SAP, and creating the order there.

When setting up Salesforce Connect, an authentication mechanism may be required so that Salesforce can communicate securely with the other system. This may take the form of a username/password of the user Salesforce will use to perform queries in the external system, or it may be a more sophisticated setup, such as using **Open Authentication** (**OAuth**) with an external authentication service, such as Microsoft Azure Active Directory.

External data retrieval using the OData 2.0 or OData 4.0 adapters

OData is a protocol built upon **Representational State Transfer** (**REST**). As defined at `https://www.odata.org`, OData is described as *an open protocol to allow the creation and consumption of queryable and interoperable REST-ful APIs in a simple and standard way.*

If an external data source can be exposed as an OData RESTful web service, then the OData 2.0 or OData 4.0 Salesforce Connect adapter can be used to allow for its display in the Salesforce UI.

External data retrieval using the Cross-Org adapter

It is possible to pull in data from another Salesforce instance using the Cross-Org adapter for Salesforce Connect. This uses the Lightning Platform REST API to access data stored in another Salesforce instance (also referred to as an *org* or *organization*), although the implementation is hidden from the Salesforce administrator setting up the Salesforce Connect Cross-Org adapter. It's therefore possible to pull data held in one Salesforce instance to another.

If, for instance, your company acquired another company that also used Salesforce, yet it was decided that the acquired company would continue to have a degree of independence and keep their separate Salesforce system, then the opportunity data could be pulled into your Salesforce instance so that a more complete set of sales data could be reported on.

External data retrieval using a custom adapter

In scenarios where an existing adapter isn't suitable, a custom adapter can be created in Apex, using the Apex Connector Framework. The knowledge of coding such an adapter isn't in the scope of the exam or this book, but documentation can be found here: `https://developer.salesforce.com/docs/atlas.en-us.234.0.apexcode.meta/apexcode/apex_connector_top.htm`.

A custom adapter is generally required when an external data source isn't OData 2.0 or OData 4.0 compatible, and the external data source also isn't another Salesforce instance. In these scenarios, a custom adapter is required for communication with the external data source so that its data can be presented, searched, and queried right within the Salesforce UI.

With an understanding of the various methods on how to construct the golden record data through relationships to data held in other systems (the system identifiers), let's explore how we can consolidate data attributes from those systems.

Consolidating data attributes from multiple sources

When designing an MDM strategy, we need to determine what data attributes constitute the golden record, along with the source of the data attributes. Where multiple sources may contain the same attribute, it may be necessary to implement a cleansing and de-duplication process in order to ensure that the same data attribute values are preserved throughout the enterprise. Depending on the MDM implementation method being used, it may be necessary to allow any source system to facilitate the update of a data attribute to the golden record, which then invokes a process to push that update down to all source systems for that data attribute. Therefore, when implementing the golden record for the first time, data quality and classification are crucial, and so time should be given to a data cleansing, matching, and de-duplication strategy as part of the initial golden record population. It may then be wise to consider *locking down* the source systems for new record creation by users, so that duplicate records can be caught in the system of entry, with permissions to create new records in source systems reserved almost exclusively for an integration or process user. This way, users are entering data in a single place, and are told immediately if there are data duplication issues, and source systems remain in the cleanest state possible.

Invariably, data issues may occur over time, and reporting and analytics will help deduce the cause of these. User behavior can be influenced by training and modification of the data entry system (through the use of validation and approval processes), and automated processes can be tweaked with changes to the rule-base from which they are built to operate.

With an understanding of data attribute consolidation across the multiple systems that constitute under our belts, let's now look at how to preserve traceability and context when working with our data from the golden record.

Preserving traceability and business rule context

In line with our establishment of a golden record, or single source of truth, it is important that an MDM strategy plays nicely with existing business rules, and changes to data are preserved throughout the organization. For example, the process of creating a bank account in a connected system from a Salesforce Financial Services Cloud instance would be done as a user acting on behalf of Salesforce – this provides some traceability as to what instigated that action. The rules in which records are created or updated in connected systems should still largely hold true (albeit some may need adjusting for the processes introduced by the MDM strategy).

The updating of an address for a customer in a bank may have previously been subject to an approval process in the source system. Moving up this approval process to the system of record (such as Salesforce Financial Services Cloud in our banking example) preserves the context of the business rule, so the approval still takes place. Moving business rules to the appropriate system still preserves their context, facilitating the *who did what when* nature of data management.

There are several facilities offered by Salesforce for preserving traceability and capturing metadata.

Event Monitoring

User events can be captured in Salesforce Event Monitoring, such as login/logout events, web clicks, API calls, Apex executions, and report exports. More information on Salesforce Event Monitoring can be found here: `https://trailhead.salesforce.com/content/learn/modules/event_monitoring`.

Setup Audit Trail

Setup Audit Trail is the log that Salesforce keeps of actions performed in the Setup area of Salesforce, useful in determining what actions have been taken by system administrators and those with certain setup privileges.

Field History Tracking

Field History Tracking allows for the recording and preservation of changes to specific fields on Salesforce objects (configured in Salesforce Setup). This includes the user that made the change, the date/time of the change, the old value, and the new value. By default, you can track the field history for up to 20 fields per object.

Field Audit Trail

Field Audit Trail is a Salesforce feature for defining a policy for the retention of archived field history data. This can be for 10 years from when the data was archived (as opposed to the 18 months Salesforce allows without Field Audit Trail enabled). Field History Tracking is a pre-requisite for Field Audit Trail (as the old and new values are required, for example). When Field Audit Trail is enabled, the limit of the number of fields to be tracked per Salesforce object is increased from 20 to 60. The retention policy is defined using the Salesforce Metadata API. More information can be found here: `https://help.salesforce.com/s/articleView?id=sf.field_audit_trail.htm&type=5`.

Custom metadata types and custom settings

Custom metadata and custom settings facilitate the creation and storage of metadata specific to an organization's Salesforce implementation. This may include bespoke configuration information, and the storage of values for business logic, for example.

Let's now summarize what we've covered in this chapter.

Summary

In this chapter, we covered a lot of the theory behind MDM, having a single source of truth for data records, and some methods for its implementation, along with considerations for doing so. While Salesforce is often implemented to act as the de facto source of truth, it is important to understand *why* that often drives these decisions and the benefits it gives, hence spending time on the theory of MDM. With that theory understood, it should become clear how Salesforce fits into an organization's MDM strategy.

We've looked at why data quality is important in the context of MDM, and why it is important to preserve data attributes across the systems in the enterprise that constitutes the single source of truth, or golden record.

We turned our attention to MDM implementation in Salesforce, touching on the use of middleware, and highlighting the data migration exercise that will invariably accompany a Salesforce go-live.

We have covered what a golden record is and looked at the various things to consider when determining where a golden record's data fields reside, and what data fields from source systems constitute the golden record. The architecture related to associating different systems in the IT enterprise with the golden record can have an impact on how data operations work and business rules run, so we covered the theory behind that also. We also then looked at how to preserve data quality and ensure traceability and business rule context for operations and procedures, highlighting that the system in which a process runs may change due to the introduction of a new data master in the IT estate.

In *Chapter 4*, *Salesforce Data Management*, we'll dive into how Salesforce license types affect the data model and the sharing options available to work with. We'll also look at how to govern the data on the platform, as it is crucial to designing scalable, performant solutions that combine data from one or more Salesforce instances.

Practice questions

1. A *single source of truth* is otherwise known as what?

2. What is the *source of record* MDM implementation method?

3. What's the difference between a consolidated golden record and the coexistence of the golden record when implementing MDM?

4. In a simple point-to-point integration between Salesforce and one other system, where should the ID of the record in the other system (as linked to the Salesforce record) live?

5. If no external registry is available and external system IDs are not to be stored in Salesforce, yet Salesforce is connected through a middleware to other systems, where is the ideal place to store record ID associations?

Answers

1. A golden record.

2. A single system being used by everyone for access to the same single set of information.

3. A consolidated golden record is the initiator of change in connected systems. The coexistence of the golden record means any connected system may initiate a data update (bi-directional data sync).

4. In Salesforce.

5. In the middleware.

Further reading

- *Beginners Guide to MDM*: https://www.dataqualitypro.com/blog/beginners-guide-to-mdm-master-data-management

- *What is Master Data Management (MDM)?*: https://www.mulesoft.com/resources/esb/what-is-master-data-management-mdm

- *Salesforce Connect*: https://developer.salesforce.com/docs/atlas.en-us.234.0.apexcode.meta/apexcode/platform_connect_about.htm

4

Salesforce Data Management

With a grasp of **Master Data Management** (**MDM**) concepts under our belt, we can now look at Salesforce Data Management. In this chapter, we'll look at how the Salesforce data model and Salesforce licensing work together. The license types chosen for a solution have an impact on the objects available. This can extend to record sharing facilities available in the case of Experience Cloud license types.

We'll look at what data persistence looks like on the Salesforce Platform and how that works when governing solutions on the Salesforce Platform.

Next, we'll expand on our *golden record* theory from *Chapter 3*, *Master Data Management*, to explain what a **Single Customer View** (**SCV**) looks like on the Salesforce Platform, and how data from multiple Salesforce clouds and multiple Salesforce instances can be pieced together.

Therefore, in this chapter, we'll cover the following topics:

- Analyzing Salesforce license types and access to objects
- Persisting data
- Representing a single view of the customer on the Salesforce Platform
- Pulling together data from multiple Salesforce instances

Analyzing Salesforce license types and access to objects

In this section, we're going to cover how the different Salesforce licensing options affect the objects and standard functionality available to users. Given the vast array of functionality available in Salesforce products, it is important to ascertain what the required objects and functionality will be (from both an internal and external access perspective) so that the correct licenses can be purchased. As expected, certain licenses are more expensive than others—for example, Service Cloud licenses are more expensive than Sales Cloud. In the case of Experience Cloud, this type of license not only affects the objects available for users but can affect sharing rules and role hierarchy too. We'll get to those implications further along in this section.

Because of the cruciality of getting licensing correct, an important artifact produced during the **Certified Technical Architect** (**CTA**) review board is *Actors and Licenses*. This is essentially a listing of different user types and the licenses those different user types (also known as personas) need to interact correctly with the proposed solution. As a Salesforce architect, you should therefore consider this exercise as a pillar to your solution. If it is wrong, it can have profound impacts on the way users work.

> **Important note**
>
> **Experience Cloud = Community Cloud:** Salesforce has rebranded Community Cloud to become Experience Cloud. This is intentional and represents a shift from Communities being a *lens* into your Salesforce data for external users. The technology that powers Community Cloud/Experience Cloud has evolved so much that entire digital experiences and commerce storefronts can be powered from it, hence the rebranding. For the avoidance of doubt, *Community Cloud*, *Communities*, and *Experience Cloud* are one and the same. The Salesforce documentation isn't fully updated at the time of writing, so be mindful that you may still see references to *Community Cloud* and *Communities* from time to time.

Let's now delve deeper into the different types of licensing on the Salesforce Platform.

Standard platform licensing

The core Salesforce Platform consists of several products, as follows:

- **Lightning Platform**
- **Sales Cloud**
- **Service Cloud**
- **Experience Cloud**

These products are all built around the core application framework and relational database that underpins the Salesforce Platform. In fact, Sales Cloud, Service Cloud, and Experience Cloud can all be thought of as enhancements to the core Lightning Platform. For example, Sales Cloud has (among others) the **Account**, **Contact**, **Opportunity**, and **Lead** objects. These are predefined and interrelated objects that allow for a sales process to be quickly and easily set up and facilitated. They can also be thought of as a predefined set of objects and associated functionality that build upon the foundations of the Lightning Platform—namely, a relational database and application tier.

Service Cloud builds upon the functionality available in Sales Cloud (although Service Cloud and Sales Cloud are designed to address different use cases). Service Cloud attracts a different cost model than Sales Cloud, given the difference in exposed functionality to users, and subsequently is classed as a different product license.

Experience Cloud can be thought of as a *lens* into your Salesforce data, and several Experience Cloud license types are available. These are explained in the following section. Experience Cloud only exposes access to objects on the core platform, so that includes Sales Cloud objects, Service Cloud objects (if licensed), and Custom objects.

When designing solutions that require data to reside on the Salesforce Platform, consider the Standard platform licenses that will be required for your internal users. Generally, if a standard object offered by Sales or Service Cloud is designed to hold a specific type of data or is used to perform a certain function, then it is advisable to take advantage of it for the functionality built around it.

For example, use Sales Cloud when you require prospecting functionality because this is offered by the out-of-the-box **Lead** object. There are also features such as **Lead Assignment Rules** and conversion to create an **Account, Contact**, and **Opportunity** record. It would be ineffective to reinvent the wheel to create these objects yourself. Similarly, when you have requirements for **Service-Level Agreement (SLA)** functionality for your customers cases, Service Cloud offers the **Entitlement** and **Milestone** objects for this purpose. If you wish to provide access to your customers so that they can raise support queries or have issues with the products you've sold them, Experience Cloud provides the means to do this.

Now that we've covered Standard platform licensing for your internal users, let's look at Experience Cloud licensing for external user access.

Experience Cloud licensing

Experience Cloud is the way external users (those not internal to your company) access Salesforce. In this section, we're going to look at the license types available for your external users.

Experience Cloud licensing works differently from Standard platform licensing in that each license type affects access to objects and record sharing differently. There are different types of Experience Cloud licenses to use when designing solutions—namely, these ones:

- **External Apps**. Used for custom digital experiences, including customer engagement and brand loyalty. Limited access to Salesforce objects. This license type can be used with Person Accounts.

- **Customer Community**. Used for **Business-to-Consumer (B2C)** experiences with large numbers of users that need access to the **Case** object or Salesforce Knowledge. This license type can be used with Person Accounts.

- **Customer Community Plus**. Used for B2C experiences where users need access to reports and dashboards and need advanced sharing. This license type can be used with Person Accounts.

- **Partner Community**. **Business-to-business (B2B)** experiences where users need access to **Partner Relationship Management (PRM)** objects such as **Lead** and **Opportunity**. This license type cannot be used with Person Accounts.

- **Channel Account**. B2B sites that calculate their usage based on the number of partners instead of the number of individual users.

At the time of writing, the exam covered the Customer Community, Customer Community Plus, and Partner Community license types. Therefore, those license types will be the focus of the next section.

Experience Cloud licensing and sharing

The license type used with Experience Cloud can have an impact on sharing and the way record access works for users. In a nutshell, the *Customer Community* license type doesn't support roles, and sharing sets are used instead of sharing rules. Sharing sets are used to grant record access to any record associated with an account or contact that matches the users account or contact record. Sharing sets can also grant record access using access mapping. Access mappings work by using indirect lookups from the user or target record to an account or contact record. An example of this (as explained at `https://help.salesforce.com/s/articleView?id=sf.networks_setting_light_users.htm&type=5`) is granting a Customer Community license user access to all cases related to an account, that is also the account related to the contact that is associated with the users contact record.

In addition to sharing sets, the Customer Community Plus and Partner Community license types allow for the use of owner-based or criteria-based sharing rules in order to share records with Experience Cloud users. Also, Experience Cloud users with either of these license types support external roles (three levels maximum). Think of this as a *mini role hierarchy*. These roles can then be subordinate roles of an internal role in the role hierarchy. Record access can therefore be opened up to external users through the external roles, and these in turn can be opened up to internal users.

The other main difference between the Customer Community Plus and Partner Community license types is the object access and also how reports and dashboards can be interacted with.

This is explained in the following diagram:

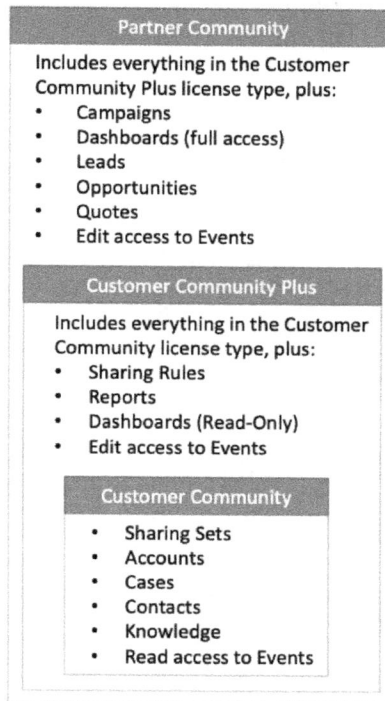

Figure 4.1 – Experience Cloud License type differences

Important note

When to use the different Experience Cloud license types: In short, there is a relatively simple way to determine which license type to use for Experience Cloud sites.

Generally, start with the Customer Community license type, and then adapt this according to your requirements, as follows:

If advanced sharing (beyond sharing sets) read-only access to reports and dashboards is required, move to Customer Community Plus licenses.

If **Lead** or **Opportunity** object access is required, or the ability to create reports and dashboards is required, choose Partner Community.

Of course, there are additional nuances (explained at `https://help.salesforce.com/s/articleView?language=en_US&type=5&id=sf.users_license_types_communities.htm`), but this should be a good way to get started when learning for the exam.

Licensing for Salesforce products not on the core platform

The *non-core* products in the Salesforce suite (such as Commerce Cloud and Marketing Cloud) are licensed differently. Their licensing is not in the scope of the exam, and therefore won't be covered in this book.

Full products versus Salesforce-managed packages

Salesforce products on the *core* platform—such as Sales Cloud, Service Cloud, and Experience Cloud—are licensed on a per-user, per-month basis. Each license opens up more functionality and access to different entities on the Salesforce *core* platform.

Certain products in the Salesforce suite are licensed separately and interact with the core platform through the use of connectors, as is the case with Marketing Cloud, Pardot, or Commerce Cloud. The exam syllabus covers core platform usage, and therefore revision should concentrate on the data entities and functionality afforded by the *core* platform products only.

Salesforce-managed packages that are built for the core platform, including (but not limited to) Financial Services Cloud, Manufacturing Cloud, and Health Cloud, are essentially licensed managed packages that install additional entities, apps, and other functionality (such as flows) onto the *core* platform.

Let's now look at package licensing, which also applies to managed and AppExchange packages.

AppExchange and package licensing

Depending on the licensing requirements of an AppExchange, managed, or unmanaged package, permission set licenses are the typical method of licensing paid packages. As you'll already know, when installing a package from AppExchange (or directly from Salesforce, in the case of an offering such as Financial Services Cloud), users will need to be given the correct permission set licenses in order to gain access to any objects or other functionality specific to that package. When designing solutions that require access to data entities and other functionality exposed by a package, one or more permission set licenses associated with that managed package will need to be given to the users that require access to that functionality.

As you now know, there are myriad licensing options available to us as Salesforce architects when it comes to producing robust, scalable solutions on the platform to deliver the right functionality to the right users. This extends to external users of the system interacting in a controlled manner to the data held within your Salesforce **Organization** (**org**). We can now turn to persisting data in a consistent manner on the Salesforce Platform.

Persisting data

Ensuring data is persisted in a consistent manner is paramount to the long-term success of a Salesforce implementation. Therefore, it is important to understand the causes of data quality issues and the techniques available to improve data quality but ideally prevent it from happening in the first place as much as possible.

Data quality issues can arise due to the age of the data, how complete and accurate the data is, whether duplicate data exists, and the consistency in the way data is used. Data quality issues can cause users to be presented with incomplete or incorrect information, causing them to spend more time gathering that information (which may require them to spend time in multiple systems or with multiple data sources). Worse still, customers may be subjected to poor customer service caused by account managers or service agents having incomplete or incorrect information. Lastly, frustrated users may be deterred from utilizing a **System Of Record** (**SOR**) and move to offline processes instead, meaning reduced or degrading system adoption. Luckily, Salesforce has several features that can be utilized in order to address these potential issues.

Starting with duplication of data, Salesforce has the ability to specify matching and duplicate rules in order to identify and merge records of a particular type, such as duplicate **leads** (such as an example of multiple **Web2Lead** captures from the same person yet existing as multiple lead records). The out-of-the-box matching and duplicate rules are built around sensible defaults, such as leads or **contacts** sharing an email address being potential duplicates. Users are presented with a notification on the Salesforce **User Interface** (**UI**) from which they can take remedial action such as discarding the record they are on (or the potential duplicate) or merging record information together.

When it comes to the inputting of data, validation rules can be utilized to ensure that formulaic conditions are met in order to prevent record creation or updates, making users adhere to a specific format when entering correct data. For example, if a lead is being progressed beyond a certain stage, validation rules can be used to ensure that a certain industry field is selected or a valid phone number has been entered (down to the format). Secondly, picklists (predefined lists of values) can be used to limit the values a user can enter against a record. When picklists are used over free-text values, users are restricted (in a good way) to selecting values from managed lists. Reporting and searching are made quicker and easier as a result. There is also the concept of dependent picklists, whereby the values in one picklist are filtered or restricted based on another. This again can be used to direct users to select from specific value sets in order to drive data quality. Those value sets can be shared across multiple picklists to ensure consistency in the values chosen (as the underlying values are shared and managed centrally).

Salesforce has declarative automation in the form of workflow rules and flows. Workflow rules can be thought of as a container for a set of instructions for automating actions based on defined criteria (which can be time-bound), such as sending emails or updating fields. These instructions can be thought of as taking an *if this*, *do that* format.

Flows can be used to perform certain record operations in order to drive consistent behavior with regard to data. For example, when an account is created, a flow can run to ultimately trigger an outbound call to a credit agency to pull in credit rating information about the company to whom the account record pertains.

Next up in the category of automation is **approval processes**. This feature of the Salesforce Platform facilitates record changes being submitted for approval by a users manager, a named user, or a group of approvers. Approvals can be configured (so that only one of a group or a whole group needs to approve the request) and provide a virtual paper trail of changes that take place. For example, a salesperson attempting to apply a discount on a quote above a certain threshold may require approval from the Sales Director. Salesforce's approval process mechanism is a perfect fit for this type of behavior.

Lastly, data cleansing may also be required. Salesforce doesn't contain native data-cleansing capabilities, but AppExchange packages and external tools exist that facilitate either the real-time cleansing, enrichment, and deduplication of data either in situ on the platform (in the case of an AppExchange package) or off-platform, where an export/import of data is required (in the case of a fully-fledged offline tool).

While data-cleansing capabilities per se aren't native to the platform, there are a few field types and configuration options that can be exploited to make life a little easier when it comes to categorizing, cleansing, and deduplicating data. These typically are picklists, checkboxes, and lookup filters.

In short, **picklists** are used to restrict input to one of a set of predefined values (which can be global value sets for org-wide uniformity in options). **Checkboxes** are for true/false value selection, and **lookup filters** can ensure that the range of values to be selected is reduced to those that are determined applicable based on filtering criteria.

When developing a data management strategy, it may be wise to consider what kinds of conventions to instill (and apply reporting and validation on if possible). For example, always abbreviate the suffix *Limited* to *Ltd* for **United Kingdom** (**UK**) companies. While this is an overly simplistic example, the principle is that consistency in which data is created, updated, and viewed ensures that confusion doesn't result when working with data and that data can be kept in a consistent state.

This then leads us nicely on to how data quality is monitored. A plan should be designed from the outset to determine how data is identified and the strategy of how it will be dealt with, down to the assignee and owner of such activities. For example, the sales team is required to ensure that all incomplete lead records are reviewed and updated to conform to data completeness or formatting requirements by the business at the end of every month. That way, the team knows that it starts each month with a better dataset than what it finished the previous month with.

Now that we've covered how data can be persisted in a consistent manner on the Salesforce Platform, we can now look at how Salesforce addresses the concept of a *single view of a customer* on its platform.

Representing a single view of the customer on the Salesforce Platform

A single view of the customer (sometimes called an SCV, but meaning exactly the same thing), represents a unified 360° view of each customer. As explained in *Chapter 3, Master Data Management*, an integration layer can be used to produce a golden record whereby it consolidates data from multiple sources (using an **Identifier (ID)** registry or IDs in Salesforce against a record). Additionally, data cleansing, deduplication, and enrichment can be included in the process of bringing customer data together.

As you may or may not know, not all Salesforce clouds are on the same underlying infrastructure, and therefore Salesforce produces various connectors and accelerators to overcome this. Examples include the following:

- The Marketing Cloud connector—connects Marketing Cloud and Sales Cloud
- The Pardot connector—connects Pardot and Sales Cloud
- MuleSoft accelerators and connectors for Commerce Cloud (B2B and B2C)

Salesforce brings various technologies and connectors together to form an offering called Customer 360. For example, a global profile can be built by consolidating data from multiple Salesforce clouds using connectors and MuleSoft as an integration platform. For example, a customer's B2C Commerce Cloud profile, Service Cloud profile, Experience Cloud profile, Marketing Cloud profile, and external system data can all be consolidated under a single global profile ID. An example of this is the *Salesforce Architecture for Retail*, found at `https://help.salesforce.com/s/articleView?id=sf.icx_b2c_solution_architecture_overview.htm&type=5`.

Let's now take a look at the different elements of the Customer 360 platform.

Elements of the Customer 360 platform

There are several areas of the Customer 360 platform that are useful for the *Data Architecture* exam. These are explained next.

Salesforce Customer 360 Data Manager

Customer 360 Data Manager is a Salesforce solution for connecting customer-centric data across Salesforce products, Salesforce instances, Commerce Cloud B2C instances, and other data sources. Data is surfaced through one view, to provide a single view of the customer.

Salesforce then layers on Einstein dashboards that provide data-validation capabilities. Source record data that has been matched to form a global profile can be managed from a single location, including editing and deleting source data.

There is also the concept of a **Cloud Information Model** (**CIM**) that maps data to a common schema. This provides a single representation of that data in connected data sources.

Salesforce technologies such as Marketing Cloud, MuleSoft, and Commerce Cloud form part of a Data Manager solution, as data points exposed in these technologies form the data points of the customer representation.

These concepts should be familiar given the concepts and theory we covered in *Chapter 3, Master Data Management*.

Next up, let's look at Customer Identity.

Salesforce Customer Identity

Salesforce Customer Identity is a name given to a suite of technologies that allow (from an **Identity and Access Management**, or **IAM**, perspective) customers and partners to access your Salesforce instance and interact with your brand. Salesforce Identity concepts apply here, with the addition of Experience Cloud sites as the means upon which your brand is interacted with. As you may already know, Experience Cloud sites can be set up to use **Open Authentication** (**OAuth**), **Single Sign-On** (**SSO**) (if not through an OAuth provider such as Facebook or Google), and passwordless login. It's also possible to use Customer Identity to embed a login experience into an existing website (such as an e-commerce site at the checkout stage). This provides a touchpoint to customers and allows for the collection of information such as an email address, currency preference, and so on.

This functionality requires External Identity or Community license types.

Lastly, let's investigate the **Customer Data Platform** (**CDP**).

Salesforce CDP

In what can be thought of as an evolution of the traditional **Customer Relationship Management** (**CRM**) system, Salesforce CDP layers on engagement information (from Marketing Cloud) and buying information (from Commerce Cloud), along with integrated data sources using MuleSoft. In a nutshell, it is used to unify and segment data so that experiences for customers that are powered by the Salesforce Platform can be targeted and personalized to them. Customers can be engaged using their preferred channels and have a personalized experience that transcends sales, service, commerce, and marketing because these technologies are all connected, and the single view of the customer is exposed through the Salesforce Platform.

Now that we've explored how we can represent a single view of the customer on the Salesforce Platform, let's now look at how an important part of that process—data from multiple Salesforce instances—can be achieved.

Pulling together data from multiple Salesforce instances

Salesforce data architects must be able to design how to effectively consolidate, process, and leverage data from multiple Salesforce instances. While there are pros and cons of using multiple Salesforce instances within the boundaries of an **Information Technology (IT)** enterprise, there are instances where knowing how to best leverage the data from those multiple instances together across the IT enterprise can unlock value for your users. Salesforce offers several options or solutions in bringing data from several instances of Salesforce. These can include the following:

- Salesforce Connect
- Salesforce to Salesforce
- Bulk API
- Batch Apex

These are explained in the following sections.

Salesforce Connect

As explained in *Chapter 3, Master Data Management,* Salesforce Connect is a method for pulling in data from external data sources, using the OAuth 2.0 protocol, OAuth 4.0 protocol, or a custom Apex adapter for external data access.

Salesforce Connect is useful for surfacing data that isn't mastered in Salesforce yet can form part of the **Single Source Of Truth (SSOT)**. Consider a financial institution that has bank account information in Salesforce. Given the relative frequency in which transactions on a bank account may occur, it may make sense to surface that data on demand rather than store the transactions in Salesforce. This is a perfect use case for Salesforce Connect.

Read more about Salesforce Connect at `https://help.salesforce.com/s/articleView?id=sf.platform_connect_about.htm&type=5`.

Salesforce to Salesforce

Salesforce to Salesforce is a technology that's used to share data across Salesforce instances. Essentially, a connection is made between Salesforce instances, and then data sharing is set up so that users can see shared data and updated information from another Salesforce instance in their own Salesforce instance. Users only have access to shared records as they are mapped to records in their own org, and therefore the original data records in the external Salesforce org aren't directly accessible to users in your org. Custom reports can be created to report on external data. Field subscriptions can also be set up to map fields in an external Salesforce instance to fields in your Salesforce instance.

Salesforce to Salesforce is useful in scenarios such as a company that has different divisions that cannot or do not share business logic. This may be since the company has made a merger or acquisition or has a group structure, such as rolling up sales data from one **Business Unit (BU)** to a parent or group BU. Salesforce to Salesforce can be one-directional or bi-directional in terms of information transfer.

More information on Salesforce to Salesforce can be found at `https://help.salesforce.com/s/articleView?id=sf.business_network_intro.htm&type=5`.

Bulk API

Salesforce Bulk API (version 2.0 at the time of writing) is a **Representational State Transfer (REST)**-based Salesforce-specific **Application Programming Interface (API)** used to asynchronously read, upload, or delete large quantities of data on the Salesforce Platform. A good rule of thumb is that any datasets of 2,000 records or more are suitable candidates for Bulk API operations. As per Salesforce's documentation at `https://developer.salesforce.com/docs/atlas.en-us.api_asynch.meta/api_asynch/asynch_api_intro.htm`, datasets of fewer than 2,000 records should be used with *bulkified* synchronous API calls (adhering to governor limits, using either REST or **Simple Object Access Protocol (SOAP)** protocols with the Salesforce Platform).

Addressing the question of using Bulk API for the bringing together of data from multiple instances, this API is a candidate for cases where large amounts of data are moved from one instance of Salesforce to another. Requests are processed asynchronously, with Salesforce returning a job ID upon accepting the request that can be queried for periodic updates of the status of the job.

Read more on getting started with Bulk API at `https://developer.salesforce.com/docs/atlas.en-us.api_asynch.meta/api_asynch/asynch_api_quickstart.htm`.

Batch Apex

Complex, long-running processes that run on the Salesforce Lightning Platform can utilize a technology called Batch Apex. Essentially, large datasets are queried, broken down into manageable chunks of data, and then processed. It is commonplace to perform whole data-type operations on a nightly basis as Batch Apex, such as processing and archiving all accounts that have had no activity past a certain date. Batch Apex utilizes the `Database.Batchable` interface and the Apex scheduler can be used to facilitate a Batch Apex class being run at certain times (such as hourly or nightly).

Batch Apex lends itself well to scenarios that call for business-logic operations that need to work with lots of data. In the UK, educational institutions and schools are regularly inspected by a regulatory body. Imagine that schools, inspectors, and information such as holidays booked by inspectors and term dates of schools are all held in Salesforce. A nightly Batch Apex job is the perfect candidate to initiate and process the data when scheduling inspections for schools, which could in theory require processing down to the area an inspector is responsible for.

Read about using Batch Apex at `https://developer.salesforce.com/docs/atlas.en-us.apexcode.meta/apexcode/apex_batch_interface.htm`.

> **Important note**
>
> **Batch Apex is an interface**: Batch Apex is exposed as an interface that requires a developer to write an implementation for. Therefore, Apex coding skills are required for Batch Apex operations as they require running queries and processing using bespoke code.

As we delved into in *Chapter 3, Master Data Management*, an SSOT approach can be defined and then used to consolidate data when presenting data to users. This may manifest itself in a *golden record*. One such example for data consolidation whereby data is brought together from multiple data sources and forms a single view of the customer is Salesforce Customer 360 Data Manager, as explained earlier in the *Representing a single view of the customer on the Salesforce Platform* section.

Summary

In this chapter, we covered a range of topics related to data on the Salesforce Platform. We started by looking at licensing and how different types of licenses affect the solutions we build as Salesforce architects. Different license types afford different object/entity access and functionality. For example, the Service Cloud license allows for entitlements and milestones, meaning it facilitates an SLA mechanism. Without this license, users don't have access to the entities for entitlements and milestones.

We also looked at external user access to the Salesforce Platform through the use of Experience Cloud license types. We covered the differences afforded in terms of object access and sharing functionality and looked at the different use cases for each license type for Experience Cloud.

You may have questioned why licensing was important to cover at the start of this chapter, but by now, you'll hopefully appreciate that licensing can have a profound impact on the data access of the solutions we architect.

Next, we looked at data persistence. We revisited the concept of an SCV on the Salesforce Platform, bringing in our knowledge from *Chapter 3, Master Data Management*, and understood how Salesforce addresses the notion of a single customer through its product suite.

We also built upon knowledge acquired in *Chapter 3, Master Data Management*, in bringing together data from multiple Salesforce instances, covering the options available to us to achieve this.

In *Chapter 5, Data Governance*, we'll look at how data on the Salesforce Platform can be safeguarded and governed, including visiting the concepts that underpin compliant solutions.

Practice questions

1. Which Experience Cloud license type is required in B2C scenarios where access to reports is required?

2. Which Experience Cloud license type exposes the **Quote** object?

3. Which Experience Cloud license type is required for access to Knowledge?

4. Which Experience Cloud license type only facilitates record sharing through sharing sets?

5. Which Experience Cloud license type allows for the creation of dashboards?

6. Which Experience Cloud license types allow for sharing rules?

7. Which Experience Cloud license type allows for the creation of reports?

8. Which Experience Cloud license type exposes the **Lead** and **Opportunity** objects?

9. Which technology is used to surface external data in **Open Data Protocol** (**OData**) 2.0 or OData 4.0 format?

10. Which technology is used to process and execute long-running Apex operations across entire datasets on the Salesforce Platform?

11. Which technology is used to read, upload, or delete large datasets on the Salesforce Platform?

12. Which technology is used to surface data in one Salesforce instance to another Salesforce instance?

13. Customer 360 is a Salesforce solution designed to provide what?

14. Marketing Cloud and Salesforce are connected using what?

15. What is the recommended technology to bring together data from external data sources on the Salesforce Platform as part of Customer 360?

Answers

1. Customer Community Plus

2. Partner Community

3. Customer Community

4. Customer Community

5. Partner Community

6. Partner Community and Customer Community Plus

7. Customer Community Plus

8. Partner Community

9. Salesforce Connect

10. Batch Apex

11. Bulk API

12. Salesforce to Salesforce

13. A 360° view of the customer

14. The Marketing Cloud connector for the Salesforce Platform

15. MuleSoft

Further reading

Salesforce Experience Cloud licensing:

`https://help.salesforce.com/s/articleView?id=users_license_types_communities.htm&type=5&language=en_US`

Setting up sharing sets:

`https://help.salesforce.com/s/articleView?id=sf.networks_setting_light_users.htm&type=5`

Salesforce data storage allocations:

`https://help.salesforce.com/s/articleView?id=sf.overview_storage.htm&type=5`

CDP:

`https://www.salesforce.com/ap/solutions/customer-360/`

Salesforce to Salesforce:

`https://help.salesforce.com/s/articleView?id=sf.business_network_intro.htm&type=5`

Introduction to Bulk API 2.0:

`https://developer.salesforce.com/docs/atlas.en-us.api_asynch.meta/api_asynch/asynch_api_intro.htm`

5
Data Governance

Being able to safeguard data on the **Salesforce** platform is a key part of the Salesforce Data Architect's role. This chapter covers the concepts *behind building compliant solutions* and how the Salesforce platform offers features that can help in the technological underpinning of an enterprise **data governance** strategy.

In this chapter, we'll cover the following topics:

- Considerations for implementing a compliant data model
- Enterprise data governance

While data governance may be perceived by some as a somewhat *dry* or boring topic, read on and you'll find out why it is important when designing *scalable*, *secure* solutions on the Salesforce platform. Data governance accounts for **10%** of the certification syllabus, so that's some valuable points that can be attained when taking the exam.

This chapter is the culmination of several topics that are interwoven when it comes to data management, security, and governance. By the end of this chapter, you'll understand the concepts and regulations behind a compliant data model, such as the **General Data Protection Regulation (GDPR)**, **Personally Identifiable Information** (**PII**), and more, and be able to articulate both what enterprise data governance is and how it relates to the Salesforce platform.

Let's begin by understanding the considerations for implementing a compliant data model.

Considerations for implementing a compliant data model

The Salesforce Certified Data Architect credential syllabus talks about implementing a **compliant** data model in the context of data governance. As Salesforce Data Architects, it is on us to ensure that we can recommend an approach for designing a data model that conforms to the **compliance standards** that are set out in regulations such as the following:

- **General Data Protection Regulation (GDPR)**, European Union
- **California Consumer Privacy Act (CCPA)**, United States
- **Personal Information Protection Act (PIPA)**, Japan
- **Lei Geral de Proteção de Dados (LGPD)**, Brazil
- **Personal Information Protection and Electronic Documents Act (PIPEDA)**, Canada

This includes going over the various options available for identifying, classifying, and protecting sensitive data.

We'll look at one such regulation now, namely the GDPR.

What is the GDPR?

The GDPR is the European data protection law that defines how personal information regarding EU individuals needs to be handled.

The GDPR is there to control how information is used by organizations or governments. Individuals have a legal right to know how their information is collected, processed, and stored. They have a right to request the information a company, government, or entity holds about them, and a right to be forgotten. If such a request is made, the organization holding the data is required to delete it, subject to the fair processing of data (which the person must have been made aware of when they freely opted into the company or entity collecting this information). Companies are legally required to collect information fairly, only use it for the specific purposes they need it for, store it securely, and erase it when it's no longer needed. If a company falls foul of the GDPR, the greater figure out of a maximum of €20 million or 4% of their annual global turnover is what the fine could be (this is according to the GDPR itself).

The impacts of complying with the GDPR from a software application perspective include ensuring that the application data model can record consent and privacy preferences. As we already know, Salesforce includes several standard objects to assist with recording preferences and consent (such as the `Individual` object). Additional custom objects can be added for specific requirements.

The Individual object

According to the Salesforce documentation available at `https://developer.salesforce.com/docs/atlas.en-us.api.meta/api/sforce_api_objects_individual.`

htm, the `Individual` object *represents a customer's data privacy and protection preferences. Data privacy records based on the Individual object store your customers preferences. Data privacy records are associated with related leads, contacts, person accounts, and users.*

When the `Individual` object is enabled, it can be exposed to users by adding the `Individual` field to the **Lead**, **Contact**, and **Person Account** page layouts.

> **Important note**
>
> Enabling the `Individual` object: The `Individual` object is available if **Data Protection and Privacy** is enabled in Salesforce. This can be done by selecting **Make data protection details available in records** under **Data Protection and Privacy** in **Salesforce Setup**.

Dealing with GDPR data

Personal data and sensitive personal data are covered by the GDPR and need to be **identified, classified,** and **protected**. How does Salesforce help address data protection? Well, Salesforce includes several features to assist with protecting data from unauthorized access, including the following:

- Classic and platform Shield Encryption
- Data masking
- Field-level security
- Sharing settings
- Event Monitoring
- Session security
- Field history tracking

Let's look at these topics in detail.

Classic encryption

Included with a base license, **classic encryption** provides encryption for data at rest for custom fields (a distinct custom field type) using the 128-bit **Advanced Encryption Standard** (**AES**). Users will need the **View Encrypted Data** profile permission enabled within their profile or via an assigned permission set to read encrypted field values. Classic encryption facilitates masking encrypted fields from users who don't have permission to read the values. They will be presented with a series of asterisks instead. Encrypted fields that use classic encryption cannot be searched or used in automation such as Flow, approval processes, workflow updates, and so on. Therefore, consider classic encryption when encrypting certain data fields that simply store data in a manner that is masked to those who shouldn't see it when viewing the record. If the field requires data to be encrypted at rest, needs to be searchable by users, or readable in automation scenarios such as Flow, consider Shield Encryption instead.

> **Important note**
> Classic encryption is effectively *free*: it is available with any base license, so it doesn't incur an extra fee.

Shield Encryption

Available for an additional fee, **Shield Encryption** provides encryption at rest using 256-bit **AES**. While Shield Encryption doesn't provide data masking of values, it does allow for the encryption of both standard and custom fields, not requiring a special field type. When configuring the fields, encryption parameters can be set. Fields encrypted using Shield Encryption can be searched and used in automation facilities such as **Flow**. Additionally, **Salesforce Shield** allows you to encrypt **Files and Attachments**. You can read more about the differences between classic encryption and Shield Encryption at `https://developer.salesforce.com/docs/atlas.en-us.securityImplGuide.meta/securityImplGuide/security_pe_vs_classic_encryption.htm`.

> **Important note**
> Shield Encryption works on standard objects: classic encryption doesn't extend to standard objects. Therefore, if the need to encrypt data on standard objects arises, you'll need to invest in Shield Encryption.

Field-level security

As covered in *Chapter 2, Data Modeling and Database Design*, **field-level security** is set at the profile and permission set levels, and simply determines if users should be able to see a field, read the values, or edit the values in that field. Field-level security is a de facto way to determine if users should have access to a field, and if they should, whether that access is read-only or read/write.

Sharing settings

As also covered in *Chapter 2, Data Modeling and Database Design*, **sharing settings** such as **Org-Wide Defaults (OWDs)** can be used to state the default level of access users should have to a Salesforce instance's data.

Event Monitoring

As part of the Salesforce Shield suite, **Event Monitoring** enables access to an API-only object called **EventLogFile**, the **LoginEvent** object, **Transaction Security**, and an **Event Monitoring Analytics** app.

With Event Monitoring enabled, it is possible to understand events and act on them, either through the API or by visually looking at event types using a Tableau CRM app. When acting on the events using the API, it is possible to determine usage such as impossible journeys. Impossible journeys are logins or page requests close together in time yet from locations far apart, making access from those locations within a specific time impossible and potentially malicious.

You can read about how to enable Event Monitoring at `https://help.salesforce.com/s/ articleView?id=000339868&type=1`.

Session security settings

It's possible to configure settings related to the security of a users session for when they are accessing Salesforce to safeguard access to your org data held on the platform.

Session settings cover a wide range of topics, including **timeout settings, caching, multi-factor authentication**, and **high-assurance sessions** for accessing sensitive data.

You can read more about session security at `https://help.salesforce.com/s/ articleView?id=sf.admin_sessions.htm&type=5`.

Field history tracking

Lastly (but by no means least), **field history tracking** is a powerful tool for understanding who made what change to a custom subset of object fields. Certain field changes may be required for tracking by your company – for example, who changes the **Stage** picklist on **Opportunities**, recording the old and new value, who made the change, and when. Field-level security allows for 20 fields per object to be tracked *out-of-the-box* with Salesforce, although Shield (which incurs a separate subscription/ charge) can raise this limit to 60 fields per object. Additionally, with Shield, the field history data is archived after 18 months and stored for 10 years.

You can read more about field history tracking at `https://help.salesforce.com/s/ articleView?id=sf.tracking_field_history.htm&type=`.

Now that we've looked at how to implement a compliant data model (looking at the various tools and techniques available on the Salesforce platform to do so), let's turn our attention to enterprise data governance.

Enterprise data governance

As data architects, we must look at the various approaches and considerations when designing an enterprise data governance strategy for implementation within an organization.

To understand this better, the following diagram shows the components of an enterprise data governance strategy:

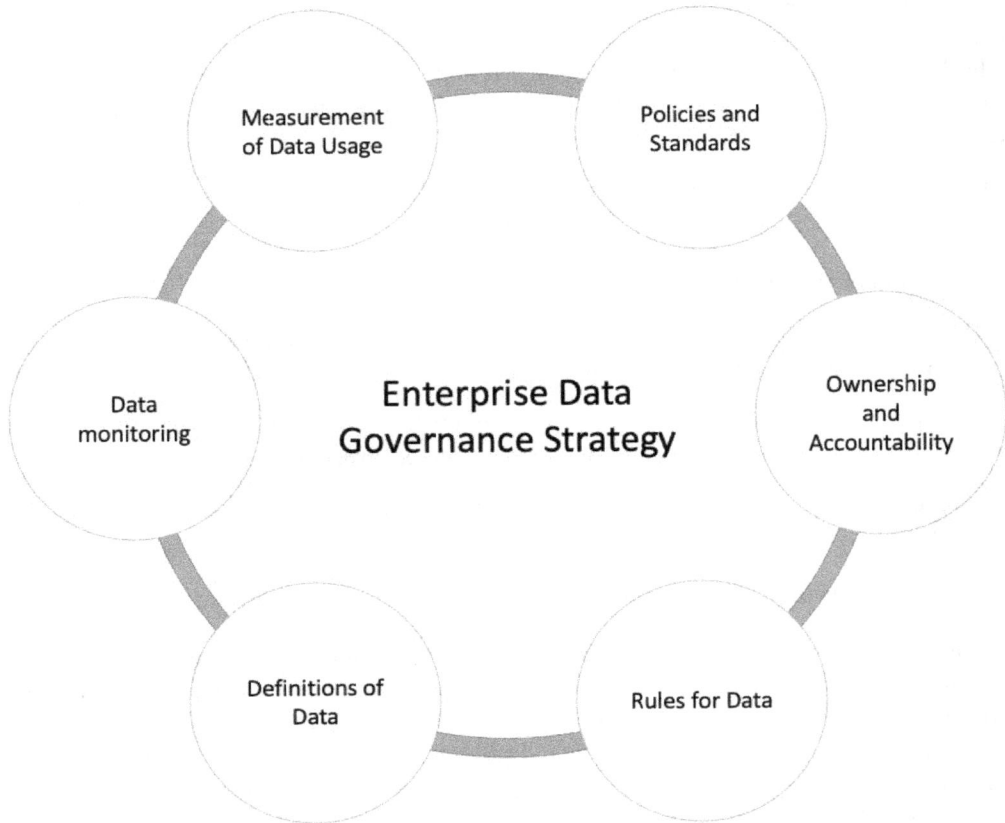

Figure 5.1 – Components of an enterprise data governance strategy

An enterprise data governance strategy contains several key things, including the following:

- **Policies and standards for data:**

  - What external policies, rulings, or standards must data adhere to? For example, is the business a financial services organization, and therefore are there regulatory body requirements that need to be considered for the governance of data?

  - What internal policies must data adhere to? For example, are there internal policies relating to PII?

- **Ownership and accountability of data**:

  - Who owns the data?

  - Who is accountable for the data?

- **Rules for data**:

  - What rules are in place surrounding the data?

  - What rules need to be put in place?

  - Who oversees those?

- **Definitions of data**:

  - Where is the data dictionary defined, stored, and managed?

- **Data monitoring**:

  - What monitoring is in place for the data?

  - What systems need to be monitored?

  - What is the monitoring for?

- **Measurement of data usage**:

  - What measures or **Key Performance Indicators** (**KPIs**) is data usage measured against?

Having introduced these enterprise data strategy components, it should be clear that the questions posed contribute to the importance of having a sound data governance strategy in the first place. Given how valuable data is to an organization (and the laws and regulations that ensure it is treated as such), governing that data from collection to definition, usage, monitoring, and measurement is paramount to safeguarding what some may argue is its most valuable asset.

Now, let's take a look at some roles and responsibilities involved in data governance.

Roles and responsibilities

An enterprise data governance framework may contain different roles and responsibilities, which is why each organization will have differing requirements. Each company needs to implement a suitable data governance model based on its specific requirements.

Let's visualize the roles as they would sit in a data governance framework:

Steering Committee		
C-Suite/Senior Management	Business Domain Owners	CIO and/or CISO

Data Owner	Data Owner	Data Owner	Data Owner	Data Owner	Data Owner

Data Stewards

Figure 5.2 – An enterprise data governance role framework

There is typically commonality in the following role across data governance frameworks:

- The steering committee
- Data owner
- Data steward

Let's look at each role in more detail.

Steering committee

A **steering committee** is a forum of senior management, those accountable for certain business functions (such as Sales or Service), and C-level individuals (almost certainly the **Chief Information Officer** (CIO) and sometimes the **Chief Information Security Officer** (CISO).

This committee has several responsibilities, which include setting the data governance strategy, working with the data stewards, and ensuring the data governance function is held to account (which may include various programs or projects of work that have specific deliverables, outcomes, and deadlines).

Data owner

A **data owner** is a person or team responsible for ensuring information within a data domain is governed across the systems in the organization's IT enterprise and business functions, such as sales. Data owners may be part of the steering committee (if the data owner is also a C-level member or in charge of a business function, such as Service). Data owners are typically responsible for the following:

- Approving the data definitions (the descriptions or metadata about the data).

- Ensuring the accuracy of information across the entire enterprise.

- The quality of the data.

- Contributing to, reviewing, refining, and approving the business approach to master data management. This can include reviewing or defining plans and other additional work items or artifacts that affect the master data management approach and its implementation.

- Working with the other data owners to collaborate on data issues across the enterprise and resolve them.

- Working with the steering committee, particularly to input on solutions (where the data owners have SME knowledge to offer). Additionally, they must give input on the selection and use of software and define and review policies or other regulatory requirements of their data domain (an example of a financial services organization in the United Kingdom is the **Financial Conduct Authority** (**FCA**), which has strict requirements around handling data).

Data steward

Data stewards are accountable for the day-to-day management of the data in the enterprise. They are the **Subject Matter Experts** (**SMEs**) who can both understand and communicate the meaning, definitions, and uses of the data in their business domain (and additionally, other related information across their business line). Data stewards work with other data stewards across the business to make decisions around the governance of the business data.

In a nutshell, data stewards are responsible for the following:

- Being the SMEs for their particular data domain

- Identifying, working through, and resolving issues with their and other data stewards data

- Reporting to the data owner and other applicable stakeholders within a particular data domain

- Working across the entire business to ensure that their data is managed and understood by other data stewards and data owners

As you now know, there are different roles, each with discrete responsibilities, under an enterprise data governance framework. Communication is the key driver in ensuring these roles work well together. This is why the steering committee is of such importance to hold data owners and data stewards to account.

Let's summarize what we've learned in this chapter.

Summary

Data governance accounts for 10% of the Salesforce Certified Data Architect exam testing criteria.

First, we looked at compliance and how it must be considered (using the GDPR as an example) when implementing a data model in Salesforce. Some companies and industries need to demonstrate compliance when safeguarding people's data according to a particular regulation or act of law. For example, a UK bank needs to adhere to the GDPR to safeguard customer data. If their Salesforce solution weren't implemented with a consideration of the GDPR, they may be subject to fines and forced to take remedial action. Then, we covered practical tips on how we can adhere to certain data standards or regulations, such as using classic encryption or Shield Encryption.

After that, we turned our attention to enterprise data governance, diving into the various roles and responsibilities that are involved in how organizations safeguard, process, and manage data.

When combined with the theory we covered in *Chapter 4*, *Salesforce Data Management*, you can now understand how vital effectively managing and governing data is crucial to building scalable yet compliant data solutions on the Salesforce platform, and how there are a plethora of Salesforce features available to facilitate this.

In *Chapter 6*, *Understanding Large Data Volumes*, we'll look at how data on the Salesforce platform can be safeguarded and governed, including visiting the concepts that underpin compliant solutions.

Practice questions

Test your knowledge of the topics covered in this chapter by answering the following questions:

1. What is the name of the function that has responsibilities that include setting the overall data governance strategy?
2. Which role in the enterprise data governance model is responsible for identifying data issues and working with like-minded individuals to resolve them?
3. Which Salesforce encryption technology allows Standard object fields to be encrypted?
4. Which Salesforce encryption technology allows Custom object fields to be masked with asterisks?
5. How many fields on a given object can be tracked with Field History Tracking by default?

6. How many fields on a given object can be tracked with Salesforce Shield Field History Tracking?

7. Which Salesforce object is designed to capture a contact's data privacy preferences?

8. The European Union data privacy regulation is known by what acronym?

9. How is the `Individual` object enabled for use in Salesforce?

10. Which enterprise data governance role is responsible for approving data definitions?

11. How is the `Individual` object exposed to users?

12. What Salesforce security measure controls a users default access to an object?

13. What is the Event Monitoring Analytics app?

14. Two login events from locations a large distance apart within an extremely small time frame is known as what?

15. Which enterprise data governance role is responsible for data quality?

Answers

The following are the answers to the previous questions. How many of them were you able to answer correctly? Check your answers to the previous questions here:

1. The steering committee

2. Data stewards

3. Shield Encryption

4. Classic encryption

5. 20

6. 60

7. The `Individual` object

8. The GDPR

9. By enabling **Data Protection and Privacy** in **Salesforce Setup**

10. The data owner

11. By adding it to the **Lead**, **Contact**, and **Person Account** page layouts

12. OWDs

13. A Tableau CRM app that reads data from the **LoginEvent** and **EventLogFile** objects

14. An impossible journey

15. The data owner

Further reading

See the following resources for more information on what was covered in this chapter:

- *The Individual Object*: https://developer.salesforce.com/docs/atlas. en-us.api.meta/api/sforce_api_objects_individual.htm

- *Salesforce Shield Encryption versus Salesforce Classic Encryption*: https://developer. salesforce.com/docs/atlas.en-us.securityImplGuide.meta/ securityImplGuide/security_pe_vs_classic_encryption.htm

- *Enabling Salesforce Shield Event Monitoring*: https://help.salesforce.com/s/ articleView?id=000339868&type=1

- *Session Security*: https://help.salesforce.com/s/articleView?id=sf. admin_sessions.htm&type=5

- *Field History Tracking*: https://help.salesforce.com/s/articleView?id=sf. tracking_field_history.htm&type=5

6

Understanding
Large Data Volumes

While the Salesforce platform can cope with large amounts of data, some considerations apply to larger/massive amounts of data (referred to as **Large Data Volumes** (**LDV**)) and how performance on the platform is affected. This chapter covers LDV considerations and mitigations, as well as scalable data model design and data archiving strategies.

In this chapter, we will cover the following topics:

- Designing a scalable data model
- LDV performance mitigation strategies
- Data archiving strategies

Unlike traditional applications that utilize a database, Salesforce stores all data in a few, large database tables. Therefore, traditional performance tuning techniques associated with databases don't necessarily apply to the Salesforce platform. Instead, we, as data architects, must design our Salesforce implementations to handle large amounts of data. This is best achieved by understanding LDVs, their impact on Salesforce performance, and how impacts caused by LDVs can be mitigated. In this chapter, we'll dive into some of the things that can affect performance and discuss their mitigation techniques.

Designing a scalable data model

As Salesforce implementations grow in size and complexity, so does the volume of data. Salesforce, being a multi-tenant architecture, handles the scaling up automatically, but as the volume of data grows, the processing time for certain operations increases too.

Typically, two areas are affected by different data architectures or configurations on the Salesforce platform:

- Loading or updating large amounts of records. This can be through the UI (directly) or with one or more integrations.
- Extracting data, be it through reports or other views into the data or querying the data.

Optimizing the data model generally involves doing the following:

- Only hosting data that truly needs to reside on the Salesforce platform based on business purpose and intent
- Deferring or temporarily disabling sharing change processing and other business rule logic when performing certain data operations
- Choosing the best (most efficient) operation for a given task or job related to data

Before we delve into how we can identify and mitigate based on LDV, it's worth revisiting some of the theory behind how Salesforce organizes and queries data.

In *Chapter 2, Data Modeling and Database Design*, we looked at how Salesforce doesn't have physical database tables for each object in our instance of Salesforce, but instead virtualizes storage of standard and custom object fields based on a few (very) large physical database tables.

Instead of managing the changing data structures for each customer's Salesforce instance on its multi-tenant platform, Salesforce uses this virtualization technique. Traditional performance tuning techniques associated with databases don't necessarily apply to the Salesforce platform, because the underlying data structure for your Salesforce instance is different from the perceived data structure presented to your users and admins. **Account** and **Contact** are perceived as two distinct data entities, which would be separate tables in a traditional **Relational Database Management System (RDBMS)**. However, in Salesforce, they are virtualized from large tables shared with other Salesforce orgs on the same node, such as EU6. If you try to apply RDBMS performance-tuning techniques based on the virtualized data and schema of your Salesforce org, you won't see the effect you expect on the actual, underlying data structures of your instance (or the Salesforce node for that matter). A full list of Salesforce nodes can be found at `https://trust.salesforce.com`.

Now, let's look at searching for data, understanding indexes, and how they affect search performance.

Searching for Salesforce data

In a nutshell, **searching** is the act of querying two records based on free-form text (that is, putting a string into the search engine and having results returned). The Salesforce search architecture differs from where your object and record data are stored. It uses its own data store in the Salesforce application architecture, which is specifically designed for searching for free-form text. This is essentially how free-form text search operations are facilitated on the Salesforce Platform.

As a Salesforce Data Architect, you may already be familiar with the various ways in which search capabilities are surfaced to the users of your instance. Salesforce provides search capabilities in several places throughout the application, including the following:

- Global Search
- Advanced Search
- Lookup fields
- Duplicate processing (based on matching rules)
- Knowledge Base
- Suggested Solutions
- Web2Lead
- Web2Case
- **Salesforce Object Search Language (SOSL)**, used with Apex and via an **Application Programming Interface (API)**

Let's look at indexing data, and how Salesforce uses those indexes when performing searches.

Indexing data

To search for data in Salesforce, the data must be indexed. Salesforce has a separate set of search indexing servers for **indexing** operations that, when new or modified data events occur, generate and process queue entries for the indexing operations. Therefore, search indexing is an asynchronous operation. Salesforce suggests (according to `https://developer.salesforce.com/docs/atlas.en-us.salesforce_large_data_volumes_bp.meta/salesforce_large_data_volumes_bp/ldv_deployments_concepts_search_architecture.htm`) that it could take 15 minutes (or even longer, depending on how much data has been created or modified) for the text being indexed to become searchable.

How Salesforce performs indexed searches

When a user runs a search through the UI, the API, or through an action requiring a search to be invoked using Apex code, Salesforce will search the indexes that have been created for the appropriate records. Taking those results, Salesforce will then apply access permissions, search limits, and any other filters or filter logic to narrow down the results into a *result set*. This will typically contain the most relevant results for the user or operation invoking the search. When the *result set* reaches a pre-determined size, as specified internally by the Salesforce query optimizer, the remaining records from the search results are discarded. The *result set* is then used to invoke the actual database query to return the records that the user will see, or the operation will return to a calling process (in the case of a record search invoked by the Salesforce API or through Apex code).

Now that we have seen how Salesforce queries data, let's look at how operations related to records can be affected by too many child records of a single parent record, otherwise known as data skew.

Data skew and its impacts on performance

When thinking about and designing a record ownership strategy in Salesforce, always keep the number 10,000 at the front of your mind. When *more than 10,000* child records belong to the same parent record in Salesforce, an issue known as **data skew** arises.

Data skew comes in three not-so-delicious flavors:

- Account data skew
- Ownership skew
- Lookup skew

We'll explore each type of data skew in more detail shortly but remember that if you design a data strategy that facilitates distributing record ownership so that no one record is the parent for more than 10,000 child records, then you don't have to worry about data skew affecting the users of your Salesforce instance.

Account data skew

Certain Salesforce standard objects, including the **Account** and **Opportunity** objects, have a special data relationship that maintains parent and child record access under a private sharing model. **Account data skew** is where one account has too many child records. Therefore, when thinking about your account record ownership strategy, think about distributing records appropriately. Don't create a generic *unassigned* or *bucket* parent account record and think that will be enough as when the magic 10,000 child record number is reached, your users won't be happy. Two main issues occur when account data skew makes its presence known, namely *record locking* issues and *sharing* issues.

Think about updating a lot of child records that belong to the same account (such as contacts or opportunities). Because Salesforce maintains integrity in the database, it will lock both the record being updated and the parent account when updates are made to the child record. When updating lots of records that all are children of the same account, those locks can result in errors, where one record update has locked the parent account. This means that other child record updates may not occur and your users will be presented with an error instead. Not good.

Now, let's turn our attention to sharing issues that may occur when changing the sharing of either the parent account or the child record. Because Salesforce will re-calculate access to either the parent account or the child records, this sharing re-calculation will take time. Guess what? Those records will all be locked during that sharing re-calculation too. When we factor in recalculations that consider role hierarchy and sharing rules, these locks can be in place for longer than anticipated and cause errors to be returned to users.

Ownership skew

In situations where lots of records (think of our magic number 10,000) of the same object type (such as Contact) are owned by a single user, this causes a performance issue known as ownership skew. Every record in Salesforce is required to have an owner (due to the ownership-based data model), so this can cause performance issues when sharing calculations are required to manage the visibility of all of those records owned by the same user. Again, this is another reason to try and plan to avoid generic *single-unassigned* or *bucket* parent records as much as possible.

When the user causing the ownership skew exists in the role hierarchy, operations such as record deletes or record ownership changes require the Salesforce platform to remove the sharing of the record from the (skew-causing) owner and all parent users of the owner, as specified within the role hierarchy, and then finally from all users given access by sharing rules. Record ownership changes are already considered a *costly* operation in that they lock records and take a lot of time while sharing is recalculated. Ownership skew exacerbates that process.

Where ownership skew can't be avoided, Salesforce suggests not giving that user a role. This way, the role hierarchy is effectively removed from any sharing or permissions calculations, meaning performance is less affected as a result when performing these operations.

Lookup skew

Lookup field types in Salesforce should be thought of as akin to foreign key relationships between objects. Every time a user inserts or updates a record, the Salesforce platform locks the records that are referenced by each lookup field on that record (for example, a parent account for a Contact record being created or updated). By locking the referenced records, Salesforce ensures that when the inserted or updated data for the record is committed to the database, the referential integrity between those records is maintained. Therefore, 10,000 records or more looking up to a single record can slow things down or cause errors due to contention where Salesforce is locking records to maintain database integrity.

Since lookup skew is harder to spot, it's easier to plan to distribute records appropriately to avoid more than 10,000 child records looking up to a single parent to avoid lookup skew in the first place.

With data skew and its impact on performance now covered, let's turn our attention to data virtualization.

Data virtualization

A key question data architects should be asking themselves is, *do I need to store this data in Salesforce?*

While Salesforce provides a scalable architecture to allow your users to access the data they need to perform their business activities, access to constantly changing or large amounts of data can be served by allowing Salesforce to present data held on an external system to users as and when they need it. Think bank account transactions, line items from an ERP, or customer-purchase transactions. This technique is known as **data virtualization**.

Salesforce provides several solutions for accessing data held on external systems. Depending on the technology used, users of your Salesforce instance can interact with a report on the data held in an external system as if that data were stored on the Salesforce platform. This has the benefit of keeping your users in one system, interacting with your enterprise data in a common way.

Salesforce provides different options for virtualizing data, including (but not limited to) **Salesforce Connect** (using the standard **OData** 2.0/4.0 adapters or a custom adapter implementation), **Heroku Connect**, or a custom integration using request/reply. Typically, it depends on the integration capabilities of the system that is having its data surfaced in Salesforce before you can decide on the technology to use to surface the data in Salesforce. The Salesforce Connect adapter supports OData 2.0 and 4.0 and requires relatively little setup, making it a low barrier to getting external data in front of your users if the system being queried supports OData.

Salesforce supports two types of lookup relationships to associate the data held in the external system with the data held within Salesforce. An **external lookup** is for situations where the external object data is the parent for your child records held in Salesforce (such as service garage records related to an external record representing a vehicle). An **indirect lookup** is for situations where your Salesforce data is the parent of the external object data (such as a bank account in Salesforce and transactions from an external system). You can revisit these special relationship types by going back to *Chapter 2, Data Modeling and Database Design*.

Now that we've looked at factors that affect performance (including data skew), let's look at performance mitigation strategies for dealing with large amounts of data.

LDV performance mitigation strategies

There are several tools available to us as data architects when it comes to working with data and keeping things running as optimally as possible. Of course, we should first question what data needs to reside in Salesforce. How often should we consider moving data off-platform to reduce performance impacts due to having large amounts of data available? Typically, data of a certain age (determined by business requirements or regulatory requirements in some instances) should be archived regularly to ensure that users are only interacting with the data that makes sense to be hosted on the Salesforce platform.

With data that may need to reside on Salesforce, some other techniques are available that can improve performance:

- Custom indexes
- Skinny tables
- Selective filter conditions
- Divisions

Let's take a look at them.

Custom indexes

To speed up query performance, Salesforce supports the creation of **custom indexes**. Think of an index as a way of sorting records in an order that's based on the parameters that form the index. By using a sorted index, record retrieval speed can be increased. Custom indexes are enabled by contacting **Salesforce Support**. Before considering doing so, it's worth touching on which fields are automatically indexed by the Salesforce platform for most objects:

- `RecordTypeId`
- `Division`
- `CreatedDate`
- `Systemmodstamp` (`LastModifiedDate`)
- `Name`
- `Email` (for `Contact` and `Lead` records)
- Foreign key relationships (`Lookup` and `Master-Detail`)
- The (unique) Salesforce record ID, which is the primary key for each object

> **Important note**
> Custom indexes can be created on almost all types of fields, except for multi-select picklists, text areas (long or rich), non-deterministic formula fields, and encrypted text fields. External ID field types cause an index to be created on that field by default, but only Auto Number, Email, Number, and Text types are supported for the creation of external ID field types.

Salesforce's underlying database architecture makes the actual data table for custom fields unsuitable for traditional database indexing (because we're essentially talking about a large single physical table that contains all the fields for the objects in your Salesforce instance). To overcome this indexing limitation, Salesforce creates a separate index table (for each Salesforce infrastructure node running the Salesforce application) that essentially contains a copy of the object field data in that node, along with information about the data types of the object fields. Salesforce then can (through its application layer) build and maintain a traditional database index on this separate index table. The index table places upper limits on the number of records that an indexed search can effectively return, as only those indexed records are considered to be returned to the process or the user issuing the query before defaulting to a much wider (and therefore less performant) non-indexed search.

By default, the index tables do not include empty records (sometimes known as null records, although Salesforce support can enable custom indexes that contain null records if desired). If custom indexes are created on custom fields, then you must explicitly enable and rebuild the indexes to get the empty-value rows included in the index.

It is also worth knowing that the Salesforce query optimizer (a feature of the Salesforce application layer) maintains a separate database table that contains statistics about the distribution of object and field data in each index. Salesforce's query optimizer uses this table to perform pre-queries when an automated process, user, or report issues a query to determine whether using an index can speed up the query (and therefore increase performance).

Standard indexed fields

Salesforce's standard indexed fields are used when a SOQL query filter matches less than 30% of the first million returned records in the database and less than 15% of additional records in the database, up to a total of 1 million records.

For example, a standard index is used in the following cases:

- When a SOQL query is issued against an object table with 2 million records, and the filter matches roughly 450,000 or fewer records (as 30% of 1 million is roughly 300,000 and 15% of the remaining 1 million is roughly 150,000)

- When a SOQL query is issued against an object table with 5 million records, and the filter matches roughly 900,000 or fewer records (as 30% of 1 million is roughly 300,000 and 15% of the remaining 4 million is roughly 600,000)

With standard indexed fields covered, let's look at custom indexed fields and when they are used.

Custom indexed fields

Unlike standard indexes, custom indexes are used when a SOQL query filter matches less than 10% of the total records, up to a maximum of 333,333 records.

For example, a custom index is used in the following cases:

- When a SOQL query is executed against an object table with 500,000 records, and the filter matches 50,000 or fewer records (as 10% of 500,000 is 50,000)

- When a SOQL query is executed against an object table with 5 million records, and the filter matches 333,333 or fewer records (as 10% of 5 million is 500,000, yet the upper limit is 333,333 records so the value of 333,333 is used)

For more information about some of the intricacies concerning indexes, see `https://developer.salesforce.com/docs/atlas.en-us.salesforce_large_data_volumes_bp.meta/salesforce_large_data_volumes_bp/ldv_deployments_infrastructure_indexes.htm`.

Now that you have understood indexing, let's focus on a solution that helps us avoid joins in tables for optimizing read-based operations.

Skinny tables

To speed up the performance of certain read-only operations on a single object, **skinny tables** can be created to avoid joins across the standard and custom fields. When skinny tables are enabled, they are used automatically where appropriate. You can't create, access, or modify skinny tables directly since this is done by Salesforce Support. In essence, you work with them to define what the skinny table should contain when optimizing read-only queries to, say, accounts for specific fields. If the report, list view, or query you're optimizing (and therefore getting the skinny table created for) changes (such as adding a new field to respond to business users needing an extra value in a report), you'll need to contact Salesforce to update your skinny table definition.

It's also worth noting that skinny tables don't contain soft-deleted records, so they won't be available when queries are using the skinny table over the broader object data in the standard underlying tables.

Read-only operations that reference only those fields defined in a skinny table won't require an extra join across the standard and custom object field tables, and therefore they can perform better. According to Salesforce (at `https://developer.salesforce.com/docs/atlas.en-us.` `salesforce_large_data_volumes_bp.meta/salesforce_large_data_volumes_bp/` `ldv_deployments_infrastructure_skinny_tables.htm`), the use of skinny tables is best employed with Salesforce objects containing millions of data records to improve the performance of read-only operations on those records, such as executing reports and dashboards or list views.

Skinny tables can be created on all custom objects and the following standard objects:

- `Account`
- `Contact`
- `Opportunity`
- `Lead`
- `Case`

Some other considerations apply to skinny tables. For example, skinny tables can contain a maximum of *100 columns*, and they cannot contain fields from other objects. Think of them as optimized tables for read-only operations for a single object.

Let's look at a visual example of a skinny table:

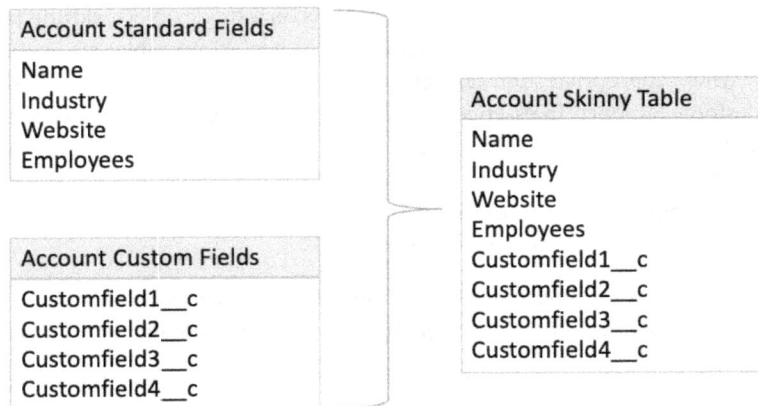

Figure 6.1 – Example of a skinny table

They are created to remove joins across standard and custom fields when issuing read-only queries to read data from a single object.

Selective filter conditions

Selective filter conditions can be used in your **Salesforce Object Query Language** (**SOQL**) queries to improve performance. Within the Salesforce application logic, the Salesforce platform's query optimizer feature makes this decision and determines the filter condition selectivity for an issued SOQL query (including those required for reports and list views) when queries are run.

When dealing with relatively simple SOQL queries, you can easily determine whether a specific filter condition is selective by gathering statistics on it using several tools, but the humble **Developer Console Query Editor** will do just fine. After you apply an index to a selective field, queries with related filter conditions will perform more efficiently.

By confirming that filter conditions in reports, SOQL, and list views are selective, then by applying indexes to those fields, the Lightning Platform query optimizer doesn't have to perform full dataset scans when looking for target data. This means that the performance will be optimal in such use cases.

Divisions

Divisions can be used to partition data and reduce the number of records returned by SOQL queries, therefore increasing performance for the user or process calling the query. Salesforce provides special support for partitioning data by divisions (which can be thought of as logical sections of data), but this needs to be specifically enabled by contacting Salesforce Customer Support.

Now that we've looked at LDV mitigation methods, let's look at the various methods for archiving data. As we covered earlier in this chapter, optimally, we only have the right, relevant data on the platform. With that said, let's explore the strategies for data archiving.

Data archiving strategies

Just as we have data on Salesforce for our users, there are situations where data needs to be archived off the platform. This may be due to various reasons, such as regulatory compliance (where certain data needs to be retained), or to keep the optimum amount of data in the platform (such as only the data that is being used being kept on the platform, and automatically archiving data over a certain age). Luckily, various options are available for archiving Salesforce data, such as using on-platform solutions such as big objects or storing data off-platform in an external system or data warehouse. We'll take a look at these options in the following subsections.

Big objects

As covered in *Chapter 2, Data Modeling and Database Design*, **big objects** are used to store and manage huge amounts of data (up to 1 million records by default, though this can be scaled up at an additional cost to tens of millions or even billions of records).

Big objects provide consistent performance no matter how many records are loaded into them, which is useful in auditing an archiving use case that big objects are suited to. Anything that requires consistent performance when working with hundreds of millions or billions of records is the use case that big objects are designed for.

Big objects work using a separate, distributed database to the main Salesforce platform, and are not transactional. As a reminder, sharing isn't supported on big objects other than object and field permissions. Additionally, this means that automation (for example, workflows, flows, and triggers) is not supported on big objects.

Data Loader

The humble Salesforce Data Loader can be used for both importing and exporting data. This will be covered in more detail in the next chapter, *Chapter 7, Data Migration*, but for now, we know that the Salesforce Data Loader supports getting data in and out of Salesforce using two different modes, **Serial** and **Bulk**, which support different batch sizes and concurrency options. While Data Loader is generally a manually invoked tool, it can be used as a simple solution for archiving data by exporting Salesforce data as one or more CSV files that can be stored or ingested off-platform, such as on a local server, shared drive, or data warehousing tool.

ETL

Extract, Transform, Load (ETL) tools can be used to automate the archival of data using the Salesforce REST, Partner, and/or Bulk APIs. As part of a regular nightly job, an automated process or scheduled job from a middleware solution such as **MuleSoft** can run, whereby a query is issued to retrieve data that meets the archival criteria since the last successful run of the job. This data can then be saved to an offline data store or inserted into an **Enterprise Data Warehouse** (EDW).

Summary

In this chapter, we dug deep into the data architecture and its potential pitfalls and mitigation strategies. Understanding why data skew happens helps us design better parent/child record ownership strategies. Also, understanding the way Salesforce uses indexes ensures that we can create reports, list views, and build queries that work with the constraints of the multi-tenant architecture nature of the platform, not against them. Due to this, we looked at LDV issues and mitigation strategies, understanding how concepts such as selective filter conditions and skinny tables can be used to ensure we can work with our large amounts of data effectively.

Next, we turned our attention to data archiving strategies and the various options we have at our disposal, ensuring that we are keeping to regulatory requirements for data retention and archival (if appropriate) and ensuring that we only use the data that is relevant to our users.

In *Chapter 7, Data Migration*, we're going to build upon our knowledge of how the data on the Salesforce platform is indexed and organized so that we can start building effective strategies to get data in and out of the platform.

Practice questions

Test your knowledge of the topics covered in this chapter by answering the following questions:

1. What does LDV stand for?

2. Which type of Salesforce object is used to store 1 million or more records?

3. One account that contains over 10,000 child records is known as what?

4. More than 10,000 records looking up to a single parent record is known as what?

5. Utilizing data hosted on an external system is a technique known as what?

6. What can be used to partition data and reduce the number of records returned by SOQL queries and reports?

7. What can be used to avoid joins within queries to data held within a single object and speed up read-only operations?

8. More than 10,000 child records belonging to the same parent record is known as what?

9. Specify the type of index that's used in the following scenarios:

  - When a SOQL query is executed against object data where that object contains 400,000 records, and the filter matches 40,000 or fewer records

  - When a SOQL query is executed against object data where that object contains 15 million records, and the filter matches 333,333 or fewer records

10. Can custom indexes be created on multi-select picklists?

Answers

The following are the answers to the previous questions. How many of them were you able to answer correctly? Check your answers to the previous questions here:

1. Large Data Volume
2. Big object
3. Account skew
4. Lookup skew
5. Data virtualization
6. Divisions
7. Skinny tables
8. Ownership skew
9. Custom index
10. False

Further reading

See the following resources for more information on what was covered in this chapter:

- *Salesforce Trust*: https://trust.salesforce.com
- *Search Architecture*: https://developer.salesforce.com/docs/atlas.en-us.salesforce_large_data_volumes_bp.meta/salesforce_large_data_volumes_bp/ldv_deployments_concepts_search_architecture.htm
- *Indexes*: https://developer.salesforce.com/docs/atlas.en-us.salesforce_large_data_volumes_bp.meta/salesforce_large_data_volumes_bp/ldv_deployments_infrastructure_indexes.htm

- *Skinny tables*: `https://developer.salesforce.com/docs/atlas.en-us.salesforce_large_data_volumes_bp.meta/salesforce_large_data_volumes_bp/ldv_deployments_infrastructure_skinny_tables.htm`

7
Data Migration

Data migration is essentially the process of taking data from one or more systems, performing operations upon it (such as cleansing, transformation, and enrichment), and then subsequently loading that data into one or more systems.

Typically, when implementing Salesforce, data migration is treated as a discrete workstream with questions to answer. How do you get good-quality data into the Salesforce Platform? How do you ensure loading large amounts of data is smooth, reliable, repeatable, and timely? How do you effectively export data from the Salesforce Platform? What's the right set of steps to follow when importing or exporting data to or from the Salesforce Platform? Where do you begin?

In this chapter, we will learn the methods available to import data into the Salesforce Platform, including tuning and optimization techniques. Then, we'll explore some of the concepts and processes that need to be considered and understood when undertaking any large data movement in or out of the Salesforce Platform. We'll also learn how to effectively export data from the Salesforce Platform.

Data migrations are needed due to several reasons, such as when a new system (such as Salesforce) has been implemented to serve as a single customer view or a company may have acquired another and is merging data into another system. Another example is when data is regularly purchased or acquired, and that data needs to be migrated into a company CRM. Therefore, data migrations are an important, ongoing process.

Data migrations are seen by some as big, scary, and best left to someone else, but once the concepts are understood, migrating data in or out of the Salesforce Platform needn't be feared. Data migration accounts for 15% of the exam outline. By understanding the material in this chapter, you will be equipped to understand the process, concepts, and intricacies surrounding data movement and the Salesforce Platform.

In this chapter, we will cover the following topics:

- Understanding data movement and its considerations
- Loading high-quality data
- Migrating Large Data Volumes to Salesforce
- Exporting data from Salesforce

Understanding data movement and its considerations

In this section, we'll cover the various stages involved in data migration, and why it is important to invest time in the definition phase of data migration. When considering moving data from one system or another, it is important to ask yourself the following questions:

- Is it appropriate to move the data?
- What will I gain by moving the data?
- Is the data of sufficient quality?
- How would the data be maintained in the long term?
- What governance or other processes should be put in place?

By tackling the questions, we've essentially started our data migration process. While one system in the IT enterprise may store a certain part of the data, it may not always make sense to move the data if it is being moved into a target system for the sake of it, just because that system is a shiny new piece of the IT enterprise. For example, I worked with a client in the past who invested in Salesforce to provide better marketing and customer service and, as part of the implementation, immediately believed that all of the data from their repair management system needed to be migrated into Salesforce. This client produced physical devices for measuring the weights of fresh produce, such as fruits and vegetables. When these devices developed issues, their inspection and repair processes would be carried out using a cloud-based system that only support staff and repair engineers had access to. When Salesforce was introduced as the new system of record for customer data in the IT enterprise, time was taken to assess the systems Salesforce was to interact with to see what data needed to be surfaced for marketing, sales, and support agents to interact with what was being termed *the connected customer*. Essentially, we're talking about Salesforce pulling together data from several data sources (sound familiar? We covered the concepts behind this scenario in *Chapter 4, Salesforce Data Management*).

When speaking with the client, they wanted to redefine their service process, so we decided that, with Salesforce being the new customer master, we would implement a case-based workflow. For the existing repair data, we decided not to import data from a system that was going to be put into a read-only state before eventually being decommissioned in several years. To meet this requirement, we decided to use external objects to surface the repair data but leave it in the existing system. However, what we actually decided to do was pull in the information relating to the service entitlement and contract for support, which will be driven from Salesforce going forward. Essentially, the client was looking to provide better service through Salesforce by migrating only the needed data. By allowing existing records to be surfaced in Salesforce, only the required data was moved across.

The point of the questioning exercise at the start of the process of migrating data led us to the design I've explained here in terms of what data will be moved.

The next stage in questioning the data migration process is to understand if the data is of sufficient quality. When talking to clients, some are quite open about there being lots of duplicates or incomplete fields in their primary systems. Others may not have an honest answer as to how good their data quality is. Luckily, we can work with clients to define the metrics that will underline what quality data means to them. For example, what fields are considered necessary? When profiling data, we can quickly determine what fields, as an overall percentage of the total record count, have no value in them or only a very low percentage have been populated. We should be questioning whether these fields are required to build a picture of what our quality dataset looks like. We should also look at the completeness of data, duplicate counts, and so on. We'll look at this in more detail in the next section. For my client, the data wasn't too bad before it was migrated. Field completeness was good, but about 5% of the migrated records were duplicates. Therefore, the client had a decision to make – fix the duplicates before or after migrating the data. They decided to fix them afterward, once the migration was complete.

Before we're done with our considerations for migrating data, we need to think about data maintenance in the long term. Do any controls or procedures need to be put in place during or after migration? What happens to source systems in terms of access and modification rights to data? Does a process need to be put in place to process or enrich data at regular intervals? Is this a manual or automated exercise? What metrics make that process successful? This falls slightly into the governance aspects of data migration since, often, the processes surrounding maintaining data will form part of a wider governance structure. For my client, they decided that the Salesforce matching and de-duplicating functionality would serve as the main entrance to avoid duplicate Account and Contact records being entered into the system. They would monitor the process using Salesforce's reporting functionality and decide to procure a suitable tool, should data quality issues occur in the future.

Now, let's learn how to define a process for migrating data. In the next section, we will cover the steps we'll take throughout the rest of the data migration process.

Defining a process for migrating data

Once the questioning as to the *what* and *why* of data migration has been done, a more formalized process can be considered. The following sequence of steps is typical in data migration from one or more systems to another, and some steps can be omitted or moved, depending on certain requirements – for example, deduplicating data before or after migration.

I've used the following sequence of steps in several data migration workstreams as part of a Salesforce implementation:

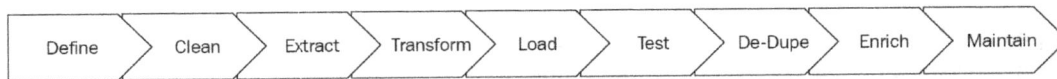

Figure 7.1 – A data migration process

Next, let's explore each of these stages to understand what's typically involved.

Define

We begin by defining the target data model and **Customer Relationship Management (CRM)** data hierarchy. This is very likely to be done as a result of capturing and validating requirements concerning how best to support target business processes. With the target data model defined, we can turn our attention to defining where the masters of data are in the IT enterprise. As alluded to previously in this chapter, profiling data is useful for determining the quality and completeness of data held in the source systems from which data is being migrated.

Next, it is necessary to understand the as-is data models from the source systems so that the data structures can be understood when we get to the Extract phase of the process. Imagine migrating from another CRM system such as Dynamics 365. Even though Dynamics 365 has the concept of Accounts, Contacts, and Opportunities, it is built upon SQL Server, so it follows a more traditional SQL database for storing data. When inspecting the as-is data model, the SQL Server database schema for the instance needs to be understood. Our data dictionary should be started in the Define phase. As we learn more about the data sources and target data structure, the data dictionary that defines the types and formats of fields (including any rules that need to be applied) can be produced.

With our source systems, data structures, selected entities, and fields identified, we can start mapping the data. We do this by defining how the source entities and fields will be mapped to the target data model, including any transformations that may need to be applied. Next, the strategy for cleaning, de-duplicating, and enriching data (if required) can be defined, including where in the process those steps should take place (pre- or post-extraction, for example).

Clean

Data cleaning can be defined simply as the act of performing data cleansing exercises, either as a manual process or by using automation and software tools. The definition of what cleansing means in terms of the data will be different for each IT enterprise; for example, ensuring that no contact name contains invalid characters. The activities that are typically involved in all cleansing activities include defining any tools to be used to assist in the process, as well as any matching rules and scoring thresholds.

Extract

Extracting data involves taking the defined source data from source systems. Therefore, to extract data effectively, it is necessary to have the source systems, as-is data models, and any other relevant information well defined and understood. It may be desirable to combine all extracted data into a staging area if any cleansing, de-duplication, or enrichment activities are to be done once all the data has been extracted.

Transform

Once the data has been extracted, or after the extraction phase of a fully automated **Extract, Transform, Load** (ETL) process, it is usually necessary to transform the data before it can be loaded into the target system. For this to be successful, it is necessary to know about any entity mappings, field mappings, and other rules, conditions, or logic to be applied at transformation time.

Load

We're now at the stage of the process where we can load data into the target system. With all of that definition and careful attention paid to preparing the data that's being loaded, we can choose a tool to use for the loading activity, such as the humble Salesforce Data Loader. You might be surprised at just how much can be automated when scripting Data Loader to run on the command line or as part of a wider automated process. We also need to consider acceptable load performance. We may have millions of records to load, so doing that in an acceptable time frame may differ, depending on the parameters of the data migration exercise, client industry, and so on. For example, I oversaw the data migration process for a bank, which naturally could only take place (and needed to be completed) when the bank wasn't open for business. Luckily, we tested the process several times, so that was a relatively straightforward Friday evening in terms of getting the data loaded promptly.

Test

There are generally two types of testing applicable to data migrations:

- Testing to specification
- Testing for intent

Simply put, testing to specification involves ensuring the right amount of data is loaded. For example, the extract gave us 1,000 company records, so we loaded 1,000 Account records into Salesforce. If the load count was 990, then 1% of the data hadn't loaded in and we needed to investigate why. This should ideally be identified and rectified as part of testing, but I appreciate that on the day of the production data migration, this may not always be the case.

Testing for intent can be thought of as **User Acceptance Testing (UAT)** for data. Does the data loaded stand up to real-world use? Will our users be able to carry out their duties as desired with the data loaded? Do the data relationships correlate correctly?

Something else to consider in the testing part of the process is the reconciliation strategy for data. How can we ensure that the sets of data from the various source systems and the target system are in agreement, accounting for the transformations we've applied? With specification, intent, and reconciliation covered, we should be in a position to say that we've loaded the correct amount of records that work as intended for the users and are correct in their desired end state, as dictated by the transform logic.

De-duplicate

As mentioned previously, the de-duplication step of a data migration process may take place earlier in the process but can take place after migration if it is deemed more suitable. When de-duplicating data, a suitable tool can be used to facilitate the process. This is typically given a set of rules that determine what criteria are used to match data. This is, in turn, used to generate a score of the likelihood of data being a duplicate and therefore should be considered for removal. For example, it isn't entirely unreasonable to build a rule that matches Contact records that have the same email address and postcode. It's likely these are the same person, so they can be flagged for intervention (in this case, marked for deletion). If you're migrating data to a new data master, it may be worth considering the intended behavior concerning propagating data changes and sending duplicate records to downstream systems.

Enrich

Once the data has been loaded and is in a clean state, it may be desirable to enrich the data by incorporating a one-time or ongoing process. For example, Salesforce has a plethora of AppExchange packages available to it that can provide enriched company address and employee information, credit scoring information, and so on. If there is a desire to enrich data, it generally makes sense to do this on a cleansed, de-duplicated dataset.

Maintain

So far, we've defined a process, carefully mapped our data, and built and executed that process by extracting, transforming, and loading data. We've cleansed, de-duplicated, and enriched the data along the way. But before we're done with this process, we need to cover the last step (and some may argue the hardest one): we need to consider how we're going to maintain the data we've spent so long and so much effort on getting into our target system in the right way. Maintenance naturally takes a different form, depending on the characteristics of the business that owns the target system. Salesforce provides tools (even down to basic reporting) that can help ensure the data stays in as good a shape as possible. This includes how data is added over time as users adopt and use the system.

With our data migration process and steps now understood, let's dive a bit deeper into loading high-quality data.

Loading high-quality data

When users interact with data, the data must be of good quality for it to be effective. For example, salespeople may go to look at a Contact record in Salesforce to make a call to try and up-sell or cross-sell to that customer. If users are presented with multiple Contact records for the same person (duplicates), and those records are at different levels of completeness, they may end up very annoyed. Due to this, those users may not have all of the information for a Contact or, worse, are still jumping between records to deduce the correct phone number to call or email address to use.

As mentioned previously, practical steps can be taken as part of a data migration process. When preparing data before loading it, or once the data has been loaded into the target system, cleansing, de-duplication, and (optionally) enrichment must take place. When thinking about the quantity of data as well as its quality, it may make sense for some enterprises to perform the cleansing, de-duplication, and enrichment activities before loading it. This way, the smallest, most complete, and duplicate-free dataset will be loaded.

Turning our attention to what can be done in Salesforce to facilitate loading high-quality data, we have several tools at our disposal. Validation rules can be used to enforce the correct format of field values. This can ensure that records are at a baseline level of completeness. This includes ensuring certain fields are filled in (such as not being able to set an Opportunity to a particular stage unless certain fields relating to the sale have been completed). We also have matching and duplication rules, which are used to flag up and assist users in preventing the creation of duplicate records. Salesforce reports can be produced off the back of the matching rules in the system to highlight those records that require attention. Lastly, Flow can be used to perform operations in an automated fashion when creating and updating data records. When processing records en masse, automation should generally be turned off. When working with one record at a time from day to day, automation such as Flow can be used to drive up the completeness of data on records or related records.

Now that we've covered various aspects related to data quality, let's look at migrating **Large Data Volumes (LDVs)** to Salesforce.

Migrating Large Data Volumes to Salesforce

When loading LDVs (hundreds of thousands or millions of records) into Salesforce, there are various tools and considerations to keep in mind. Firstly, the **Application Programming Interface (API)** used to load the data into Salesforce can make a huge difference. The Bulk API can be used to load lots of data in parallel (by setting it to parallel mode). This can cause record-locking issues, whereby records cannot be loaded as their parent is locked. However, typically, this results in a faster load time compared to loading data in one batch at a time (known as serial mode). A way to reduce the likelihood of getting record-locking issues is to order the records to be loaded by the parent record

IDs. Thinking purely in terms of performance, the Bulk API in parallel mode is the fastest way to load millions of records into Salesforce in the shortest amount of time. An external ID field can be used to avoid duplicates while importing records, as the external system ID is used to identify records. This can be particularly useful when performing, for example, scripted data loader tasks as the external ID can be used as the key for associating parent and child records.

Next, think about the operation that will be used to create and update data. Salesforce provides **insert**, **update**, and **upsert** operations. Insert is used for data creation, update is used for updating existing records, and upsert is used for updating existing records, or creating a new record if no record can be found to update. As you can imagine, an upsert operation is costlier to perform in terms of Salesforce resources as the calculation is done on the fly for every record when determining the operation to perform. Therefore, the best practice is to use the insert and update operations when migrating LDVs to the Salesforce Platform as they are faster than upsert.

Lastly, it is important to keep in mind that data storage on Salesforce is finite and generally linked to the number of user licenses purchased. If you keep loading millions upon millions of records into Salesforce, eventually, your data storage will run out. However, the limits are quite generous when a Salesforce environment is provisioned. Typically, data storage is set at 10 GB (for Salesforce orgs provisioned from late March 2019) plus either 20 MB or 120 MB per licensed user, depending on the Salesforce edition purchased (so a 20-user org on Salesforce Professional Edition will have 10.4 GB of data storage).

> **Important note**
> More details on data allocation and storage limits can be found at `https://help.salesforce.com/s/articleView?id=sf.overview_storage.htm&type=5`.

This leads us nicely to the next section, where we'll look at exporting data from Salesforce.

Exporting data from Salesforce

As much as we may want to maximize the investment our clients make in Salesforce by moving data into it, we should consider the requirements surrounding exporting data from Salesforce. This may involve exporting certain data (for example, to a data warehouse platform), which typically involves an automated process being performed at a scheduled interval (such as every night). As expected, several techniques can be used to accomplish this task.

Data Export

Salesforce offers two methods for exporting data out of the box. The first is the Data Export service, which is accessible from within the Salesforce setup. Data Export can be used to manually export data weekly or monthly (depending on the edition of Salesforce you have), as well as to schedule regular data exports weekly (every 7 days) or monthly (every 29 days).

The second method for exporting data is the humble Data Loader application from Salesforce. This can be used to extract object data and can use queries to filter the data if desired, such as for filtering all Accounts by the last modified date of the current day. Data Loader can be scripted for export operations as well since it supports a command-line interface that's only available on the Windows operating system.

Bulk API

Salesforce's Bulk API can be used just as effectively for exporting data as it is for importing data when working with millions of records. For example, a Bulk API Query can be used to efficiently query large amounts of data (up to 15 GB), split into (up to 15) 1 GB batches. The query must return within 2 minutes (otherwise, a QUERY_TIMEOUT error is returned). If the results are within the 1 GB batch size limit, and the batch was processed within a 10-minute time limit, then the batch is processed, and results are returned. Salesforce will try 15 batch attempts (hence the 15 GB limit), so if this is breached, the batch is considered unsuccessful and a **Retried more than 15 times** error is returned.

PK chunking

Added to the Bulk API back in 2015, **Primary Key (PK)** chunking is used to increase the performance of large data downloads from the Salesforce Platform. All custom objects and most standard objects are supported by PK chunking (a complete list is available at https://developer.salesforce. com/docs/atlas.en-us.234.0.api_asynch.meta/api_asynch/async_api_ headers_enable_pk_chunking.htm).

The way PK chunking works is that when enabled in a Bulk API request, along with a chunk size (say 250,000), Salesforce gets the minimum and maximum IDs for the dataset to be returned, and then creates a set of SOQL statements that each contains a WHERE clause to retrieve records for the given chunk size. Salesforce combines all the results and returns a complete dataset. If we take an example whereby we select all email addresses for every contact in Salesforce, we'd write a SELECT SOQL statement, as follows:

```
SELECT Email FROM Contact
```

Now, suppose we have 1 million contacts in Salesforce and we set a chunk size of 100,000. Here, Salesforce would generate 10 SOQL statements, similar to what's shown in the following code block (where the <ID of record x> placeholders would be replaced with the actual record IDs):

```
SELECT Email FROM Contact WHERE Id >= <ID of record 1> AND Id <
<ID of record 100,000>
SELECT Email FROM Contact WHERE Id >= <ID of record 100,000>
AND Id < <ID of record 200,000>
SELECT Email FROM Contact WHERE Id >= <ID of record 200,000>
AND Id < <ID of record 300,000>
```

```
SELECT Email FROM Contact WHERE Id >= <ID of record 300,000>
AND Id < <ID of record 400,000>
SELECT Email FROM Contact WHERE Id >= <ID of record 400,000>
AND Id < <ID of record 500,000>
SELECT Email FROM Contact WHERE Id >= <ID of record 500,000>
AND Id < <ID of record 600,000>
SELECT Email FROM Contact WHERE Id >= <ID of record 600,000>
AND Id < <ID of record 700,000>
SELECT Email FROM Contact WHERE Id >= <ID of record 700,000>
AND Id < <ID of record 800,000>
SELECT Email FROM Contact WHERE Id >= <ID of record 800,000>
AND Id < <ID of record 900,000>
SELECT Email FROM Contact WHERE Id >= <ID of record 900,000>
AND Id < <ID of record 1,000,000>
```

The reason PK chunking is faster than a straight export is that, by dividing the query into several subqueries, the Salesforce Platform Query Optimizer processes the queries more efficiently. This is because queries will be below the selectivity threshold.

Now, let's summarize what we've covered in this chapter.

Summary

In this chapter, we learned how to migrate data, covering each step in detail to ensure you have the requisite knowledge to answer questions on these topics in the exam. Next, we looked at the Salesforce perspective on loading high-quality data, including considerations for LDVs being migrated to the Salesforce Platform. Lastly, we looked at exporting data from Salesforce while covering the various techniques available for us to do so, including Data Loader, Data Export, and the Bulk API, including PK chunking.

This effectively wraps up the theoretical side of the exam content. In the next chapter, we will cover the design aspects of the exam, and we will begin with Accounts and Contacts.

Practice questions

Test your knowledge of the topics covered in this chapter by answering the following questions:

1. What does LDV stand for?

2. What does the *PK* in the term PK chunking stand for?

3. What is the name of the in-browser tool used for manual or scheduled weekly or monthly data exports?

4. What method is used to speed up the performance of large `SELECT` SOQL queries when exporting large amounts of data from Salesforce?

5. What data API facilitates the asynchronous processing of data in parallel batches?

6. Ordering records to be imported by their parent record ID reduces the likelihood of what happening?

7. True or false: upsert is considered good for performance when loading large amounts of data.

8. PK chunking is a feature of which Salesforce API?

9. What's the first step in any data migration process?

10. Why is PK chunking considered faster than a straight *Export All* operation?

Answers

The following are the answers to the previous questions. How many of them were you able to answer correctly? Check your answers to the previous questions here:

1. Large Data Volume

2. Primary key

3. Data Export

4. PK Chunking

5. Bulk API

6. Parent record locking

7. False. Use insert and then update as separate operations.

8. The Bulk API

9. Define

10. Because by breaking the query down into sub-queries, the Salesforce Query Optimizer threshold isn't reached and therefore the performance of each query is optimal.

Further reading

See the following resources. For more information on what was covered in this chapter:

- Data Export options from Salesforce: `https://trailhead.salesforce.com/content/learn/modules/lex_implementation_data_management/lex_implementation_data_export`

- PK chunking in Salesforce: `https://developer.salesforce.com/docs/atlas.en-us.234.0.api_asynch.meta/api_asynch/async_api_headers_enable_pk_chunking.htm`

- Data allocation and storage limits: `https://help.salesforce.com/s/articleView?id=sf.overview_storage.htm&type=5`

- Bulk API Query: `https://developer.salesforce.com/docs/atlas.en-us.api_asynch.meta/api_asynch/asynch_api_bulk_query_intro.htm`

Section 2: Salesforce Data Architect Design

Turning our attention to the effective design of solutions on the Salesforce platform that focus on data, this part of the book covers topics regarding the core data model, the effective use of Apex, knowing what options exist to get data in and out of the platform, tuning for performance, and territory management. Much like the first part of this book, the topics outlined will become a handy reference in your day-to-day job as a Salesforce Data Architect.

This section comprises the following chapters:

- *Chapter 8, Accounts and Contacts*
- *Chapter 9, Data APIs and Apex*
- *Chapter 10, Tuning Performance*
- *Chapter 11, Backup and Restore*
- *Chapter 12, Territory Management*

Accounts and Contacts

Two of the core objects in core platform clouds (such as Sales Cloud and Service Cloud) are Account and Contact. These two objects deserve a chapter of their own to describe the special behavior that the Salesforce platform gives to them.

In this chapter, we will cover the Account and Contact model, including Person Accounts and the Contacts to multiple Accounts enablement implications, Account Skew, and the implications this has on the performance of queries and reports. We'll also look at the objects in the standard Salesforce data model that are associated with Accounts and Contacts.

By the end of this chapter, you'll understand the Account and Contact data model, including what happens when personal accounts are enabled. You'll also understand the implications and considerations for enabling the Contacts to multiple Accounts feature. Furthermore, you'll understand the objects that are associated with Account and Contact. Lastly, you'll understand Account Skew in terms of what it is and how it impacts your users.

In this chapter, we will cover the following topics:

- Understanding the Account and Contact model
- Introducing person accounts
- Exploring the Contacts to multiple Accounts feature
- Exploring objects associated with Accounts and Contacts
- Putting it all together
- Revisiting Account Skew

Understanding the Account and Contact model

The **Account** object is at the heart of many Salesforce core platform cloud products, such as Sales Cloud, Service Cloud, Financial Services Cloud, and Experience Cloud. The **Contact** object represents a person that is associated with an Account record.

At its most basic interpretation, an **Account record** represents a company or similar entity from which one or more Contact records can be associated, such as employees. Therefore, an Account record can be thought of as a company or business. An Account record can have many Contact records, representing the employees of that company or business.

Let's look at how this simple structure is represented diagrammatically:

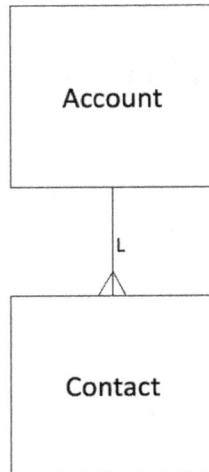

Figure 8.1 – Simplified Account and Contact object relationship

As you would expect with Salesforce originally being focused on sales teams/selling (hence the company name), the Account object contains many useful standard fields that can be utilized with minimal customization.

These standard fields include the following:

- **Industry**: A picklist of industries the account may belong to, such as agriculture or transport
- **Shipping address**: The mailing address
- **Billing address**: Where invoices and paperwork are sent
- **Number of employees**
- **Ownership**: Denoting if the company ownership structure is private, public, limited, and so on
- **Standard Industry Classification (SIC) code**
- **Ticker symbol**: The public stock ticker trading code – for example, **Customer Relationship Management (CRM)** for Salesforce as it trades under the CRM symbol
- **Website**: The website's address

Other standard fields are available, which you can find out more about in the Account object documentation available at https://developer.salesforce.com/docs/atlas.en-us. object_reference.meta/object_reference/sforce_api_objects_account.htm.

Now that we understand the Account object, let's explore Account Hierarchies.

Account Hierarchies

Account records can also have parent Accounts, representing hierarchies of companies. For example, you may have a company called *MadeUp* that has Account records for MadeUp Incorporated (the global group entity), MadeUp North America, MadeUp **Europe, Middle East, and Africa (EMEA)**, and country-specific Account records for the MadeUp entity for that country.

Let's visualize our Account Hierarchy with the following diagram:

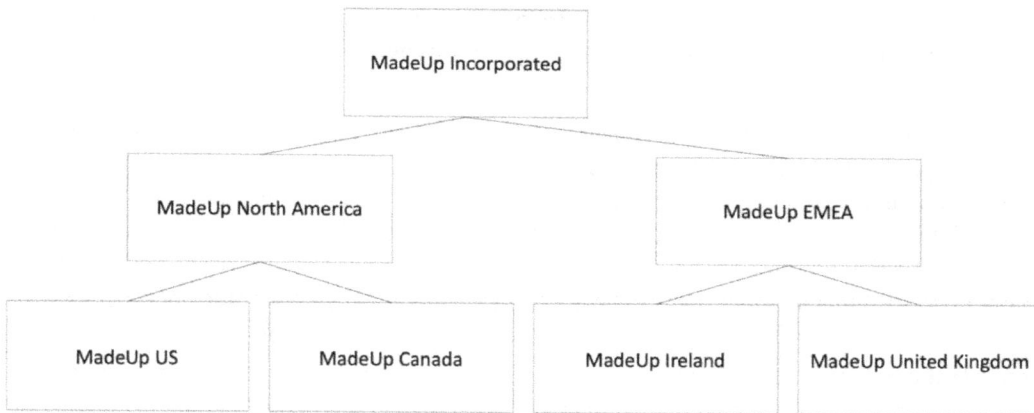

Figure 8.2 – An Account Hierarchy visualized

Account Hierarchies can be achieved by having an Account record with its ParentId field populated with the parent Account record's Salesforce ID. This is a standard field that requires no feature enablement or customization.

Having looked at the business view of Accounts and Contacts, let's look at Person Accounts.

Introducing Person Accounts

In the business view of Accounts and Contacts, where an Account is a company and a Contact is an employee of that company, the business deals (Opportunities) are related to the Account record. When selling to individual people, such as a banking client in the case of a Financial Services Cloud implementation, we need to associate Opportunities with those people as if they were Account records. This is where the Person Account concept comes in.

A **Person Account** is a special type of Account record that pulls through some, but not all, information of a single associated Contact record onto it. This allows the information about the person (from the associated Contact information) to be represented when associating a business deal (Opportunity) with that person. The Opportunity is still associated with the Account record to form the Person Account.

When enabling a Person Account, the Account and Contact **Organization-Wide Defaults (OWDs)** need to be set to Private or Contact needs to be set to Controlled by Parent. When enabled, a Person Account record type is available for use. Other Person Account record types can then be created as needed for page layout/profile assignment and other features necessary for the correct experience for your users.

To enable Person Accounts, a case needs to be raised with Salesforce Support. When enabled, Person Accounts cannot be disabled. Additionally, this has a permanent effect on the sharing model. Given that when you enable Person Accounts a prerequisite is to set the **OWD** of Contact to be either Controlled By Parent or Private, consider the permanent effects of enabling such a far-reaching sharing setting. Contacts that do not form part of a Person Account will need to be shared explicitly with users following the other sharing features of Salesforce, such as Role Hierarchy and Sharing Rules.

> **Important note**
>
> It is possible to have Person Accounts enabled and use Account and Contact records as before. Taking the example of a bank with Financial Services Cloud that requires Person Accounts to be enabled, the bank can create Opportunities against both companies and individual people, as represented by their Account and Person Account records, respectively.

When using Person Accounts, consider that Leads (which represent people) are not converted into a separate Account, Contact, or Opportunity. Instead, you must convert the Lead into a Person Account and an Opportunity.

Additionally, the Parent Account field won't be present on the Person Account, as you can't represent Account Hierarchies using Person Accounts. When diagramming and visualizing Person Accounts, I prefer to draw a dashed box around the combined Account and Contact, as shown in the following diagram:

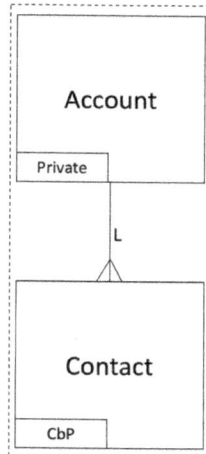

Figure 8.3 – A diagrammatic representation of a Person Account

Now that we've covered Person Accounts, let's learn how to associate a Contact record with more than one Account record in Salesforce.

Exploring the Contacts to multiple Accounts feature

As you would expect, the Contacts to multiple Accounts feature allows a Contact record to be associated with more than one Account record. When Contacts to multiple Accounts is enabled, Contact records essentially have a primary Account record relationship and zero or more indirect Account relationships.

> **Important note**
> Disabling the Contacts to multiple Accounts feature will effectively delete all indirect Account relationships for your Contact records.

When enabled, the Account object's standard Contacts-related list can be replaced on page layouts with the **Related Contacts** list instead. Contact page layouts can have the **Related Accounts** list added to them. Person Accounts can have both related lists added to their page layouts.

> **Important note**
> By default, any activities associated with a Contact record will roll up to the primary Account record for the contact. It is possible to disable this default behavior by unselecting the **Roll up activities to a contact's primary account** option in **Activities Settings** in **Salesforce Setup**.

Now, let's explore the wider object model that surrounds the Account and Contact objects.

Exploring objects associated with Accounts and Contacts

Despite having an explicit relationship between each other, where multiple Contact records can belong to the same Account, there are a couple of additional objects that allow for context to be given to the relationship between the records of these two objects.

Now, let's explore the various Account and Contact object associations, starting with `AccountContactRelation`.

AccountContactRelation

We described the Contacts to multiple Accounts feature earlier in this chapter, thus covering how a single Contact record can be associated with more than one account. Well, the `AccountContactRelation` object is the underlying data model entity that facilitates this Salesforce feature.

The `AccountContactRelation` object essentially acts as a junction object between Account and Contact. Some standard fields are used to provide context about the relationship a Contact has to an Account. These can include things such as Start/End dates for when the Contact relationship with the Account started and ended. They may also include the Roles they may play on the Account, where more than one can be selected. Other fields may include denoting information such as if the relationship is active, and if the relationship is to the Contacts primary account (using the `IsDirect` field).

The underlying data model for this entity can be visualized as follows:

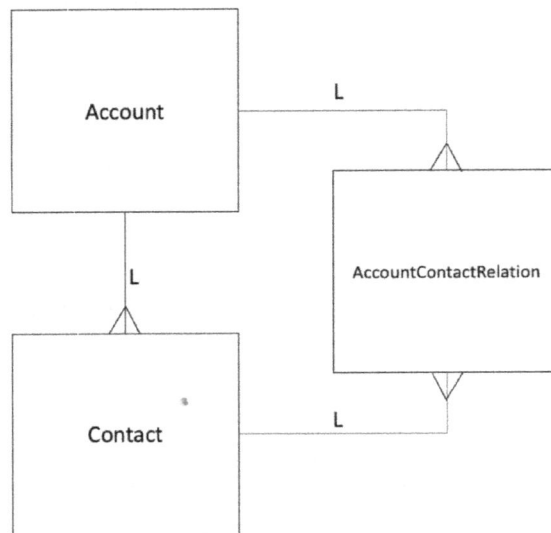

Figure 8.4 – AccountContactRelation as it fits within the standard
Salesforce data model (OWDs intentionally omitted)

Now, let's learn how to provide context to the relationship between related Accounts and Contacts.

AccountContactRole

To represent the actual role that a particular Contact record plays against an Account record, such as Decision Maker, Buyer, and so on, the `AccountContactRole` object is a lightweight way of associating Contacts in a way that provides context.

Imagine that you are a salesperson using Salesforce and are selling to a particular company (Account). Knowing who (the Contact records) does what (the `AccountContactRole` records) makes selling more targeted and helps ensure you can have the right conversations with the right people.

The `AccountContactRole` object is a junction object, in that it contains lookups to the Account and Contact objects – that is, the `AccountId` and `ContactID` fields, respectively. As you'd expect, it is also the object that's used to capture the role the Contact performs. This is represented by the `Role` field.

This junction object can be represented in a data model with Account and Contact as follows:

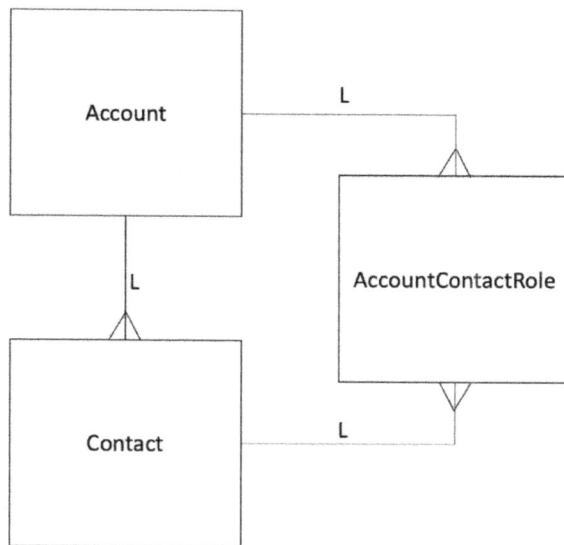

Figure 8.5 – AccountContactRole as it fits within the standard
Salesforce data model (OWDs intentionally omitted)

With the `AccountContactRole` object covered, let's look at Account Teams.

Account Teams

Account Teams represent the Salesforce users that play a role in the Account. For example, when selling to or serving an Account, you may have Salesforce users in your organization that are responsible for managing the relationship, being a point of escalation, and so on.

Account teams provide a way of associating your Salesforce users to Accounts in addition to what's offered by the sharing model that's already been configured in Salesforce for your organization. For example, you may have a private Account, Contact, and Opportunity sharing model, as well as a Role Hierarchy set up, that has sales team members in the same place of that Role Hierarchy. By default, those users would not automatically have access to all Account records. They would need to be explicitly shared using a Sharing Rule or Manual Sharing, for example. Account teams provide a way of opening up access to Accounts and other objects (including Contact, Opportunity, and Case). This access can be specified on a per-Account Team Member basis.

The Salesforce entity responsible for this functionality is called `AccountTeamMember`. As well as lookups to User and Account, this object provides `AccountAccessLevel`, `CaseAccessLevel`, `ContactAccessLevel`, and `OpportunityAccessLevel` picklist fields. These fields can have the `None`, `Read`, and `Edit` values and can be used to set the respective access level.

> **Important note**
>
> The `AccessLevel` picklist values must be set to values higher than the **Organization-Wide Defaults (OWDs)** for the respective object. For example, `AccountAccessLevel` must be set to **Edit** if the OWD provides Public Read-Only by default.

A representation of the `AccountTeamMember` object in the data model is as follows:

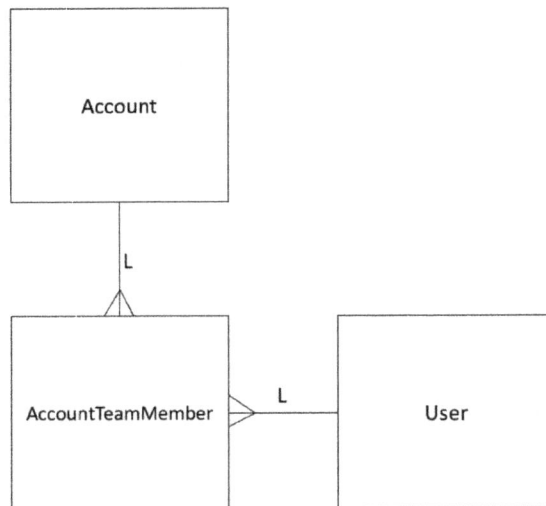

Figure 8.6 – AccountTeamMember as it fits within the standard
Salesforce data model (OWDs intentionally omitted)

Now that we've covered the associated objects around the core Account and Contact data model, let's look at an example where we can bring everything in this chapter together.

Putting it all together

Let's put what we've learned throughout this chapter together using a practical example from the Account and Contact concepts we have covered in this chapter.

Let's imagine that there's a fictitious bank that deals with both individuals and businesses (and therefore the people that work for that business). The fictitious bank has sales teams that deal with corporate clients, personal bankers that deal with non-corporate banking clients, and certain customer individuals who can be privy to the dealings of more than one company, such as a legal professional. Let's imagine how the Account and Contact parts of the data model can be visualized:

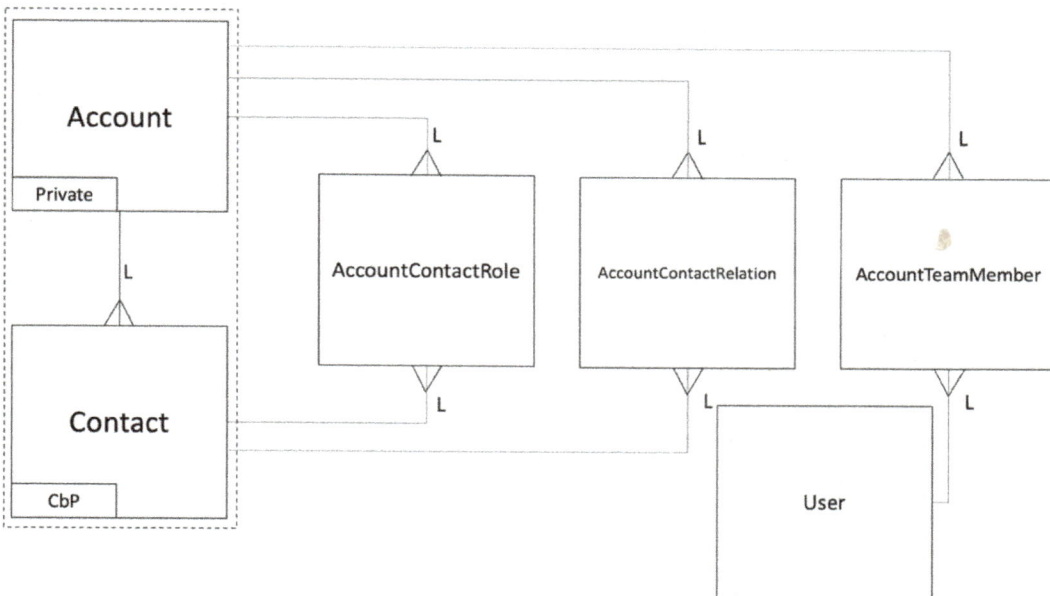

Figure 8.7 – An example data model

Here, we can see how several different relationship types between Accounts and Contacts can be achieved using the Person Accounts feature and three join objects. Our fictitious bank can deal with businesses using separate Account and Contact records (much like the out-of-the-box Salesforce functionality), or with individuals using Person Accounts.

The roles that Contacts play in Accounts are represented using the AccountContactRole object, so multiple people can be dealt with by the same corporate client.

For the requirement relating to legal professionals that deal with multiple companies, the `AccountContactRelation` object can be used.

Lastly, the requirement for teams of users dealing with corporate clients is possible using the `AccountTeamMember` object.

While the object model focuses purely on Accounts and Contacts (since no OWDs are included), it's possible to see how several business requirements can be achieved in a straightforward manner using standard Salesforce objects.

Now that we've covered an example that brings everything together, let's revisit a performance issue that affects Accounts and Contacts: Account Skew.

Revisiting Account Skew

As introduced in *Chapter 2, Data Modeling and Database Design*, **Account Skew** is the result of an Account record containing 10,000 or more child records. This causes performance and record locking issues.

When updates are made to the child record of an Account, Salesforce locks the parent Account record to maintain record integrity in the database. Updating a large number of child records under the same Account record may cause issues since each of those child record operations will be trying to lock the parent's Account record.

Additionally, when updates are made to an Account record that affects sharing, such as a seemingly harmless action such as changing the record owner, then all sharing for that Account will have to be recalculated. This goes for all child records of the account. This can cause many inter-connected processes to fail since sharing rules, Role Hierarchy calculations, and other sharing operations will have to take place. If any of these operations lock a record or take too long, contention may occur.

Mitigating Account Skew

The simple rule for mitigating Account Skew is to distribute child records across multiple parent Account records. Remember, 10,000 is the maximum advised number of child records for a particular account record before Account Skew may occur.

With Account Skew revisited, let's summarize what we've covered in this chapter.

Summary

In this chapter, we dug deep into the Account and Contact model, understanding its position at the center of the wider data model for many core Salesforce cloud products. First, we looked at the nuances involved in enabling Person Accounts and looked at the Contacts to multiple Accounts feature. The wider data model that surrounds the Account and Contact objects was also explored. Finally, we revisited Account Skew to understand its importance in terms of performance.

In *Chapter 9, Data APIs and Apex*, we will cover the practical aspects of the exam.

Practice questions

Test your knowledge of what we've covered in this chapter by attempting to answer the following practice questions:

1. Which object is responsible for managing the role a Contact has with an Account, where that Contact may be associated with more than one Account?

2. Which object is responsible for managing the role a Contact has with an Account, where the Contacts to multiple Accounts feature hasn't been enabled?

3. What term describes an Account record that behaves like a Contact, yet can be associated with Opportunities?

4. Which object associates User records with an Account outside of the ownership and configured org-wide sharing model?

5. On Account records, what is the `ParentId` field used for?

6. True or false? It is possible to use Person Accounts and Business Accounts side by side.

7. True or false? Once Person Accounts are enabled, they cannot be disabled.

8. True or false? After enabling the Contacts to multiple Accounts feature, a Contact's activity history will roll up to the designated primary Account record for the Contact.

9. When using Account Teams, what must the **AccessLevel** picklist value be set to?

10. What is Account Skew?

Answers

How did you get on answering the practice questions? Check your answers here:

1. `AccountContactRelation`

2. `AccountContactRole`

3. Person Account

4. `AccountTeamMember`

5. Account Hierarchies

6. True

7. True

8. True

9. Values higher than the org-wide defaults for the respective object

10. Record locking, sharing, or other long-running processes that may fail as a result of an Account record having too many child records

Further reading

The following resources will help bolster what you've learned in this chapter:

- The Account object API documentation: `https://developer.salesforce.com/docs/atlas.en-us.object_reference.meta/object_reference/sforce_api_objects_account.htm`

- The Contact object API documentation: `https://developer.salesforce.com/docs/atlas.en-us.object_reference.meta/object_reference/sforce_api_objects_contact.htm`

- *Enable Person Accounts*: `https://help.salesforce.com/s/articleView?id=sf.account_person_enable.htm&type=5`

- *Set Up Contacts to Multiple Accounts*: `https://help.salesforce.com/s/articleView?id=sf.shared_contacts_set_up.htm&type=5`

- *Comparing Contacts to Multiple Accounts to Other Options*: `https://help.salesforce.com/s/articleView?id=sf.shared_contacts_comparison.htm&type=5`

- AccountContactRelation API documentation: `https://developer.salesforce.com/docs/atlas.en-us.object_reference.meta/object_reference/sforce_api_objects_accountcontactrelation.htm`

- AccountContactRole API documentation: `https://developer.salesforce.com/docs/atlas.en-us.object_reference.meta/object_reference/sforce_api_objects_accountcontactrole.htm`

- AccountTeamMember API documentation: `https://developer.salesforce.com/docs/atlas.en-us.object_reference.meta/object_reference/sforce_api_objects_accountteammember.htm`

9
Data APIs and Apex

In this chapter, we're going to explore the various Salesforce **Application Programming Interfaces** (**APIs**) that relate to data operations. Understanding the various APIs and Apex operations is important in rounding out your knowledge of the programmatical capabilities of the Salesforce platform as it relates to data operations. When taking the exam, you may get quizzed on hypothetical scenario questions that involve answering based on use of a Salesforce API or the use of Apex code to achieve a certain data operation. Therefore, this is crucial in rounding out your knowledge as a Salesforce Data Architect. In this chapter, we're also going to look at Apex facilities relating to data, including database operations, working with batch data methods, and asynchronous Apex.

In this chapter, we will cover the following topics:

- How to call an API

- Lightning Platform Data APIs

- Apex Database operations

- Batch Apex

- Asynchronous Apex

By the end of this chapter, you'll be in a good position to understand the appropriate ways to deploy each of the topics covered when designing solutions involving data operations on the Salesforce Lightning Platform. Let's begin with understanding how to call an API.

How to call an API

While the design and implementation of APIs is out of the scope of this book, we'll briefly cover how to call an API, namely the Salesforce REST API. At a high-level, an API is essentially a request to an endpoint (a URL) with an XML or JSON body (known as the request payload). The endpoint will return a response payload, which may be XML or JSON depending on how it is configured.

Let's cover what calling a REST API looks like, and examine the request and response payloads as we do. For this, we're going to use an online utility called Workbench, which is a free-to-use web application for interacting with your Salesforce instance. Note that it is not an official Salesforce product, and therefore support is limited.

To begin, open a web browser and navigate to the URL https://workbench.developerforce. com/login.php

Next, click the checkbox to agree to the terms and conditions, and click the **Login with Salesforce** button:

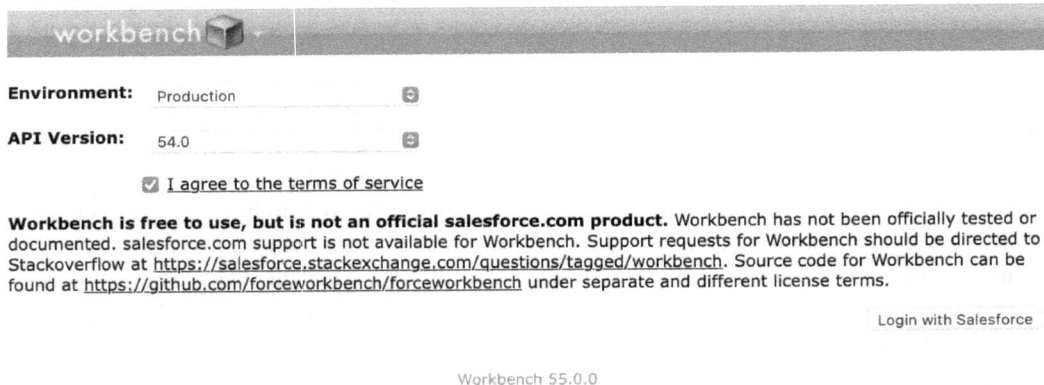

Environment: Production

API Version: 54.0

☑ I agree to the terms of service

Workbench is free to use, but is not an official salesforce.com product. Workbench has not been officially tested or documented. salesforce.com support is not available for Workbench. Support requests for Workbench should be directed to Stackoverflow at https://salesforce.stackexchange.com/questions/tagged/workbench. Source code for Workbench can be found at https://github.com/forceworkbench/forceworkbench under separate and different license terms.

Login with Salesforce

Workbench 55.0.0

Figure 9.1 – The Workbench application login page

Log in to your developer edition org, and you'll be returned to the Workbench application in your browser:

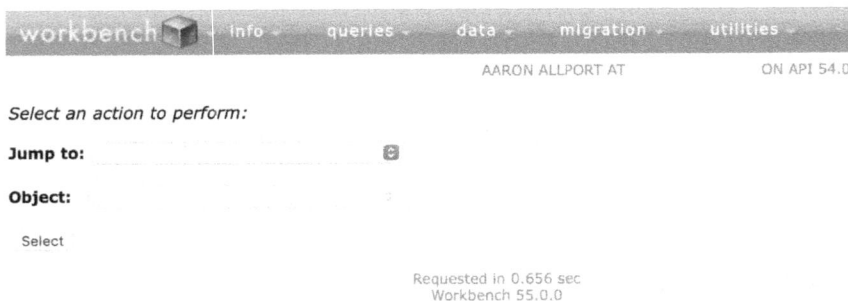

Select an action to perform:

Jump to:

Object:

Select

Requested in 0.656 sec
Workbench 55.0.0

Figure 9.2 – The Workbench application once logged in

In the **Jump to** picklist, choose **REST Explorer** and click the **Select** button. Next, put *URL /services/data/v54.0/query?q=SELECT+Name+FROM+Account* in the text box and click the **Execute** button:

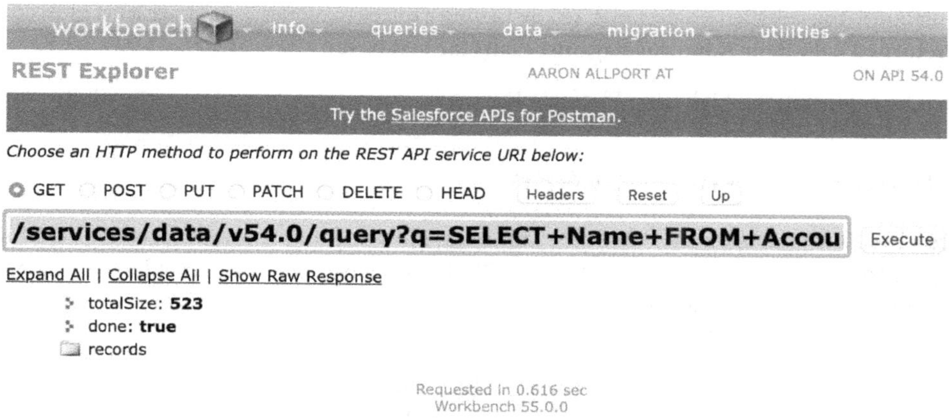

Figure 9.3 – Issuing a REST API query through Workbench

Lastly, hit the **Show Raw Response** tab. You will be able to see an array of Account records, with their names returned:

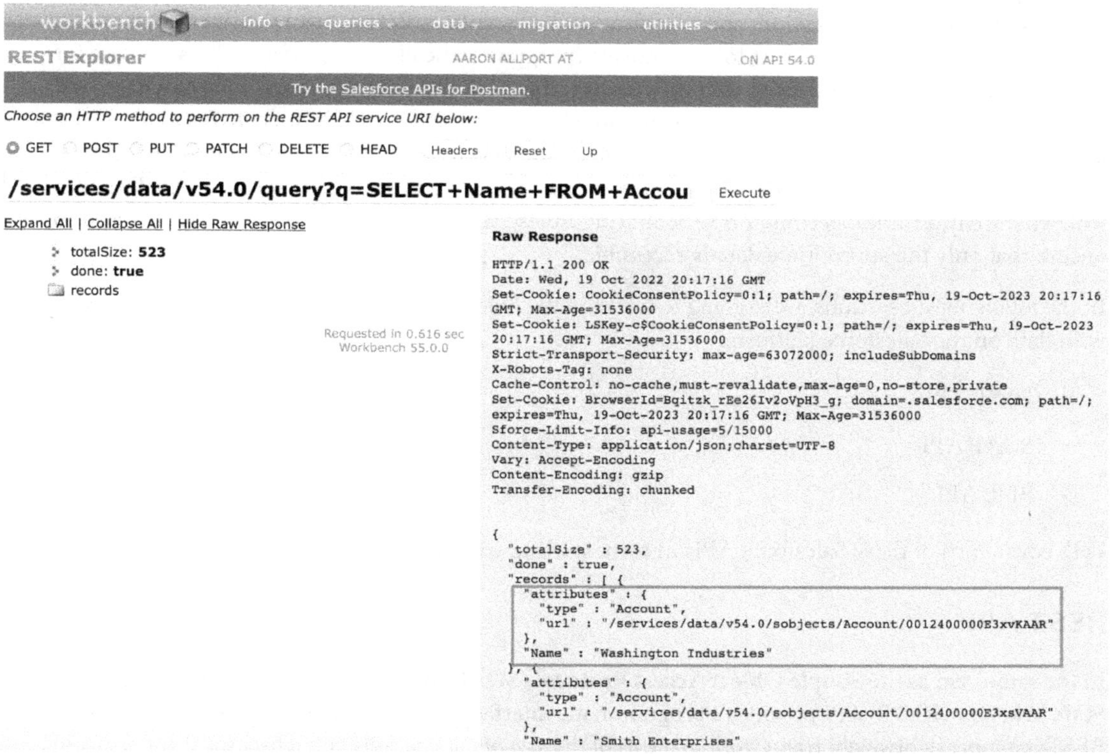

Figure 9.4 – The raw (JSON) response from our issued REST API query

Congratulations! You've called a Salesforce API by issuing a query (a request) and have a list of Account records returned with their Name field against each (the response).

Let's begin by exploring the Lightning Platform Data APIs.

Lightning Platform Data APIs

There are 11 APIs available on the Salesforce Lightning Platform that cover all sorts of operations, including working with metadata (the Metadata API), building user interfaces that let users interact with Salesforce records (the User Interface API), and for use when building custom development modules or applications (the Tooling API).

I appreciate that not everyone reading this book will be a software engineer and therefore understand the intricacies of how APIs work. However, understanding how Salesforce programmatically exposes data-related operations is necessary. This will give you a more complete understanding of how data can be affected by operations on the Salesforce platform outside of general user interface interaction.

In a nutshell, an API provides a means by which two software applications can talk to each other. Typically, one of the applications exposes a select set of operations that other applications can invoke. APIs also support authentication, and Salesforce is no exception. Before invoking operations with a Salesforce API, it is a requirement to authenticate (programmatically) to Salesforce. As is the case for users interacting with Salesforce using the user interface, all API operations are done as a user, and therefore it is subject to the same permission model as other users. I've seen specific *Integration User* accounts set up for this purpose. The upshot of the same permission model applying to user accounts used by other software tooling means that the same permission facilities (Organization-Wide Defaults, Role Hierarchy, Profiles, Permission Sets, Sharing Rules, Manual Sharing, and so on) can be used to ensure that only the appropriate data is accessible.

In the following subsections, we're going to focus on the following APIs because they allow us to work with data on the Salesforce platform:

- REST API
- SOAP API
- Bulk API

Let's cover each of these Salesforce APIs in turn, starting with the REST API.

REST API

In the same vein as the **Simple Object Access Protocol (SOAP)** API, the Salesforce **Representational State Transfer (REST)** API provides a programmatic interface for interacting with Salesforce. Because REST is a more lightweight framework in terms of the size of data packets going backward and forward to Salesforce, it is preferred for mobile applications.

Important note

REST involves utilizing a standard set of HTTP methods for getting data or pushing data to and from an endpoint. REST API calls are stateless, in that each call is treated as a discrete operation. REST supports JSON or XML for the payload format.

SOAP is a bit more heavyweight than REST but allows for more flexibility in determining the methods to be called when invoking operations on a particular endpoint. SOAP API calls are stateful in that the state of the operation or data is passed backward and forward each time. SOAP uses XML for the payload format.

Salesforce provides the same underlying data model and the same governor limits apply to operations, irrespective of being called using the REST or SOAP API.

Using the REST API, Salesforce data queries can be invoked as part of a request to the query endpoint, where the SOQL query can be passed as part of the request. For example, invoking a `GET` operation on the following endpoint would return all `Account` record `Name` values, in accordance with the REST API specification: `https://login.salesforce.com/services/data/v54.0/query?q=SELECT+Name+FROM+Account`.

To create a record, invoke a `POST` operation on the endpoint for the object you are creating the record for (such as `/services/data/v20.0/sobjects/Account/`, with a payload of field name and value mappings). This could look as follows:

```
{

    "Name": "Packt",
    "Industry": "Publishing"

}
```

It is worth noting that the Salesforce REST API is stateless, in that the calling application needs to have all of the information necessary in the request to Salesforce for Salesforce to understand how to process that request. If you develop with the Salesforce REST API, you'll quickly notice that it works using generic HTTP methods (GET, POST, and so on), and therefore all resources and operations are accessed using a generic interface.

The REST API supports authentication to Salesforce using the OAuth 2.0 protocol, which is a well-documented method for authenticating RESTful applications to Salesforce.

Now that we've been introduced to the REST API, let's explore the relatively similar SOAP API.

SOAP API

The SOAP API works similarly to the REST API in that you can work with object data using web service calls. The SOAP API is not as lightweight in use as the REST API as state is transferred backward and forward with each request and response. SOAP web service calls must use XML as the payload data format and can be used by any programming language that supports web services.

SOAP web services are defined by consuming a **Web Service Description Language** (**WSDL**) file, which describes the methods available to be executed, any parameters, and example requests and responses to calls to those operations. The WSDL for your Salesforce instance can be downloaded from **Setup** and typing API in the search box, then selecting the API menu item returned. Then, you can download one of two WSDL files:

1. `Enterprise WSDL`: This is specific to your Salesforce instance and takes the customizations you have made into account (such as the creation of custom objects).

2. `Partner WSDL`: This is a WSDL file that works using generic types (all objects are interacted with through Object operations, rather than operating directly on an Account entity, Contact entity, and so on).

   When working with the SOAP API, you'll first invoke an operation to log in to Salesforce as the user under whom you wish to execute the operations, which generates a session identifier. This session identifier is then used in all subsequent requests.

   Taking our example of creating an Account record from the *REST API* section of this chapter, a SOAP representation would look as follows (it's assumed that the login operation has been done):

```
<soapenv:Envelope xmlns:soapenv="http://schemas.xmlsoap.
org/soap/envelope/" xmlns:urn="urn:enterprise.soap.
sforce.com" xmlns:urn1="urn:sobject.enterprise.soap.
sforce.com" xmlns:xsi="http://www.w3.org/2001/XMLSchema-
instance">
  <soapenv:Header>
    <urn:SessionHeader>
      <urn:sessionId>[sessionId retrieved from a login()
call]</urn:sessionId>
    </urn:SessionHeader>
  </soapenv:Header>
  <soapenv:Body>
    <urn:create>
      <urn:sObjects xsi:type="urn1:Account">
        <Name>Packt</Name>
<Industry>Publishing</Industry>
      </urn:sObjects>
```

```
    </urn:create>
  </soapenv:Body>
</soapenv:Envelope>
```

As you can see, compared to the REST example, the SOAP API call is a lot more descriptive. The `<urn:create>` tag specifies that this is a SOQL insert operation, the `<urn:sObjects xsi:type="urn1:Account">` tag specifies that this is an `Account` object, and then the child tags specify the fields. The REST API, by POSTing to an Account endpoint, assumes the same thing.

While this section has been technical, the SOAP and REST APIs have parity in terms of database operations. The difference is in the way they are interacted with. Suffice it to say, database operations can be executed programmatically. Given that all operations run under the context of a user, then the Salesforce permission model applies.

With the SOAP API now covered, let's look at the Bulk API.

Bulk API

The Salesforce Bulk API is used for two main purposes: to ingest and query. To simplify those terms, you can use the Bulk API to perform insert, update, upsert, or delete operations (ingest), or you can retrieve data (query). The key reason the Bulk API is used is due to the size of the data being ingested or queried. Any operation that involves more than 2,000 records is a suitable candidate for the Bulk API.

When performing an ingest operation, the Bulk API divides the operation into a set of smaller batches to improve performance. When starting an ingestion batch job, first, you must create a CSV file that represents the records to process (much like you'd use with Salesforce Data Loader). The job specifies what the operation is (insert, update, upsert, or delete), and the object to operate on, such as Account or Contact. When you start the job, Salesforce will take care of optimizing the job to reduce the likelihood of performance issues, timeouts, and batch failures.

When performing a query operation, the Bulk API will return the records as per the specified query. Again, Salesforce will optimize the job for performance and reduce the likelihood of timeouts or failures as much as possible.

When performing an ingest job, Salesforce will divide the data into batches for every 10,000 records (there is a daily limit of 150 million records). Salesforce attempts to process each record in a batch, but if a batch doesn't complete within 10 minutes, the batch fails. Salesforce will retry any failed batches up to 10 times. If a batch still fails after 10 retries, the whole batch job is marked as failed. In this scenario, you'd use the results returned from calling either the Failed Record Results or Unprocessed Record Results endpoints of the Bulk API to retrieve those records that were not processed and start a new job using those, after correcting any errors or issues first.

Query jobs are naturally a lot simpler to manage, as the data is returned once the job completes. If, however, a query job retries more than 15 times, it will fail. The simplest workaround in this scenario is to apply filter criteria to the query to improve performance and reduce the number of records that are returned.

Now that we've looked at the Bulk API, let's look at Apex Database Operations next.

Apex Database operations

In Apex code, it is possible to interact with the Salesforce database in one of two ways: as **Database Manipulation Language (DML)** statements or using Apex Database class methods. DML statements take the form of insert, update, upsert, or delete operations. Take the following example of a DML insert statement:

```
public class dmlStatementTest {
    public void testStatement() {
        List<Account> accounts;
        accounts.add(new Account(Name='Packt UK'));
        accounts.add(new Account(Name='Packt India'));


        insert accounts;
    }
}
```

Database Apex methods work slightly differently because rather than using a keyword such as insert or update, you call a method of the Database class instead. I'd argue that this offers more flexibility at the expense of more verbose code for the equivalent DML operation. This is because the Database class methods allow for an argument to specify whether to attempt partial record processing if errors are encountered. The same example that we used previously but using the Apex Database class can be represented as follows:

```
public class apexDatabaseClassTest {
    public void testStatement() {
        List<Account> accounts;
        accounts.add(new Account(Name='Packt UK'));
        accounts.add(new Account(Name='Packt India'));

        Database.SaveResult[] accountSaveResult = Database.
insert(accounts, false);
        // You would iterate through the
```

```
        // Database.SaveResult list here
    }
}
```

The second argument to the `Database.insert` operation is a Boolean that specifies whether to attempt partial record processing. If a value of true is passed, then as soon as one record cannot be processed, all remaining records are not attempted and an exception is thrown. If a value of false is passed, all records are attempted, and the status for each record is returned to the `Database.SaveResult` array. This can be iterated on and action can be taken as appropriate.

To determine the most appropriate Apex approach to use, think about whether you need exceptions to be thrown and immediately interrupt the execution of your code. If this is desired, then using a DML statement would be appropriate. If you wish to allow some records to be processed and take action on all records based on their status without interrupting the flow of your code, then consider an Apex `Database` class method call instead.

> **Important note**
>
> Database transaction control and the ability to roll back database operations are only available in the Apex `Database` class. In addition, the Apex `Database` class allows you to empty the recycle bin and convert a Lead (using the `convertLead` method).

Now that we've covered database operations using Apex, let's turn to another Apex data working facility called batch Apex.

Batch Apex

As its name suggests, batch Apex is used to invoke and process a potentially large number of records in batches, where the number of records is determined by issuing a query to Salesforce. This execution typically lends itself well to situations where a potentially large number of records could need processing, yet the exact number of records isn't known, such as updating records as part of an overnight batch procedure.

batch Apex classes must implement the `Database.Batchable` interface and therefore the `start`, `execute`, and `finish` methods. A bare-bones Apex class for implementing the `Database.Batchable` interface would look similar to the following:

```
public class myBatchClass implements Database.Batchable {
    public Database.QueryLocator start(Database.BatchableContext
info){}
    public void execute(Database.BatchableContext info,
List<sObject> scope){}
```

```
    public void finish(Database.BatchableContext info){}
}
```

The `start` method is used to define the query. The returned `Database.QueryLocator` is used to effectively retrieve the results of the query in the batch size specified (which is 200 if not specified).

The `execute` method is used to define the bulk of the Apex class logic and process the records that are returned in that record batch.

The `finish` method is used for any post-processing logic. I use this in nightly batch job class definitions to invoke an email summarizing the statistics from the job (number of total processed records, success, and failures).

To invoke a batch Apex class, it must be scheduled. This can be done in the Developer Console, as an anonymous Apex execution:

```
Id batchJobId = Database.executeBatch(new BatchClass(), 150);
```

In this example, our batch Apex class is called `BatchClass`, and we're executing it with a batch size of 150 records at a time (so 150 records are processed by the `execute` method of our batch class with each batch).

As an example, let's write a batch class that returns all Account records in our Salesforce instance that were created today, and append the phrase *processed* to *each*. Then, we'll invoke with the default batch size of 200:

```
public class appendAccountNameBatch implements Database.
batchable{
    public Database.QueryLocator start(Database.
BatchableContext info) {
        return Database.getQueryLocator('SELECT Id, Name FROM
Account WHERE CreatedDate = TODAY');
    }

    public void execute(Database.BatchableContext info,
List<sObject> scope) {
        List<Account> accounts = new List<Account>();
        for(sObject s : scope) {
            Account act = (Account)s;
            act.Name = act.Name + ' processed';
            accounts.add(a);
        }
```

```
        update accounts;
    }

    public void finish(Database.BatchableContext info) {
        // Do nothing
    }
}
```

This class will be invoked as follows:

```
Id batchJobId = Database.executeBatch(new
appendAccountNameBatch());
```

Batch Apex jobs can be viewed (and stopped) in Salesforce Setup by typing Apex Jobs into the quick-find box. If a job is **Completed**, then it means it ran without errors. Jobs that have a status of **Aborted** or **Failed** require investigation because they have not been executed successfully.

It's entirely possible to schedule batch Apex jobs to run according to a schedule, say every night. To do that, you need to create a wrapper class for your batch Apex class that implements the Schedulable interface, and then schedule that class to be executed according to a schedule, defined by using the Unix-like cron format.

> **Important note**
>
> The **Unix** cron format is used to specify a frequency for which schedulable jobs are to be run. It has origins in the cron utility on Unix operating systems. It follows a format of six values for day/time (with an optional seventh for the year). It is represented as a string, such as 0 0 17 * * ?, for a daily execution at 5 P.M. More information on the format of the cron string can be found at https://developer.salesforce.com/docs/atlas.en-us. apexcode.meta/apexcode/apex_scheduler.htm.

For example, let's wrap our appendAccountNameBatch class to allow it to be scheduled:

```
public class scheduledAppendAccountmeBatch implements
Schedulable {
   public voi execute(SchedulableContext sc) {
   appendAccountNameBatch b = new appendAccounNameBatch (); //
your batchclas
   database.executebatch(b);
   }
}
```

Then, we can call this schedulable class using anonymous Apex:

```
System.schedule('Nightly scheduledAppendAccountNameBatch  Job',
'0 0 1 * * ?', new scheduledAppendAccountNameBatch());
```

This would cause our batch class to run every night at 1 A.M. By understanding how the Apex code is invoked and how the batching of records facilitates us working within governor limits, we can effectively process lots of records using Apex code.

With batch Apex now under our belts, let's explore asynchronous operations using Apex on the Lightning Platform.

Asynchronous Apex

Apex code can be run in an asynchronous manner using batch classes, and subsequently queued or scheduled. Apex code can also be written to run in the background when it's asynchronous by using the `@future` annotation on methods. All Apex web service callouts are `@future` methods, with a `callout=true` parameter, in that they are forced to run asynchronously, and in the background, user interface operations are not held up by their invocation.

Another way to think about asynchronous Apex is that it essentially executes in its own time. A bonus of using `@future` methods is that the governor limits are higher, meaning SOQL query size and heap size limits are more generous as the execution is in its own time, on its own system thread.

When writing Apex methods that are annotated using `@future`, they must be static and only return a void return type – that is, return nothing.

Here's an example of a bare-bones asynchronous Apex class:

```
public class asyncClass {
    @future
    public static void anAsyncMethod() { }
}
```

With asynchronous Apex now understood, let's summarize what we've covered in this chapter.

Summary

In this chapter, we explored the more programmatic elements of the Salesforce platform when it comes to manipulating data. We looked at the REST and SOAP APIs before looking at the Bulk API. Then, we turned our attention to Apex `Database` class operations, batch Apex, and asynchronous Apex using `@future` annotations. With these concepts understood, you, as a Salesforce Data Architect, are now well versed to make decisions on programmatic behavior affecting the state of a solution.

In the next chapter, we'll explore more of the concepts around how you can mitigate **Large Data Volume (LDV)** concerns through practical examples and how to load massive amounts of data.

Practice questions

Test your knowledge of the topics covered in this chapter by answering the following questions:

1. What is the only data format that's suitable for SOAP API requests?
2. What are the two job types that the Bulk API is used for?
3. What type of resource is used to describe the operations that are offered by a SOAP API that can be imported by calling applications?
4. How many retries are attempted by a Bulk API Query operation?
5. What batch size are records divided into when running a Bulk API Ingest operation?
6. What operations are supported as part of a Bulk API Ingest job?
7. What interface is extended when writing an Apex batch class?
8. What annotation is used for asynchronous Apex methods?
9. The Apex `insert` statement, followed by a list of records of a particular object type, is an example of what type of approach when working with the Salesforce database?
10. The Apex `Database` class's insert/update/upsert/delete methods have a Boolean parameter that does what?

Answers

The following are the answers to the previous questions. How many of them were you able to answer correctly? Check your answers to the previous questions here:

1. XML
2. Ingest and Query
3. WSDL
4. 15
5. 10,000
6. Insert, update, upsert, delete
7. `Database.Batchable`
8. `@future`
9. A DML statement
10. Determine whether to allow partial processing of records

Further reading

See the following resources for more information on what was covered in this chapter:

- *OAuth 2.0 with Salesforce*: `https://developer.salesforce.com/docs/atlas.en-us.api_rest.meta/api_rest/intro_oauth_and_connected_apps.htm`

- *Batch API*: `https://developer.salesforce.com/docs/atlas.en-us.api_asynch.meta/api_asynch/asynch_api_intro.htm`

- *Bulk API 2.0 – How requests are processed*: `https://developer.salesforce.com/docs/atlas.en-us.api_asynch.meta/api_asynch/how_requests_are_processed.htm`

- *Batch Apex*: `https://developer.salesforce.com/docs/atlas.en-us.222.0.apexcode.meta/apexcode/apex_batch_interface.htm`

- *Executing Batch Apex*: `https://help.salesforce.com/s/articleView?id=000328480&type=1`

- *The Apex Batchable Interface*: `https://developer.salesforce.com/docs/atlas.en-us.apexref.meta/apexref/apex_interface_database_batchable.htm#apex_Database_Batchable_execute`

- *The Apex Schedulable class*: `https://developer.salesforce.com/docs/atlas.en-us.222.0.apexcode.meta/apexcode/apex_scheduler.htm`

- *Future methods in Apex*: `https://developer.salesforce.com/docs/atlas.en-us.222.0.apexcode.meta/apexcode/apex_invoking_future_methods.htm`

- *The Apex Database Class*: `https://developer.salesforce.com/docs/atlas.en-us.apexref.meta/apexref/apex_methods_system_database.htm`

10
Tuning Performance

In this chapter, we'll cover the various methods available to tune performance when designing Salesforce applications on Lightning Platform. We'll revisit several concepts we've already looked at, diving a little deeper into some scenarios to demonstrate the practical application of the techniques highlighted. By the end of this chapter, you'll know of the various performance tuning techniques available when designing scalable solutions on the Salesforce Platform, with particular regard to data performance.

In this chapter, we'll cover the following topics:

- Skinny tables and other **Large Data Volume** (**LDV**) mitigation techniques
- Query and search optimization
- Task locks
- **Primary Key** (**PK**) chunking to improve performance
- Loading massive amounts of data

We'll begin by looking at LDV mitigation techniques and tuning our Salesforce implementations when working with massive amounts of data.

Skinny tables and other LDV mitigation techniques

Skinny tables are an LDV mitigation technique that is useful when users experience slow read operations for queries against the Salesforce database. This is since the underlying (virtual) database schema for a standard object is actually a join across two tables. There are standard object standard fields and standard object custom fields. For example, a query for data from a standard object such as Account that includes both standard and custom fields of the Account object may benefit from skinny tables when performance is impacted.

As mentioned in *Chapter 6, Understanding Large Data Volumes*, skinny tables are for read operations only, in order to speed up queries for the fields that the skinny table contains. Whether a query should use a skinny table or not is determined behind the scenes by the Salesforce application layer. Skinny tables do not contain any soft-deleted records, and therefore can only be used to speed up the performance of read-only queries against records that aren't deleted.

Skinny tables are enabled by Salesforce support upon the creation of a support case, requiring you to provide the appropriate justification. Salesforce support won't simply create a skinny table without first trying to understand why the performance is slow, so they may indeed work with you to determine why that is first. It's also worth noting that skinny tables can only contain up to 100 columns.

Skinny tables can be created on all custom objects and on the following standard objects:

- `Account`
- `Contact`
- `Opportunity`
- `Lead`
- `Case`

Let's revisit our visual example of a skinny table to show how the skinny table construct works:

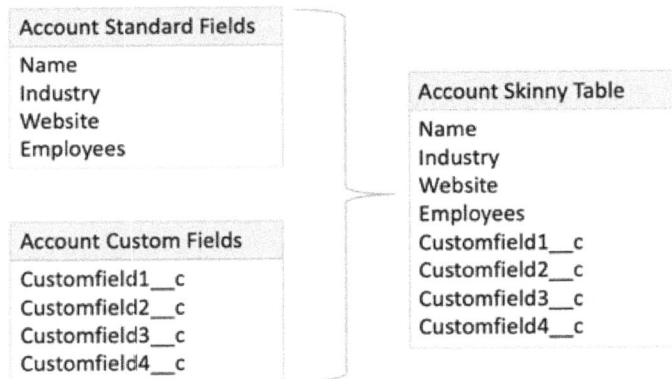

Figure 10.1 – Skinny table construct

As we can see, skinny tables are created to remove joins across standard and custom fields when issuing read-only queries to read data from a single object. Skinny tables are best enabled when a table has tens of millions of records and are useful for speeding up report performance for your users.

With skinny tables now covered, let's look at selective filter conditions and how they can be used when working to improve **Salesforce Object Query Language** (**SOQL**) query performance.

Selective filter conditions

In order to improve SOQL query performance, selective filter conditions can be utilized. You can determine whether a specific filter condition is selective by running it in the Developer Console and looking at the query statistics. You can work with Salesforce support to apply an index to a selective field in order to speed up query and reporting performance. In short, queries will perform more efficiently when indexes are applied to selective filter condition fields. Within the Salesforce application logic, the Lightning Platform query optimizer determines filter condition selectivity for a SOQL query, report, or list view when queries are issued.

By confirming that filter conditions in reports, SOQL, and list views are selective, then by applying indexes to those fields, the Lightning Platform query optimizer doesn't have to perform full dataset scans when looking for target data. It means that the performance will be optimal in such use cases.

Divisions

Divisions are a special Salesforce data performance feature that can be used to partition data and reduce the number of records returned by SOQL queries. This effectively increases performance for users running data queries and running reports. In order to enable Divisions, you need to raise a case with Salesforce support.

With skinny tables and other LDV mitigation techniques now revisited, let's look at the optimization of searches and queries.

Query and search optimization

As we explored in *Chapter 6, Understanding Large Data Volumes*, consider that Salesforce performs searches in a two-part process. The first part is the creation of a result set that is used to then perform the actual search. Let's quickly remind ourselves how a result set is produced. When a search is invoked (be it through the Salesforce user interface, a Salesforce API, or Apex code), Salesforce will first search the indexes that have been created for the appropriate records. Taking those results, Salesforce will then apply access permissions, search limits, and any other filters or filter logic to narrow down the results into a result set. That result set is then used to perform an actual search for records in the underlying database.

The way to speed up searches is to think carefully about the indexing of fields that are used when searching in order to speed up the performance of those searches. As seen in *Chapter 6, Understanding Large Data Volumes*, several indexes are automatically applied out of the box. When combined with custom indexes (which are enabled with assistance from Salesforce support), search performance can be increased.

As a reminder, when Salesforce performs an indexed search, standard indexes are used if the filter condition of the query matches less than 30% of the first million records (and less than 15% of additional records), up to a maximum of 1 million records.

Custom indexes (you would have worked with Salesforce support to enable these) are used where the query filter matches less than 10% of the total records, up to a maximum of 333,333 records.

Now we've covered the optimizations we can make to queries and searching, let's next look at task locks.

Task locks

When loading data, record locking can occur due to several issues. When dealing with tasks, it's worth noting a few conditions where records associated with the task records are locked. Specifically, these are as follows:

- When a task is inserted, the Account record, along with the records referenced by the WhoId and WhatId fields, is locked, but only if the status of the task record is not **Completed**, and the activity date is set (it's not equal to null).

- When a task is updated, the Account record, along with the records referenced by the WhoId and WhatId fields, is locked, irrespective of task record values.

- When a task is deleted, the Account record, along with the records referenced by the WhoId and WhatId fields, is locked, irrespective of task record values.

When we break down the record associations available for a task record, there are two main fields in play—namely, the WhoId and WhatId fields. WhoId is a Contact or a Lead record, and WhatId is any other type of record, such as Account or Opportunity.

With WhoId referencing a Contact record, a parent Account record is referenced through the relationship between the Contact and Account records. WhatId, if not referencing an Account record directly, will be another object record that ultimately resolves to an Account record. With this information understood, task records can be organized by the ultimate referencing account and loaded in discrete batches in parallel using the Bulk API.

Another way to load tasks, which may well be applicable if the ultimate parent Account record is the same, is by means of a serial job (one that is processed sequentially). This will be necessary when there are more than 10,000 task records associated with a single Account record, or where lock contentions may occur due to the relationships between referenced objects.

If jobs are being scheduled as part of a nightly batch or similar, the Salesforce best practice would be to ensure that there is a time buffer built into the batch job executions. This is to ensure that record overlaps with scheduled jobs that run too close together don't lock records and cause contention.

With task locks now looked at, let's turn to querying large amounts of data and how PK chunking can be used to improve performance.

PK chunking to improve performance

PK chunking is designed as a mechanism to allow entire Salesforce table data to be extracted—for example, as part of a backup routine. PK chunking effectively adds record IDs as a WHERE clause parameter to query data from a Salesforce entity in batches.

In general, if an object in Salesforce has more than 10 million rows, you should use PK chunking when exporting its data. If you are finding that querying for data times out regularly, use PK chunking.

Given that PK chunking effectively separates one big query into separate queries by adding a WHERE clause and using a range of ordered IDs, the batch size can be set. This is defaulted to 100,000 (as in, 100,000 records will be returned by default for each batch) but can be as high as 250,000. Therefore, for a 10 million-row entity, a batch size of 250,000 would result in 40 data batches being returned.

In *Chapter 7, Data Migration*, we walked through a practical example of how PK chunking works. It should be noted that it is possible to use filtered queries with PK chunking (as in, they already have a WHERE clause). In such scenarios, records returned from each sub-query may be less than the specified batch (or chunk) size. It's also worth noting that because the query is across the whole table, it will return (but omit) soft-deleted records. Given these are omitted from the result for a given query, the batch size returned may be smaller than the specified chunk size for that particular sub-query.

When viewing a PK-chunked job in Salesforce, it will have an initial state of NOT_PROCESSED. Any batches that fail will have a state of FAILED, but subsequent batches will still be processed as part of the overall job.

> **Important note**
>
> When filtering as part of your job where PK chunking is enabled, using either an ORDER BY clause or any form of ID field effectively disables PK chunking, and no performance benefit will be realized.

To start a PK-chunked batch job, send the Sforce-Enable-PKChunking header with the programmatic request. Here's an example of this:

```
Sforce-Enable-PKChunking: chunkSize=250000;
startRow=001A0000000abcdef
```

In this example, the chunk size has been set to 250000, and the starting ID of the query is 001A0000000abcdef.

With querying of large amounts of data and how PK chunking can be used to improve the performance of such operations now understood, let's look at getting massive amounts of data moving the other way into Salesforce.

Loading massive amounts of data

When loading lots and lots of data into the Salesforce Platform, we're essentially concerned with how we can get as much data as possible into our Salesforce instance, reliably, in the shortest time possible. Let's imagine we have 20 million records to load. Thinking in terms of serial versus parallel processing, we can view our loading scenario in two ways:

- Loading 20 million records sequentially (serial)
- Loading 20 million records in parallel, by breaking down the 20 million records into smaller batches, inserting them in parallel, and taking less time

To load lots of data quickly, we need to optimize our parallel data loads. There are several steps we can take before loading any data to speed up the load operations. Deferring sharing calculations until after the load operation completes will mean sharing recalculations will be run once rather than on every record batch being processed. Disabling any logic that may run when the data is loaded—such as workflow rules, flows, and triggers—will ensure that valuable processing time won't be taken running these automations when loading data. Of course, there is a reliance on the data being inserted in a preprocessed state as the automations not running mean that certain field value updates and the like won't be invoked and therefore will need to be processed offline manually.

Next, let's think about the types of skews that may occur. For example, are we going to have an individual `Account` record with more than 10,000 child records? Are we going to have an owner of more than 10,000 records? Are we going to have more than 10,000 lookups to an individual record?

By thinking about the various types of skews, we can plan for and mitigate these potential skews when loading our data. We can have several `Account` records to mitigate Account Skew and several record owners for ownership skew mitigation and remove the role for those owners (although don't do this without a proper impact analysis), and so on. Planning for the known effects resulting from our expected resultant state of data helps massively when loading lots of data.

Record locks should be considered next. Knowing how records will be locked depending on the type of record being loaded means source data can be divided up, ordered, and loaded in discrete, parallel batches. Pay attention to task-locking behavior and the behavior of detail records for Master/Detail relationships.

Lastly, batch sizes can be tweaked depending on the amount of data. For example, loading 20 million records as a sequential operation versus 200 batches of 100,000 records will result in varying degrees of performance, record-locking behavior, and data skew. With the correct planning and considerations of disabling automation, deferring sharing calculations and so on, millions of records can be loaded using the `Bulk` API to great effect.

Now we've looked at the techniques that can be used when loading massive amounts of data into Salesforce, let's summarize what we've covered in this chapter.

Summary

In this chapter, we've covered a lot of varying concepts, all related to the improvement of performance when working with data in Salesforce. We started with revisiting LDV and covering skinny tables. We then moved on to the optimization of search and queries, and then looked at task locks and their impact on performance.

Looking at moving large amounts of data out and into Salesforce was next on our agenda for this chapter. To that end, we covered PK chunking and then looked at moving data into Salesforce in a performant way despite loading millions of records.

In the next chapter, we'll look at how data movement in and out of Salesforce can be used in data backup and restore scenarios.

Practice questions

Test your knowledge of the topics and concepts covered in this chapter by attempting to answer the following questions:

1. Which data API facilitates the asynchronous processing of data in parallel batches?
2. Which LDV mitigation technique can be used to partition data and reduce the number of records returned by SOQL queries?
3. Which header is required for PK chunking to be enabled?
4. Which is considered the fastest mode for data loads with the Bulk API—**Serial** or **Parallel**?
5. When Salesforce performs an indexed search, standard indexes are used if the filter condition of the query matches what?
6. Custom indexes are used where the query filter matches what?
7. When mitigating ownership skew for users that must have a role, where should that role reside in the role hierarchy?
8. True or false? Salesforce support is needed to enable skinny tables.
9. True or false? When mitigating ownership skew, you should consider removing a role associated with users owning 10,000 records or more.
10. True or false? When loading lots of data, it is not considered best practice to disable automation such as workflow rules and triggers.

Answers

How did you get on attempting the practice questions? Check your answers here:

1. The `Bulk API`
2. Divisions
3. `Sforce-Enable-PKChunking`
4. **Parallel**
5. Less than 30% of the first million records (and less than 15% of additional records), up to a maximum of 1 million records
6. Less than 10% of the total records, up to a maximum of 333,333 records
7. At the top
8. True
9. True
10. False

Further reading

To learn more about the concepts covered in this chapter, check out the following resources:

- PK chunking: `https://developer.salesforce.com/docs/atlas.en-us.api_asynch.meta/api_asynch/async_api_headers_enable_pk_chunking.htm`
- Skinny tables: `https://developer.salesforce.com/docs/atlas.en-us.salesforce_large_data_volumes_bp.meta/salesforce_large_data_volumes_bp/ldv_deployments_infrastructure_skinny_tables.htm`

11
Backup and Restore

Whilst Salesforce is fabulous at providing a platform and underlying data facility for working with customer data and custom data, consideration should be paid to how data can be backed up from and restored to the Salesforce platform. We're going to investigate the various methods available to perform both data backup and data restore operations.

In this chapter, we'll cover the following topics:

- Methods for backing up and restoring data on the Salesforce Lightning Platform
- AppExchange and external software that facilitates data backup and restoration

Before we get into the contents of this chapter, let's be clear that we're going to investigate backing up and restoring both data and metadata. Metadata is data that describes data and is the format your customizations to the Salesforce platform take. Data is the actual data stored in your Salesforce org for customers and opportunities.

Let's begin our exploration of backup and restoration by investigating the methods available to us when working with data backup and restoration on the Salesforce platform.

Methods for backing up and restoring data on the Salesforce Lightning Platform

Before we jump into methods for backing up and restoring data, let's elaborate on the two data definitions we're covering in this chapter, namely data and metadata, as both are interacted with differently when it comes to backup and restoration. Let's start with metadata.

Introduction to metadata

Metadata is data that describes data. When we think of an **eXtensible Markup Language** (**XML**) file, that essentially is a file with data (the values) and metadata (the tags). For example, see the following:

```
<?xml version="1.0" encoding="UTF-8" standalone="yes"?>
<person>
  <firstname>Aaron</firstname>
  <lastname>Allport</lastname>
</person>
```

The code example shows a simple XML structure for a person with a first name and last name. Here, we can use the metadata (the person and the `firstname` and `lastname` tags) to infer that we are representing a person called Aaron Allport.

Salesforce represents the customizations to make to your instance as a set of metadata files. For example, a public group XML is represented as follows:

```
<?xml version="1.0" encoding="UTF-8"?>
<Group xmlns="http://soap.sforce.com/2006/04/metadata">
    <doesIncludeBosses>true</doesIncludeBosses>
    <fullName>Packt</fullName>
    <name>Packt</name>
</Group>
```

Here, we can infer from the XML that there is a group called *Packt* that allows records shared with that group to be shared with managers of group members.

Salesforce represents the vast majority of customizations as XML, and as such, they can easily be extracted and stored.

Now that we have covered how metadata is used to describe data, and, indeed, its use for your customizations on the Salesforce platform, let's now look at what data is.

What is data?

In the realm of Salesforce, data is defined as the record data for the standard objects you have customized and the custom objects you have created stored in your instance. Whereas the metadata for the contact record may define a field for `FirstName`, the value stored in that field for each record is the data of the record. When data is imported or exported from the Salesforce platform, it is usually represented in the **Comma-Separated Value** (**CSV**) format, where the first row of the file provides the fields and the following rows are the data for each record (with each record represented as a row in the file).

Other formats are possible using some transformation logic with middleware and the like. An example CSV file would look like the following for exporting a couple of *contact records*::

```
Id,FirstName,LastName,Email
003abcdefghi123456,Aaron,Allport,aaron@aaronallport.com
003jklmnopqr789012,John,Smith,j.smith@example.com
```

Having understood the difference between data and metadata, let's question why we should back up data and metadata in the first place.

Why back up data and metadata?

Let's quickly touch upon why backing up data and metadata is important. First, Salesforce doesn't automatically back up your data for you. Therefore, if there were to be a situation in which a user or automated process accidentally caused an unintentional loss of data from your Salesforce instance, it would make sense to have a copy of data from which a restore operation could take place. It's considered good practice to take regular backups of your data in case of unexpected data loss or in case a data export is required for business operational reasons.

Just like backing up your data is considered good practice, Salesforce offers the ability to back up your metadata, effectively allowing you to save most (but not all) of the configuration of your org. This is especially useful in the development of metadata changes from Salesforce sandbox environments, in addition to ensuring you keep a backup of your Salesforce environment configuration.

Now we've covered some scenarios for backing up data, let's explore the various methods to export and import data and metadata. We'll begin with backing up data.

Backing up data

Salesforce offers three platform-native ways to export your data. Whilst middleware can facilitate more advanced data retrieval and transformation, the relatively straightforward requirement to back up data can be facilitated using the following:

- The Data Export service
- Data Loader
- Report Exports

Let's explore each of these in turn, starting with the Data Export service.

The Data Export service

The Salesforce Data Export service can be used to export data from Salesforce on demand or a weekly or monthly basis. Available from the Salesforce setup menu under **Data Export**, it's possible to include all the data in the Salesforce instance. The user who scheduled the export will receive an email when Salesforce has finished processing the export, containing a link to the zip file of the export, which contains a CSV file for each object of data.

> **Important note**
> Data Export is not possible in sandbox environments.

Now we've understood the Data Export service and how it facilitates backups of data, let's turn to Data Loader.

Data Loader

The Data Loader application facilitates exports of the data contained within objects on a per-object basis, saving the contents of the export in CSV format. It's entirely possible to choose the field data to include when configuring the export by specifying the **Salesforce Object Query Language (SOQL)** query for Data Loader to execute when running the export.

> **Important note**
> Data Loader doesn't support exporting attachments.

As Data Loader requires the user to log in to Salesforce to perform actions on their behalf, the user exporting the data will therefore need read access to the records they are exporting. Bear in mind how permissions will affect the export. For example, the **Organization-Wide Defaults (OWDs)** being set to Private, with no other sharing configured, will mean that by default, only the records owned by the user will be included in the export.

With Data Loader covered, let's now look at report exports.

Report Exports

Report Exports are probably the simplest and easiest way to export data from Salesforce but are contextual only to the data contained within the report. Essentially, when a report is run by a user, and that user has the Export Reports permission assigned to them through their profile or a permission set, they can choose to export the report using one of two options:

- A formatted report, which exports to Excel (.xlsx) format only. This type of export includes headings and retains the report format as it appears at the time of initializing the export.

- A **Details Only** report, which exports all report rows without any formatting. This format supports choosing an export file type, such as Excel (both `.xls` and `.xslx`) and CSV.

Report Exports are downloaded immediately upon invoking the export.

With the methods of exporting data now covered, let's explore how to import data into the platform as a means of restoring data.

Importing data

To import data into the Salesforce platform natively, there are, of course, the APIs that we have covered in other chapters, such as the Bulk API. However, it's worth briefly mentioning the Data Loader application and the Data Loader facility in the Salesforce user interface.

Importing data using the Data Loader application

Just as the Data Loader application can be used to export data from your Salesforce instance, it can also be used to import data. To do so, CSV files for the object data must be prepared in advance to serve as the data to be imported. When invoking the Data Loader application to import data, the columns of the CSV to be imported can be mapped to the fields of the object being imported.

Importing data using the Data Loader facility through the Salesforce user interface

Salesforce setup supports importing data into an object using a CSV file, much in the same way that the Data Loader standalone application does, including the mapping of columns for the destination object.

Now we've covered importing data, let's move on to exporting metadata.

Backing up metadata

When it comes to backing up the metadata for a Salesforce instance, there are several methods that can be exploited to do so. These include the following:

- Sandbox refreshes
- Change sets
- SFDX
- The Ant Migration Tool

Let's explore each of these in turn.

Sandbox refreshes

Probably the easiest way to back up metadata from your production Salesforce instance is by initiating a sandbox refresh. This facility either creates or refreshes a designated sandbox environment with a copy of the production metadata (but depending on the sandbox environment type, data may or may not be present).

With sandbox refreshes covered, let's investigate change sets.

Change sets

Change sets are often the first way that many Salesforce administrators and developers learn to move selective metadata changes from a sandbox environment to the production environment. Change sets are non-developer friendly and essentially act as the de facto way for non-developers to move sets of metadata between Salesforce environments. Whilst most change set usage is for moving changes up into the production environment, change sets can also be used for moving changes from the production environment to a specific sandbox environment.

Having understood how change sets are used for selective metadata movement between environments, let's touch upon **Salesforce Developer Experience (SFDX)**.

SFDX

A developer-focused suite of command-line utilities, SFDX allows for metadata changes to be exported and imported from the production environment or any sandbox created from the production environment to which the user has login access. Knowledge of the specifics of SFDX usage is not important for the exam but it is useful to know that it can be used by developers to export metadata from Salesforce.

The Ant Migration Tool

Much like SFDX, the Ant Migration Tool is another command-line utility for moving your Salesforce metadata between a local directory and a Salesforce instance. Again, as with SFDX, the Ant Migration Tool can be used to move Salesforce metadata from a production environment to a local directory.

Now that we've explored backing up metadata, let's move on to importing metadata.

Importing metadata

As you can probably imagine by now, all methods besides the sandbox refresh process can be used to import metadata as a way of restoring the metadata to a Salesforce instance. Let's start with change sets.

Change sets

By capturing a selected set of metadata artifacts and moving them from one Salesforce environment to another, change sets can be used to restore a set of changes from one environment to another. Imagine a Salesforce environment refreshed from production by accident – if there were another Salesforce environment that contained the updated set of metadata artifacts, then change sets could be used as a means of performing the metadata restoration.

Let's now explore SFDX as a means to restore metadata.

SFDX

With SFDX, it is possible to use a local filesystem or source code repository to store the metadata files. This is therefore a suitable means from which to perform selective metadata restoration activities to a specific environment from a local file store or repository.

With SFDX re-visited, let's briefly touch on the Ant Migration Tool.

The Ant Migration Tool

Again, much like SFDX, the Ant Migration Tool can be used to perform metadata restorations from local file directories to specific Salesforce environments, notably production in the case of a restoration scenario.

Now that we've explored importing metadata, let's now investigate AppExchange and external software that facilitates backup and restoration of data and metadata.

AppExchange and external software that facilitates data backup and restoration

When working with data backup and restoration on the Salesforce platform, naturally, there are developers and software vendors that have explored how far data backup and restoration extend beyond the native platform offerings provided by Salesforce. As is the norm for many use cases on the platform, such as industry-specific extensions to business logic for a given industry vertical, there are also AppExchange packages and full-blown external software that support data backup and restore operations.

For example, Salesforce Backup and Restore is a paid add-on to your Salesforce subscription that facilitates regular, automatic backups of the data and metadata held within your Salesforce instance. Those backups can then be used to restore data and metadata to your Salesforce instance as required, irrespective of the operations that necessitated the action in the first place, such as human error.

There are AppExchange packages that facilitate the automated backup and restoration of Salesforce data and metadata, often to off-platform facilities. These incur a separate charge to the Salesforce subscription, as they involve contracting with a different software vendor. This then allows operations to be performed using the AppExchange package as a conduit for the various operations to and from that external platform, such as data backup and restoration. To learn more about AppExchange packages that facilitate the backup and restoration of data and metadata to and from the Salesforce platform, please read more at `https://appexchange.salesforce.com/appxSearchKeywordResults?keywords=backup%20and%20recovery`.

Next, there are full-blown external software packages that support data and metadata backup and restoration, often integrating with SFDX for metadata operations. An intricate understanding of these software packages is beyond the scope of the exam (and therefore this book), but they all automate and facilitate automated sandbox provisioning and backup and restoration of data and metadata, and often integrate with automated workflows as part of a **Continuous Integration/Continuous Deployment (CI/CD)** pipeline.

Let's now summarize what we've covered in this chapter.

Summary

In this chapter, we looked at the ways in which you can back up and restore both data and metadata when working with the Salesforce platform. We started by breaking down what the difference between data and metadata is before moving on to the tools available from a native or platform standpoint when it comes to backing up and restoring metadata and data.

Next, we moved on to looking at AppExchange and external software that facilitates backup and restoration, covering what they do to facilitate and even speed up this task. Lastly, we looked at some best practices when exporting and importing data.

In the next chapter, we'll explore Territory Management to conclude our learning material.

Practice questions

Test your understanding of the concepts covered in this chapter by attempting the following practice questions:

1. Which Salesforce feature allows for selected metadata changes to be migrated from one environment to another?

2. What is the name of the standalone application that facilitates data imports and exports to and from the Salesforce platform?

3. Which report export format supports CSV, XLS, and XLSX?

4. Which facility allows for monthly backups?

5. What format is the file from a monthly backup?

6. What is metadata?

7. What metadata backup facility is used to create a production-like instance of Salesforce?

8. Which two metadata backup and restore technologies work with local or source-controlled copies of metadata?

9. What does CSV stand for?

10. In a CSV file, the first row of data is the what?

Answers

How did you get on answering the practice questions? Check your answers here:

1. Change sets

2. Data Loader

3. Details Only

4. The Data Export service

5. A zip file containing several CSVs

6. Data that describes data

7. Sandbox refreshes

8. SFDX and the Ant Migration Tool

9. Comma-Separated Value

10. The field names to which the values in the following rows pertain

Further reading

For further information about the concepts and topics covered in this chapter, please refer to the following resources:

- *Best practices to backup Salesforce data*: `https://help.salesforce.com/s/articleView?id=000334121&type=1`

- *Export data using Data Loader*: `https://help.salesforce.com/s/articleView?id=sf.exporting_data.htm&type=5`

- *Export data using report exports*: `https://help.salesforce.com/s/articleView?id=sf.reports_export.htm&type=5`

- *Export data using weekly backups*: `https://help.salesforce.com/s/articleView?id=sf.admin_exportdata.htm&type=5`

- *Create a Sandbox*: `https://help.salesforce.com/s/articleView?id=sf.data_sandbox_create.htm&type=5`

- *Ant Migration Tool Guide*: `https://developer.salesforce.com/docs/atlas.en-us.daas.meta/daas/meta_development.htm`

- *SFDX*: `https://developer.salesforce.com/tools/sfdxcli`

12
Territory Management

As we touched upon in *Chapter 2, Data Modeling and Database Design*, **territory management** is used to facilitate the automatic sharing of account records based on rules that pertain to how those records are assigned to users based on the criteria of the record. This chapter explains territory management in more detail and how it pertains to data model design on Salesforce.

In this chapter, we'll cover the following topics:

- Enterprise territory management overview
- Implications of territory management on data model design and sharing records

Let's begin our explanation of territory management with an overview.

Enterprise territory management overview

Salesforce fully supports the concept of Sales Territories to assign accounts and opportunities to individuals or teams of salespeople. With these territories set up, automatic assignment of accounts and opportunities can be set up based on rules, and management reporting in the form of reports and dashboards is possible. A feature of Enterprise Territory Management is that the built territory model can be tested before it has been activated, allowing for testing before changes are rolled out to users.

> **Important note**
> **Legacy Territory Management** (sometimes known as the original Territory Management module) was retired in the Summer 2021 release of Salesforce, and as such is not relevant to the exam. More information about this announcement is available at https://help.salesforce.com/s/articleView?id=000318370&type=1.

Under the hood, Enterprise Territory Management is a way of sharing. By that nature, Salesforce utilizes a rules engine, as determined by how you set up Enterprise Territory Management to perform sharing and associated recalculations on the fly.

Before we get into the specifics of how Enterprise Territory Management is set up, let's cover some terminology that is specific to Enterprise Territory Management, as follows:

- **Territory**
- **Territory Type**
- **Territory Type Priority**
- **Territory Model**
- **Territory Model State**
- **Territory Hierarchy**

We'll cover each of these terms, beginning with the definition of a territory.

Territory

A **territory** can be thought of as a grouping of account records and the users in your Salesforce instance that work with those account records. Territories are created from territory types. Territories can be hierarchical. For example, it's entirely possible to have a territory called the United States, with Northwest, Northeast, Southwest, Southeast, and Central Territories as children. Territory records contain several key pieces of information, such as the following:

- Assigned users to the territory
- Any assigned accounts
- Territory/Account Assignment Rules (the characteristics of an Account that mean that it will be assigned to this territory)

Next, let's look at the definition of a territory type.

Territory Type

Territory Types are used to organize and create Territories based on criteria such as account size, account billing state, or named accounts. When Territories are created, they are created from a territory type. Territory Types do not appear on the territory model Hierarchies that are created as part of the Territory Management setup.

For example, a territory called *UK County-Based Accounts* could be created whereby territories can be created based on the **UK County** value in the **state** picklist of the Account records.

With territory type now understood, let's turn to territory type Priority.

Territory Type Priority

Territory Type Priority is a custom scheme you define, and it is used to assist when creating territory records from the territory types you've defined. For example, you may have territory type Priority values of 1 through 5 to denote the priority of the territory record when it is created to align with the sales strategy of your business. This could mean that the Southwest Territory is given a priority of 1 as it is where your business expects to see the most growth this coming financial year. Essentially, Territory Type Priority is used to ensure that the right territory types are prioritized when creating new territory records.

Now that we have covered the definition of Territory Type Priority, let's explore the territory model.

Territory Model

The territory model is the representation of a complete territory management system, as defined by you for your Salesforce instance. You can have multiple territory models, but only one can be active at any given time. Salesforce provides a nice graphical hierarchy for territory models, which assists us in visualizing how Territories are organized, including the hierarchies. territory models allow you to test how Account and User record assignments will work, and as such allow you to try seeing how implementing a certain territory model will affect things before activating it.

> **Important note**
> Salesforce Enterprise Edition only allows two territory models to exist at any one time. Performance and Unlimited editions can have four territory models. The same limits apply to Salesforce Sandbox environments that are created from a production instance utilizing one of these Salesforce editions. Remember only one territory model can be active at a time.

With territory model covered, let's now look at the definition of a territory model state.

Territory Model State

Territory Models are assigned a **state** value to quickly allow the status of a given territory model. There are three values available, as follows:

- **Planning**: All territory models default to this value. It can be thought of as signifying the territory model is being developed/is in draft status.

- **Active**: The territory model is active. Remember, only one territory model can be active at any given time.

- **Archived**: A previously active territory model is archived as another territory model has been activated. Once a territory model has been archived, it cannot be reactivated.

> **Important note**
>
> When a territory model is archived (or you decide to delete a territory on an active territory model), the **Territory** field on Opportunity records is set to a blank value on Opportunity records that had a previously active territory assigned.

When activating or archiving a territory model, there may be errors that occur. If so, the status of the territory model will be set to either **Activation Failed** or **Archiving Failed**. Salesforce will send you an email containing details as to why the failure occurred.

Next, let's look at the Territory Hierarchy.

Territory Hierarchy

A **Territory Hierarchy** shows a structured view of the territory model. The Territory Hierarchy is the main interaction point with the territory model and is the place where Territories can be created, edited, and deleted. It's also where assignment rules can be executed, and Opportunities can be assigned to Territories.

With the Territory Hierarchy definition covered, let's delve deeper into how Enterprise Territory Management is set up.

Implications of territory management on data model design and sharing records

Territory management essentially facilitates the automatic sharing of records based on a rule set, as defined by the territory model that has been activated in your Salesforce instance. How **Organization-Wide Defaults (OWDs)** are set up will have an impact on the way the territory management implementation for your organization works. This is because the sharing afforded by territory management and the assignment of Accounts and Opportunities may or may not offer any further record access in addition to the sharing already in place. In such cases where there is no difference in the sharing of records, territory management essentially becomes a tool for organizing records. Territory management report types can be utilized to provide reporting based on Accounts and Opportunities being assigned to users, as per the active territory model.

In instances where the default Account and Opportunity model is set to **Private**, then territory management can be used to set the access level for Account and Opportunity records that are shared with users. For example, Accounts and Opportunities may be **Private** as per the configured OWDs for your Salesforce instance. Territory Management can be used to configure record access to be Read or Read and Edit on Opportunity records that are shared with users.

If a territory is part of a Territory Hierarchy, then Territory records above an assigned territory in the Territory Hierarchy inherit the sharing of the assigned territory. Let's put that as an example to explain it in more detail.

Let's imagine that the Territory Hierarchy shown in the following diagram has been configured. Let's assume that the OWD has been set to Private for Account and Opportunity records, and users assigned to the Territories don't otherwise have access to the records without territory management in use. The sharing denoted in the following diagram will be the sharing as set for each territory in the Territory Hierarchy:

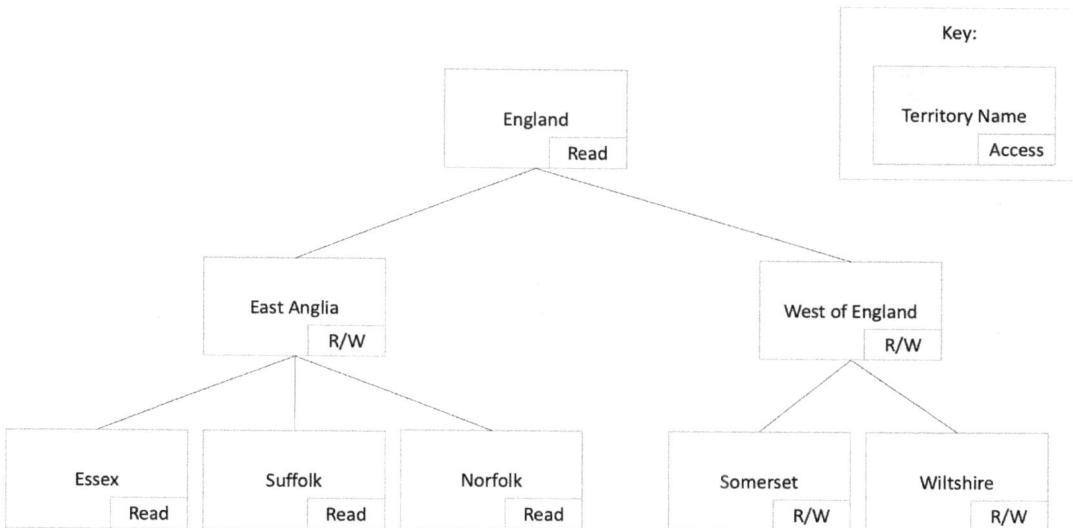

Figure 12.1 – An example territory model

In our example, users assigned to the **East Anglia** territory record will have **Read** access to the **Essex**, **Suffolk**, and **Norfolk** Territory records. Despite the access on the **East Anglia** Territory being **R/W** (Read/Write), Territory Access isn't inherited. Therefore, the access to the child **Essex/Suffolk/Norfolk** records will remain as Read-Only.

> **Important note**
>
> Automatic territory assignment to Opportunity records requires editing a generated Apex class, which requires Apex coding skills. Apex coding is outside the scope of the exam, so it won't be covered in this book.
>
> Territory assignment for Account records can be configured to run automatically as part of the declarative functionality for Account Assignment rule creation from the **Territory Model Hierarchy** screen.

Now we understand how territory management is another layer in the Salesforce sharing model for sharing Account and Opportunity records, let's take a moment to think about how territory management opens sharing to other child records associated with an Account or Opportunity.

For example, a custom object that has a **Master/Detail** lookup to an Account means that the records of that custom object that look up to an Account shared to a user through territory management will be visible by the user. This can inadvertently open record access beyond what was envisaged before territory management was implemented, and therefore consideration should be given to the territory model. Layering in criteria-based sharing rules that apply to a shared Account or Opportunity record means that other unintended side effects may occur. Therefore, testing your model is crucial for it to be successfully rolled out to an organization.

As a reminder, Master/Detail relationships mean that users inherit the access they have to the parent record when working with the child records. This can have profound implications for the design of your data model, as territory management may give unintended heightened access to other object data (such as edit access depending on the territory setup). Therefore, data model design, relationships between objects, and other factors related to the setup of the data model will be impacted by a territory management implementation.

Let's take a quick look at an example to explain some unintended side effects of implementing territory management, meaning that a data model may have to be revised:

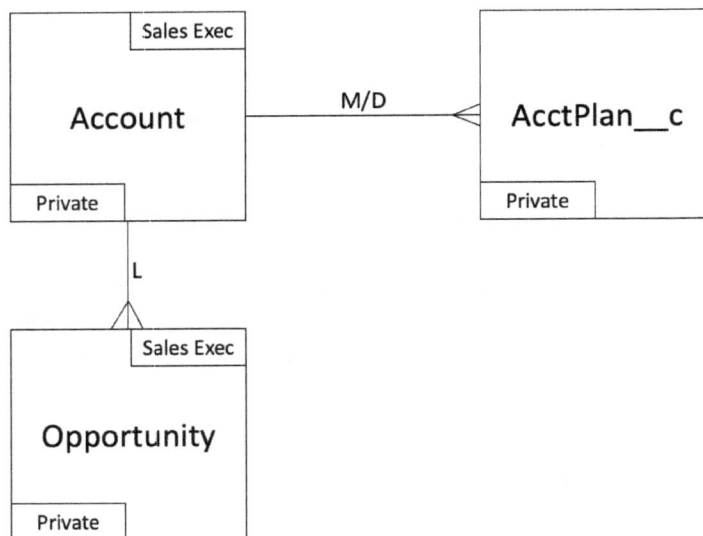

Figure 12.2 – Data model example

Using this data model example as our guide, we can see that a Private OWD is in play. Pay attention to the Master/Detail relationship from **Account** to the custom Account Plan object (denoted as **AcctPlan__c**).

Now, let's imagine we've enabled a territory model that shares (with read and edit access) Account records to certain users. Those users now have access to the Account Plan, so much so that they can edit the Account Plan records. Let's assume that only the Account Owner should ever be able to create or edit the Account Plans for the Account record. Therefore, it may have been wiser from the outset to have the relationship type set to a Lookup type from Account Plan to Account (as Lookups allow a specified sharing default to be set as per the OWDs). Of course, hindsight is a wonderful thing, but careful planning also pays dividends, particularly when dealing with the side effects of sharing. Salesforce provides other methods of sharing records, meaning that private, read-only access to Account Plan records would be possible with a territory.

Thinking back to the basics of OWDs and Salesforce instance setup, organizations that have an internal OWD of Public Read-Only or Public Read/Write for Account records won't see a record visibility increase for users. Those with Public Read-Only can use territory management to give a higher level of access to certain Account records to users if a use case for sharing lends itself to territory management.

Now that we've covered how territory management affects sharing, and how implementing territory management may affect the design of your data model, let's summarize what we've covered in this chapter.

Summary

In this chapter, we looked at Enterprise Territory Management and explored how it affects solution design and sharing on the Salesforce platform. We now understand how territory management can affect data model design and how record sharing is affected. We walked through a couple of examples to bring these points home and emphasized why it is crucial that data model design, sharing, and other factors relating to the setup of your Salesforce instance are evaluated thoroughly before implementing territory management.

With Enterprise Territory Management now under our belts, we can test our knowledge of everything we've covered in this book as we look to *Chapter 13, Practice Exam Questions*.

Practice questions

Test your knowledge of the material we covered in this chapter by attempting the following practice questions:

1. Salesforce had two types of territory management, but only one type is now supported. What is it known as?

2. What facility allows you to configure parent/child Territory associations?

3. Which feature of territory management allows for certain territory types to be prioritized when creating Territories from a territory type?

4. Let's imagine there is an active territory model that's granting selected users read/write access to Account records belonging to a Territory. The Account record has a Master/Detail relationship with a custom object that contains child records associated with the Account record. What access will the users have to the custom object records?

5. True or false? Territory Management Models can be tested before they are activated.

6. True or false? Out of the box, only Account records can be assigned using territory management in a declarative manner.

7. How are selected (that is, using a filter) Opportunity record assignments configured using territory management?

8. In its simplest definition, what does territory management do?

9. With territory management, if a user is assigned to Accounts belonging to a particular Territory with a Read-Only access level, what access do they have to the parent Territory?

10. What are the three territory model states?

Answers

How did you get on answering the practice questions? Check out your answers here:

1. Enterprise Territory Management.

2. The Territory Hierarchy.

3. Territory Type Priority.

4. Read/Write.

5. True.

6. True

7. They aren't configured as such. Territory Management Opportunity Assignment works by editing an Apex class.

8. It shares Account and Opportunity records based on criteria associated with the records to select sets of users.

9. Read-Only, as territory management propagates sharing access upwards.

10. Planning, Active, and Archived.

Further reading

To learn more about territory management, check out the *Territory Management Implementation Guide* at https://resources.docs.salesforce.com/latest/latest/en-us/sfdc/pdf/salesforce_implementing_territory_mgmt2_guide.pdf.

Section 3: Applying What We've Learned – Practice Questions and Revision Aids

With the theory learned, you can now prepare for the exam with the help of practice questions, revision aids, further reading, and learn how to take the exam.

This section comprises the following chapters:

13
Practice Exam Questions

Now, it is time to practice what has been covered throughout the book. In this chapter, test your knowledge with questions to further put into practice the theory you have learned and bolster your understanding of the topic areas of the curriculum. By the end of this chapter, you'll have had the opportunity to test your knowledge with 100 additional questions from those introduced previously.

Practice questions 1-20

1. *Universal Containers* report slow performance and timeouts in some cases when trying to export all data from their Account table. There are 15 million Account records present. Which method should be used to ensure the export can run successfully? Pick one answer:

   A. Batch Apex

   B. **Primary Key (PK)** chunking

   C. Asynchronous Apex

   D. Bulk API query with a batch size of 200

2. *Universal Containers* wish to expose the Lead and Opportunity objects to their resellers using **Experience Cloud**. Which license type is the correct one for them to purchase for those Experience Cloud users? Pick one answer:

   A. Customer Community

   B. Partner Community

   C. Customer Community Plus

   D. Experience Cloud Plus

3. What is the annotation on asynchronous Apex methods? Pick one answer:

    A. `@async`

    B. `@batch`

    C. `@future`

    D. `@istest`

4. *Universal Containers* have a generic `Account` record that is used for all `Contact` records that don't have a known parent `Account` record. Recently, performance has been sluggish with regard to operations on any of these `Contact` records or the parent record, with users complaining of onscreen errors relating to the record being locked. What is this a symptom of? Pick one answer:

    A. Contact skew

    B. Task locking

    C. Contact locking

    D. Account skew

5. *Universal Containers* management wish to have a report of open opportunities sent to them on a weekly basis. What is the most appropriate Salesforce feature to use for this? Pick one answer:

    A. Weekly scheduled report

    B. Batch Apex

    C. Flow with email action

    D. Bulk API query

6. In order to access data held in an external system and surface it within Salesforce (but not store the data in Salesforce), which Salesforce feature is typically used for this purpose? Pick one answer:

    A. Standard object

    B. Custom object

    C. Big object

    D. External object

7. Which data API facilitates the asynchronous processing of data in parallel batches? Pick one answer:

    A. Bulk API

    B. Serial API

    C. Streaming API

    D. REST API

8. *Universal Containers* have noticed that by granting access to Account objects for a select set of users, their Brand custom object (a child object of Account) is automatically visible to them. Users have the same access to this object as they do to Account objects. What type of relationship exists between Account and Brand? Pick one answer:

    A. Lookup relationship

    B. Many-to-many relationship

    C. Master/Detail relationship

    D. One-to-many relationship

9. A hierarchical relationship type is only available on which standard object? Pick one answer:

    A. Account

    B. Opportunity

    C. Contract

    D. User

10. *Universal Containers* have an Account object with Brand as a custom child object, associated using a Master/Detail relationship. What happens to Brand object records if their parent Account record is deleted? Pick one answer:

    A. The child Brand records are deleted

    B. Nothing—the Brand records remain

    C. The Account record cannot be deleted until all Brand records are deleted

    D. The Brand records are automatically re-pointed to the next available Account record

11. *Universal Containers* users are complaining of slow query performance when running reports on the `Contact` object. There are 15 million contact records, and the reports contain 80 columns of data, across standard and custom fields. Which Salesforce feature can be used to increase the performance of the reports? Pick one answer:

    A. Skinny tables

    B. Custom report types

    C. Scheduling the report and using the export instead

    D. List views

12. Which two features of skinny tables are true? Pick two answers:

    A. They are suited to object data of a few thousand rows

    B. They can contain a maximum of 100 columns

    C. They work across all standard objects

    D. They are for read operations only

13. Which of the following standard objects can be used with skinny tables? Pick three answers:

    A. `Account`

    B. `Contract`

    C. `Opportunity`

    D. `Contact`

    E. `Task`

14. Which of the following is not a **Large Data Volume (LDV)** mitigation technique? Pick one answer:

    A. Divisions

    B. Selective filter conditions

    C. Skinny tables

    D. Custom report types

15. Which LDV mitigation technique can be used to partition data and reduce the number of records returned by **Salesforce Object Query Language (SOQL)** queries? Pick one answer:

    A. Selective filter conditions

    B. Divisions

    C. Skinny tables

    D. Data virtualization

16. *Universal Containers* are seeing poor query performance with queries to their Account records, although the row count is in the hundreds of thousands. What should be done to increase query performance? Pick two answers:

    A. Run the query in the developer console to determine if there are any selective filter criteria fields

    B. Apply indexes to selective filter criteria fields

    C. Apply more fields to the WHERE clause of the query

    D. Apply indexes to as many Account fields as possible

17. Which header is required for PK chunking to be enabled? Pick one answer:

    A. -Enable-PKChunking

    B. Enable-PKChunking

    C. Sforce-PKChunking-true

    D. PKChunking=true Sforce

18. Which of the following LDV mitigation techniques can only be enabled by contacting Salesforce support? Pick two answers:

    A. PK chunking

    B. Skinny tables

    C. Selective filter conditions

    D. Divisions

19. What is considered the most foundational aspect of sharing on the Salesforce platform? Pick one answer:

    A. Role Hierarchy

    B. **Organization-Wide Defaults (OWD)**

    C. Sharing rules

    D. Manual sharing

20. Which OWD is only applicable to the Campaign object? Pick one answer:

    A. Private Read-Only

    B. Public Read-Only

    C. Public Read/Write/Transfer

    D. Public Full Access

Practice questions 21-40

1. Which OWD value does the following statement relate to? *Only the record owner or those users higher than the record owner's role in the Role Hierarchy can view, edit, and report on records of this object.* Pick one answer:

    A. Private

    B. Public Read-Only

    C. Public Full Access

    D. Public Read/Write/Transfer

2. Which sharing facility in Salesforce includes a special provision for access to cases, contacts, and opportunities outside of the OWD setup? Pick one answer:

    A. Role Hierarchy

    B. Manual sharing

    C. Sharing rules

    D. Profiles and permission sets

3. What are the two types of sharing rules? Pick two answers:

    A. Criteria-based sharing rules

    B. Ownership-based sharing rules

    C. Value-based sharing rules

    D. Profile-based sharing rules

4. Which sharing feature of the Salesforce platform is used to give specific users in Salesforce an elevated level of access to a record so that they can work collaboratively on an `Account`, `Opportunity`, or `Case` record? Pick one answer:

    A. Team access

    B. Programmatic sharing

    C. Permission sets

    D. Profiles

5. Which Salesforce sharing feature allows the use of code to build sharing settings when data access requirements cannot be fulfilled using any of the declarative means? Pick one answer:

    A. Programmatic sharing

    B. Managed packages

    C. Apex modules

    D. Programmable permissions

6. *Universal Containers* has order information held in an external system, which needs to be surfaced against `Account` records. Each `Account` record has an external ID field that is the ID of the `Account` record in the external system. Which method should be used to surface the information? Pick one answer:

    A. External object, using the ID field on the `Account` field as a lookup for the external system

    B. Big object, storing a copy of the order information, with data synchronized nightly

    C. Custom object, storing a copy of the order information, with data synchronized nightly

    D. Use the standard `Order` object, copying in the data in real time

7. *Universal Containers* users are complaining of poor account performance. The account hierarchy is set with all accounts in the system having a single, global master account. There are 30,000 `Account` records that are a child of the global `Account` record. What is this poor performance a symptom of? Pick one answer:

    A. Account skew

    B. Incorrect OWD setup

    C. Poor data archiving strategy

    D. Not enough sharing rules

8. *Universal Containers* wish to model their users managers against the user record for their employees. Which inbuilt Salesforce feature allows for this? Pick one answer:

    A. Custom field lookup to the `User` object

    B. Text field containing the ID of the users manager

    C. Hierarchical relationships

    D. Programmatic sharing

9. *Universal Containers* users are complaining that they are suffering performance issues with account records. The account hierarchy is set so that no one `Account` record has more than 10,000 child records; however, users typically own more than 10,000 `Account` records each. What is this poor performance a symptom of? Pick one answer:

    A. Lookup skew
    B. Ownership skew
    C. Account skew
    D. Relationship skew

10. *Universal Containers* are migrating data across into Salesforce to represent the history of their container leases for the last 15 years. This is about 4 million records worth of data. Which Salesforce feature can be used to store this data in a way that ensures good performance when querying the data, but in a way whereby only one instance of each record is saved to the object, thereby avoiding any duplicates? Pick one answer:

    A. Custom object
    B. External object
    C. Reuse a standard object
    D. Big object

11. *Universal Containers* are looking to provide access to external customer users using an Experience Cloud site. Customers are required to be able to run reports and dashboards, and *Universal Containers* wish their users to have access to `Order` records related to their `Account` records. Which license type is most suited to the Experience Cloud site? Pick one answer:

    A. Customer Community
    B. Customer Community Plus
    C. Partner Community

12. *Universal Containers* are looking to provide access to external customer users using an Experience Cloud site. Customers don't need to be able to run reports and dashboards, and *Universal Containers* wish their users to have access to `Order` records related to their `Account` record only. Which license type is most suited to the Experience Cloud site? Pick one answer:

    A. Customer Community
    B. Customer Community Plus
    C. Partner Community

13. Which sharing facility is only available for the Customer Community license type for Experience Cloud sites? Pick one answer.

   A. Sharing rules

   B. Sharing sets

   C. Manual sharing

   D. Programmatic sharing

14. Which technology is used to surface external data in OData 2.0 or OData 4.0 format? Pick one answer:

   A. Salesforce Connect

   B. Batch Apex

   C. Bulk API

   D. Salesforce to Salesforce

15. *Universal Containers* wish to expose quotes to customers through an Experience Cloud site. Which license type will users of the site need to see standard Quote object records? Pick one answer:

   A. Customer Community

   B. Customer Community Plus

   C. Partner Community

16. *Universal Containers* have a large amount of Container Location records that need to be updated in Salesforce on a nightly basis based on the values associated with the last Order record for each customer. Given the operation will involve querying an indeterminate number of records, what should be used to achieve such a requirement? Pick one answer:

   A. Batch Apex

   B. Bulk API

   C. Off-platform ETL job

   D. Bulk API in serial mode

17. *Universal Containers* wish to expose the `Individual` object to record their customers data privacy and protection preferences. For which objects should the `Individual` field be added to page layouts to achieve this? Pick three answers:

    A. Lead

    B. Contact

    C. Account

    D. Person Account

    E. Opportunity

18. *Universal Containers* wish to be able to detect unusual login activity such as impossible journeys (where users seemingly log in to Salesforce from multiple locations many miles apart within a short time of each other). They also wish to be able to track changes to more than 20 fields on certain objects. Which Salesforce technologies can be used to fulfill these requirements? Pick two answers:

    A. Salesforce Classic Encryption

    B. Salesforce Shield Event Monitoring

    C. Salesforce Shield Encryption

    D. Salesforce Shield Field History Tracking

19. *Universal Containers* are implementing Salesforce to act as their new data master. Which term is given to the view of customer data that users will see based on a **Single Source Of Truth** (**SSOT**) across multiple backend systems? Pick one answer:

    A. The Golden Record

    B. The Master Record

    C. The SCV Record

    D. The Customer Data Master

20. *Universal Containers* users are complaining of poor performance as they try to perform operations on the `Account` records they own. *Universal Containers* users typically own more than 10,000 `Account` records each, but they cannot reassign records to overcome ownership skew. What is the recommended next-best step for improving performance? Pick one answer:

    A. Remove the role for the users or put them in their own role at the top of the role hierarchy

    B. Use quick actions to invoke batch Apex jobs for the operations

    C. Have system administrators perform the actions on behalf of the user

Practice questions 41-60

1. *Universal Containers* are loading and updating millions of open and completed task records as part of their Salesforce implementation. They notice that task records that are not in an **Open** state (they are not set with a status of **Completed**) lock several records at a time. What is the reason for this behavior? Pick two answers:

    A. Tasks in an **Open** state that are updated will lock the Account record and the records referenced by the WhoId and WhatId fields of the Task record

    B. Tasks in a **Completed** state that are inserted will lock the Account record and the records referenced by the WhoId and WhatId fields of the Task record, but only if the Task record activity date is not blank or null

    C. Tasks in an **Open** state that are updated will lock the Account record and the records referenced by the WhoId and WhatId fields of the Task record, but only if the Task record activity date is not blank or null

    D. Tasks in a **Completed** state that are updated will lock the Account record and the records referenced by the WhoId and WhatId fields of the Task record, but only if the Task record activity date is not blank or null

2. When loading in lots of tasks, it is generally considered best practice to order Task records by which value of the record? Pick one answer:

    A. The WhoId value of the Task record

    B. The WhatId value of the Task record

    C. The account that the Task record is associated with

    D. The owner of the Task record

3. When loading in large amounts of data, what is considered the best practice for minimizing processing time as data lands on the Salesforce platform? Pick two answers:

    A. Disabling automation such as workflow rules, flow, and process builders

    B. Enabling triggers

    C. Enabling automation such as workflow rules, flow, and process builders

    D. Deferring sharing calculations

4. *Universal Containers* are loading in large amounts of data to their Salesforce implementation. What is considered best practice for the millions of records across lots of object types that they will be loading in? Pick two answers:

    A. Preprocess the data as much as possible to avoid unnecessary calculations and minimize post-load processing time

    B. Do not preprocess the data beforehand to avoid unnecessary calculations and minimize post-load processing time

    C. Defer sharing calculations to avoid unnecessary sharing recalculations on each record as it is committed to the Salesforce database

    D. Do not defer sharing calculations to avoid unnecessary sharing recalculations on each record as it is committed to the Salesforce database

5. *Universal Containers* are loading in data to their Salesforce instance using the Bulk API. Which is considered the fastest mode for data loads with the Bulk API? Pick one answer:

    A. Serial mode

    B. Parallel mode

6. *Universal Containers* wish to be able to sell to individual people as well as corporates. Which feature of Salesforce would be most suitable to leverage the out-of-the-box object model, while providing the functionality to record opportunities against individual people? Pick one answer:

    A. A custom `Individual_People__c` object, adding a look up to the `Opportunity` record to associate them to the `Individual People` object record

    B. Have a bucket account record for all individual people, with individuals represented as contacts of the bucket `Account` record

    C. The standard Account/Contact model provides this functionality already

    D. `Person` accounts

7. When enabling `Person` accounts, which OWD values are allowed for the `Contact` object prior to enabling? Pick two answers:

    A. Controlled by parent

    B. Private

    C. Public Read Only

    D. Public Read/Write

8. *Universal Containers* deal with some individuals that have associations to multiple accounts and therefore are considering enabling contacts to the **Multiple Accounts** feature for this purpose. What are the default behaviors for activity records for the contact when the **Contacts to Multiple Accounts** feature is enabled? Pick one answer:

   A. They only relate to the Account record being viewed at the time of activity record creation

   B. They are processed to relate to all Account records for the contact

   C. They roll up to the primary Account record for the contact

   D. They are all orphaned—they have no parent account

9. *Universal Containers* wish to move to a teams-based selling model. What is a feature of Salesforce that should be considered for enabling other users to access Account, Contact, and Opportunity records selectively or as part of a default sales team? Pick one answer:

   A. Account teams

   B. User hierarchies

   C. AccountContactRelation entries

   D. AccountContactRole entries

10. What must the Access Levels be set to when granting users access to an Account, Contact, or Opportunity record using account teams? Pick one answer:

    A. The AccessLevel picklist values must be set to values higher than the OWD for the respective object

    B. The AccessLevel picklist values can be set to any value other than the OWD for the respective object

    C. The AccessLevel picklist values must be set to values lower than the OWD for the respective object

11. *Universal Containers* are loading millions of Task records into their new Salesforce instance. All related objects are loaded and, as such, all relevant IDs are able to be associated with the tasks. Upon loading the tasks, record-locking issues occur. What would be the best practices to mitigate this? Pick two answers:

    A. Order all Task records by associated/ultimate parent Account ID records

    B. Batch up Task records by the associated/ultimate parent Account ID records, running multiple batches in parallel

    C. Load Task records irrespective of the associated/ultimate parent Account ID records, running multiple batches sequentially

    D. Order all Task records by associated WhatID records

12. When Salesforce performs an indexed search, standard indexes are used if the filter condition of the query matches what? Pick one answer:

   A. Less than 30% of the first million records (and less than 15% of additional records), up to a maximum of 1 million records

   B. Less than 30% of the first million records (and less than 25% of additional records), up to a maximum of 1 million records

   C. Less than 25% of the first million records (and less than 20% of additional records), up to a maximum of 1 million records

   D. Less than 25% of the first million records (and less than 25% of additional records), up to a maximum of 1 million records

13. You have enabled custom indexes for several fields on the Account object. Custom indexes are used where the query filter matches what? Pick one answer:

   A. Less than 10% of the total records, up to a maximum of 500,000 records

   B. Less than 30% of the total records, up to a maximum of 333,333 records

   C. Less than 10% of the total records, up to a maximum of 333,333 records

   D. Less than 10% of the total records, up to a maximum of 500,000 records

14. Which of the following statements is true about task-locking behavior? Pick one answer:

   A. When a task is inserted, the Account record, along with the records referenced by the WhoId (but not the WhatId) field, is locked, but only if the status of the Task record is not **Completed**, and the activity date is set (it's not equal to null)

   B. When a task is inserted, the Account record, but not the records referenced by the WhoId and WhatId fields, is locked, but only if the status of the task record is not **Completed**, and the activity date is set (it's not equal to null)

   C. When a task is inserted, the Account record, along with the records referenced by the WhoId and WhatId fields, is locked, but only if the status of the task record is **Completed**, and the activity date is set (it's not equal to null)

   D. When a task is inserted, the Account record, along with the records referenced by the WhoId and WhatId fields, is locked, but only if the status of the task record is not **Completed**, and the activity date is set (it's not equal to null)

15. What is an external lookup? Pick one answer:

   A. An external lookup is for situations where the external object data is the parent for your child records held in Salesforce

   B. An external lookup is for situations where the external object data is the child for your parent records held in Salesforce

16. Which of the following standard fields are not indexed by default? Pick two answers:

    A. `RecordTypeId`

    B. `Division`

    C. `Email`

    D. `CreatedDate`

    E. `ShippingAddress`

17. What is true of skinny tables? Pick two answers:

    A. They are read-only

    B. They contain soft-deleted records

    C. They are read/write

    D. They do not contain soft-deleted records

18. How do Divisions increase performance? Pick two answers:

    A. They are used to increase the number of records returned by SOQL queries

    B. They are used to partition data

    C. They are used to reduce the number of records returned by SOQL queries

    D. They add a filter condition to queries automatically

19. When are skinny tables best used? Pick two answers:

    A. Skinny tables are most useful with tables containing millions of records to improve the performance of read-only operations, such as reports

    B. Skinny tables are most useful with tables containing thousands of records to improve the performance of read/write operations

    C. Skinny tables are most useful with standard objects such as `Order` and `Contract` as these objects require complex queries by default

    D. Skinny tables are most useful with custom objects only to improve the performance of read-only operations, such as reports

20. What is an indirect lookup? Pick one answer:

    A. An indirect lookup is for situations where your Salesforce data is the child of the external object data

    B. An indirect lookup is for situations where your Salesforce data is the parent of the external object data

Practice questions 61-80

1. *Universal Containers* require members of their operations team to be able to see the same data, yet due to the way the role hierarchy has been set up, those team members are all in the same branch. How can `Case` records be shared with each team member so that all `Case` records owned by one member are visible to the others? Pick one answer:

    A. Ownership-based sharing rule

    B. Criteria-based sharing rule

2. *Universal Containers* require members of their L3 customer support team to be able to see all `Case` records with a value of L3 in the `Team__c` picklist. How can this be achieved? Pick one answer:

    A. Ownership-based sharing rule

    B. Criteria-based sharing rule

    C. Manually sharing the `Case` records

3. *Universal Containers* require case team members to be able to share records on demand with users in other departments as required to work on a case. The criteria cannot be clearly defined in advance, and thus a rule base cannot be built around the sharing requirements. How can this requirement be achieved? Pick one answer:

    A. Ownership-based sharing rule

    B. Criteria-based sharing rule

    C. Manually sharing the `Case` records

4. *Universal Containers* have an Experience Cloud site to allow users to be able to raise and see updates to `Case` records for their accounts. The Experience Cloud site users are complaining that they cannot see the `Case` records they raise. They are using Customer Community licenses. What can be used to remedy this? Pick one answer:

    A. Ownership-based sharing rule

    B. Sharing set

    C. Criteria-based sharing rule

    D. Manually sharing the `Case` records

5. *Universal Containers* have an Experience Cloud site to allow users to be able to raise and see updates to Case records for their accounts. The Experience Cloud site users are complaining that they cannot see the Case records they raise. They are using Customer Community Plus licenses. What can be used to remedy this? Pick two answers:

    A. Ownership-based sharing rule

    B. Sharing set

    C. Criteria-based sharing rule

    D. Manually sharing the Case records

6. The Role Hierarchy contains a special provision for access to which objects? Pick three answers:

    A. Contact

    B. Opportunity

    C. Contract

    D. Case

    E. User

7. What does the **View All** permission for an object grant a user when they are assigned to a profile or permission set with this option checked for a given object? Pick one answer:

    A. They can read any record for that object

    B. They can edit any record for that object

    C. They can create any record for that object

    D. They can delete any record for that object

8. What does the **Modify All** permission for an object grant a user when they are assigned to a profile or permission set with this option checked for a given object? Pick three answers:

    A. They can read any record for that object

    B. They can edit any record for that object

    C. They can create any record for that object

    D. They can delete any record for that object

9. What does the **View All Data** permission grant a user when they are assigned to a profile or permission set with this option checked? Pick one answer:

   A. They can read any record

   B. They can edit any record

   C. They can create any record

   D. They can delete any record

10. What does the **Modify All Data** permission grant a user when they are assigned to a profile or permission set with this option checked? Pick three answers:

    A. They can read any record

    B. They can edit any record

    C. They can create any record

    D. They can delete any record

11. What are the ways in which users record access can be restricted? Pick two answers:

    A. Restriction rules

    B. OWDs

    C. Role Hierarchy

    D. Permission sets

12. *Universal Containers* require multiple teams to be able to access the same record. Which Salesforce sharing facility is best suited to this? Pick two answers:

    A. Manual sharing

    B. Programmatic sharing

    C. Role Hierarchy

    D. Territory Management

13. Which of the following statements is true about task-locking behavior? Pick one answer:

    A. When a task is updated, the Account record, along with the records referenced by the WhoId and WhatId fields, is locked, irrespective of task record value.

    B. When a task is updated, the Account record, along with the records referenced by the WhoId and WhatId fields, is not locke.

    C. When a task is updated, the Account record, along with the records referenced by the WhoId (but not the WhatId) field, is locked, irrespective of task record values

D. When a task is updated, the `Account` record, along with the records referenced by only the `WhatId` field, is locked, irrespective of task record value.

14. *Universal Containers* sales teams are looking at introducing a mechanism whereby certain users are automatically responsible for sales deals (Opportunities) in the regions in which they are the designated owner. Which Salesforce feature is best suited to meet this requirement? Pick one answer:

A. OWDs to automatically share all `Opportunity` records with all sales team members

B. Criteria-based sharing rules for each territory as based on the `BillingState` value of the parent `Account` record

C. Role Hierarchy to automatically share all `Opportunity` records with all sales team members

D. Territory Management to share records to users based on characteristics of the Account record

15. Which statement best describes Territory Management? Pick one answer:

A. Territory Management shares records with users or groups based on the characteristics of an `Account` record

B. Territory Management shares records with users based on the owner of the `Account` record

C. Territory Management shares records with only individual users based on the location fields of an `Account` record only

D. Territory Management cannot be used to share records based on location fields of the `Account` record alone

16. *Universal Containers* wish to implement a custom backup solution utilizing their existing MuleSoft investment. Which of the following is best suited to this? Pick one answer:

A. The Get Updated REST API method for each object being backed up, which assumes a 24-hour window for data changes

B. Running a query using the REST API for each object using a WHERE clause with a timestamp

C. Running a query using the REST API for each object with no WHERE clause and processing the records in MuleSoft

D. The Get Updated REST API method for each object being backed up with a defined start and end date, as determined by the last backup

17. When mitigating ownership skew for users that must have a role, where should that role reside in the role hierarchy? Pick one answer:

A. At the top

B. At the bottom

C. A subordinate of the topmost role

18. *Universal Containers* wish to implement a solution to back up the data in their Salesforce instance but don't have a data warehouse or indeed the middleware necessary to instigate backup operations. Which options should be considered first? Pick two answers:

    A. Weekly scheduled report to act as a data export for each object

    B. Use an `AppExchange` package

    C. Run a custom SOQL query in the Developer console

    D. Use an existing cloud-based Salesforce backup solution

19. *Universal Containers* are exporting all their existing `Account` records to perform offline profiling and de-duplication activities. There are over 5 million `Account` records. What would be the most suitable export setup using existing Salesforce data export capabilities? Pick one answer:

    A. PK chunking, batch size 250,000

    B. Salesforce report, save as CSV

    C. PK chunking, batch size 100,000

    D. Bulk API read job, no PK chunking

20. *Universal Containers* have noticed some ownership skew in their Salesforce instance. Why is removing the role associated with the users that are owners of the offending records good for performance in such scenarios? Pick one answer:

    A. Sharing recalculations involving the role hierarchy are removed, and thus are quicker

    B. Users without a role are not affected by sharing recalculations

Practice questions 81-100

1. What is the maximum number of fields you can track by default with Field History Tracking? Pick one answer:

    A. 10

    B. 20

    C. 30

    D. 40

2. *Universal Containers* users are complaining that there are too many changes to the Salesforce configuration. There are several administrators making changes at any one time. Users find that sometimes, changes are reverted hours after they are made. Which Salesforce feature allows for viewing the audit log of the system administrators? Pick one answer:

   A. Setup Log

   B. Setup Admin History

   C. Setup Audit Trail

   D. Setup Config Trail

3. When Salesforce Shield is enabled, what is the maximum number of fields you can track by default with Field History Tracking? Pick one answer:

   A. 20

   B. 40

   C. 60

   D. 80

4. By default, for how long is Field Audit Trail data available? Pick one answer:

   A. 18 months

   B. 2 years

   C. 3 years

   D. 5 years

5. *Universal Containers* have an Experience Cloud site to allow users to be able to raise and see updates to Case records for their accounts. The Experience Cloud site users are complaining that they cannot see the Case records they raise. They are using Partner Community licenses. What can be used to remedy this? Pick two answers:

   A. Ownership-based sharing rule

   B. Sharing set

   C. Criteria-based sharing rule

   D. Manually sharing the Case records

6. For how long is Field Audit Trail data available when Salesforce Shield is enabled in a Salesforce instance? Pick one answer:

    A. 5 years

    B. 7.5 years

    C. 10 years

    D. 12.5 years

7. Which three features are provided by Salesforce for preserving the traceability of changes made to a Salesforce instance without additional product subscriptions? Pick three answers:

    A. Setup Audit Trail

    B. Weekly Report Exports

    C. Field History Tracking

    D. Event Monitoring

    E. Field Audit Trail

8. By default, Salesforce Connect supports which protocols? Pick two answers:

    A. OData 2.0

    B. SOAP

    C. OData 4.0

    D. OAuth

9. *Universal Containers* have two separate Salesforce instances, and they wish to connect them to show data from one instance in the other. Which technology can be used to quickly achieve this requirement? Pick one answer:

    A. Middleware, such as MuleSoft

    B. Salesforce-to-Salesforce connector

    C. The Salesforce REST API

    D. Custom Apex logic

10. Which of the following Salesforce products require connectors to read/write data to/from the core Salesforce platform? Pick three answers:

   A.   Marketing Cloud

   B.   Pardot

   C.   B2B Commerce

   D.   Service Cloud

   E.   Experience Cloud

11. Which of the following statements is true about Task record-locking behavior? Pick one answer:

   A.   When a task is deleted, the Account record, along with the records referenced by the WhoId and WhatId fields, is not locked

   B.   When a task is deleted, the Account record, along with the records referenced by the WhoId and WhatId fields, is locked, irrespective of Task record values

   C.   When a task is deleted, only the records referenced by the WhoId and WhatId fields are locked, irrespective of Task record values

   D.   When a task is deleted, the Account record, along with the records referenced by the WhoId (but not the WhatId) field is locked, irrespective of Task record values

12. *Universal Containers* have an Experience Cloud site that is available to external users. They wish for all users to have access to Events, with a subset of users having edit access to Events. Which license types are necessary to fulfill this requirement? Pick two answers:

   A.   Customer Community

   B.   Partner Community

   C.   Customer Community Plus

13. *Universal Containers* have implemented Enterprise Territory Management. Some of the territories need to be reassigned due to a change in the territory structure. Which is the best-practice procedure to follow to keep recalculations, and therefore performance impacts, to a minimum? Pick one answer:

   A.   Start with the lowest-level territory in a single branch first, and then work your way up the hierarchy

   B.   Start with the highest-level territory in a branch first, and then work your way down the hierarchy

C. Start with the lowest-level territories in the hierarchy first, and then work your way up the hierarchy

D. Start with the highest-level territories in the hierarchy first, and then work your way down the hierarchy

14. True or false? Applying inherited rules to child territories in Enterprise Territory Management improves performance. Pick one answer:

A. True

B. False

15. *Universal Containers* have filter criteria on some of their Enterprise Territory Management rules. Which are considerations for optimal performance of rule criteria? Pick two answers:

A. Define criteria on numeric fields only

B. Do not define criteria on numeric fields as text literals

C. Define criteria on string fields only

D. Only define criteria on numeric fields as text literals

16. *Universal Containers* wish to backup data from their Salesforce instance locally. Which options are available immediately (without incurring additional fees) to facilitate this requirement? Pick three answers:

A. Data Export Service

B. Salesforce Backup and Restore

C. Report Export

D. Data Loader

E. List Views

17. *Universal Containers* wish to backup metadata from their production Salesforce instance. Which options are available immediately (without incurring additional fees) to facilitate this requirement? Pick three answers:

A. Change Sets

B. Sandbox Refresh to create a sandbox from production

C. Force.com Migration Tool

D. Salesforce Metadata Export

E. Salesforce Org Backup

18. *Universal Containers* are both loading in and updating millions of records in their Salesforce instance. What are considered best practices for mitigating any performance impacts during this activity? Pick two answers:

    A. Deferring sharing calculations

    B. Disabling any automation, such as triggers and workflow rules

    C. Enabling automation, such as triggers and workflow rules

    D. Enabling sharing calculations

19. Which of the following features is Salesforce support required to enable? Pick three answers:

    A. Big Objects

    B. Skinny Tables

    C. Divisions

    D. Custom Indexes

    E. Selective Filter Conditions

20. Why do skinny tables speed up performance for objects containing millions of rows of data? Pick three answers:

    A. They avoid a join between standard and custom fields in the Salesforce database

    B. They do not contain soft-deleted records

    C. They do not contain all the fields of the object

    D. They only contain indexed fields

    E. Other fields of the object are discarded when queries are run

Summary

In this chapter, we've covered a plethora of different, exam-like questions in order to test your knowledge of the content covered in the exam. Check your answers in *Chapter 17, Answers to Practice Questions*.

In *Chapter 14, Cheat Sheets*, we'll introduce some revision aids.

14
Cheat Sheets

We've covered an awful lot throughout this book, and with the exam being a closed book format, it can be hard to remember everything! Therefore, this chapter introduces some revision aids in the form of single-page cheat sheets. These are designed to both bolster your learning and serve as a desktop reference to come back to during the day-to-day activites in your role as a Salesforce Data Architect.

In this chapter, you'll find cheat sheets for the key topics covered in this book. Let's start with data modeling and database design.

Database modeling and database design

The following resources can be used to refresh your memory on the concepts we introduced on the topic of data modeling and database design.

Let's begin by recapping the data modeling notation we introduced in *Chapter 2, Database Modeling and Database Design*:

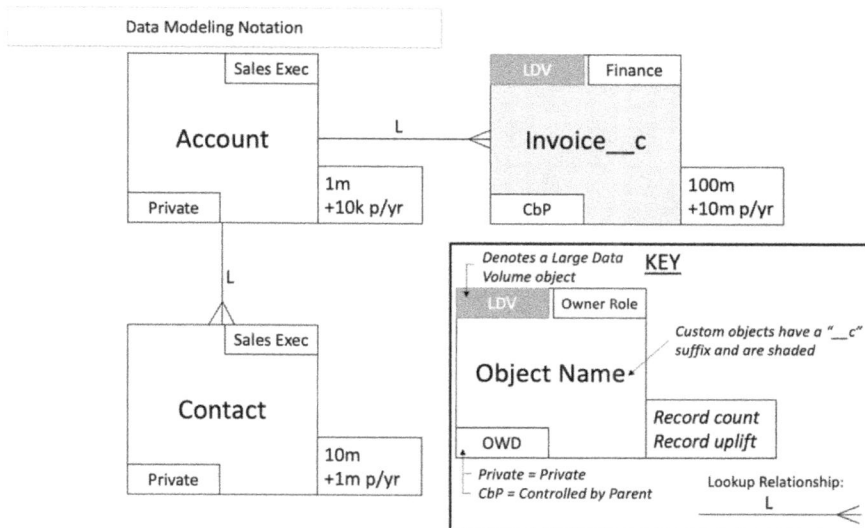

Figure 14.1 – Data modeling notation

Next, let's look at Many-to-Many relationships:

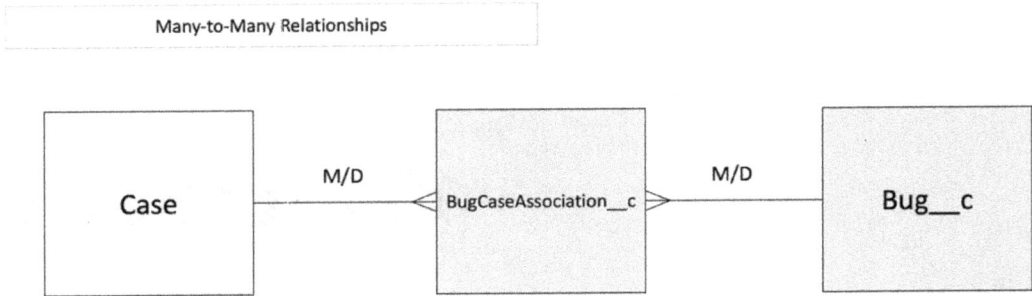

Figure 14.2 – Modeling Many-to-Many relationships

Next up is the sharing model:

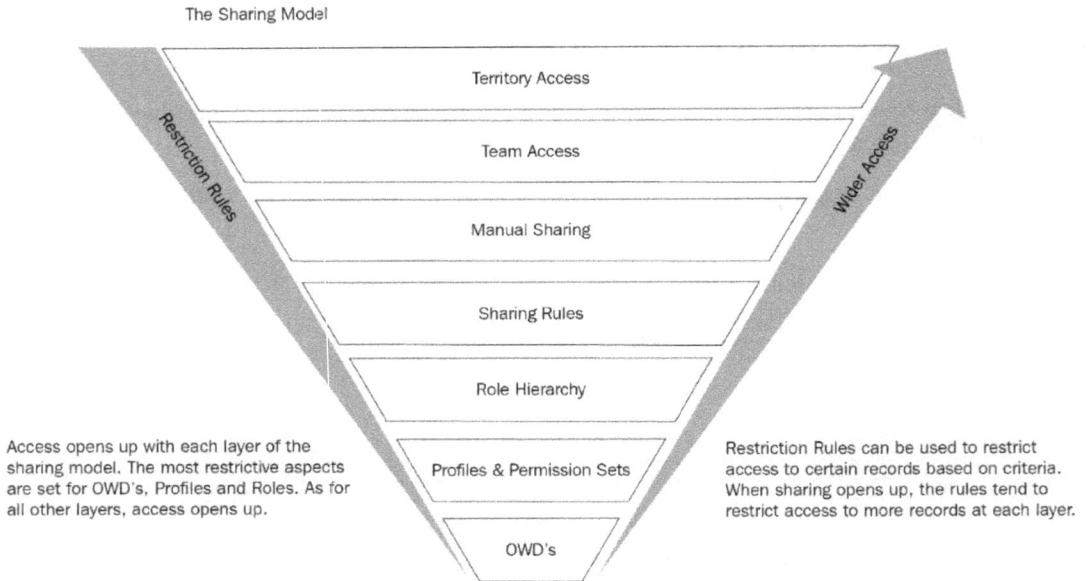

Figure 14.3 – The Sharing model

Finally, we can retouch upon object and field storage:

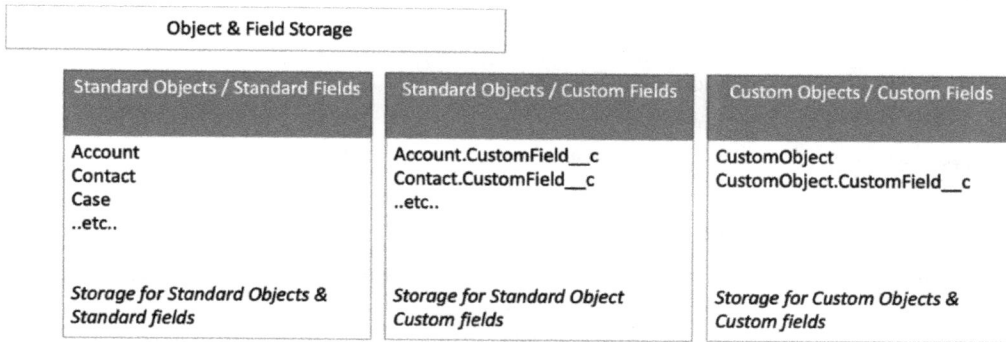

Object & Field Storage		
Standard Objects / Standard Fields	**Standard Objects / Custom Fields**	**Custom Objects / Custom Fields**
Account Contact Case ..etc..	Account.CustomField__c Contact.CustomField__c ..etc..	CustomObject CustomObject.CustomField__c
Storage for Standard Objects & *Standard fields*	*Storage for Standard Object* *Custom fields*	*Storage for Custom Objects &* *Custom fields*

Figure 14.4 – Object and field storage

Now let's move on to master data management.

Master data management

Let's now look at the diagrams we introduced on the topic of **Master Data Management** (**MDM**).

The following can be used as an aid for the topic of master data management, where we explored an MDM scenario with Salesforce as the keeper for golden record associations:

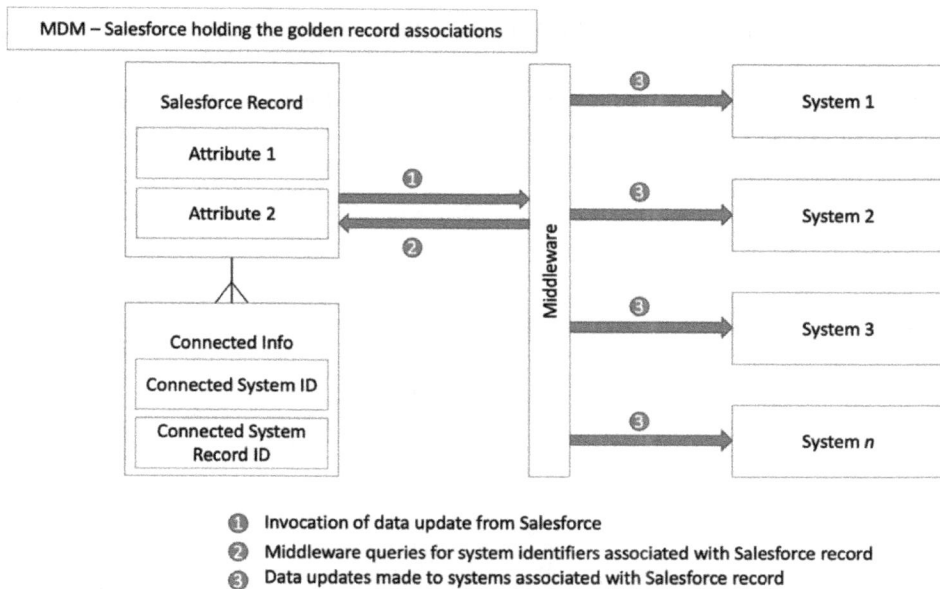

① Invocation of data update from Salesforce
② Middleware queries for system identifiers associated with Salesforce record
③ Data updates made to systems associated with Salesforce record

Figure 14.5 – Salesforce holding the golden record associations

The following can be used as an aid for the topic of MDM, where we explored an MDM scenario with middleware as the keeper for golden record associations:

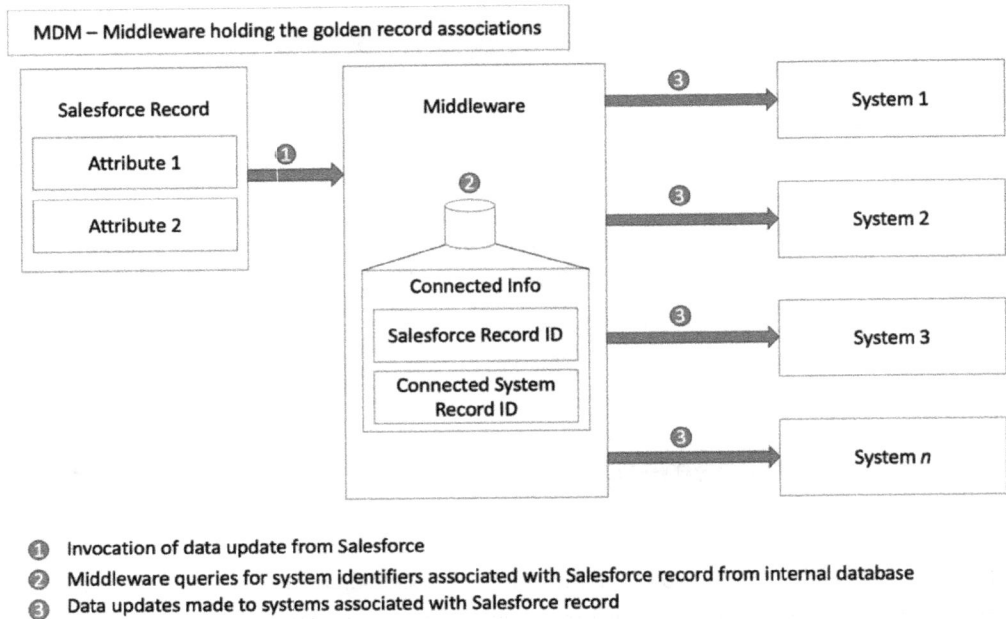

MDM – Middleware holding the golden record associations

Salesforce Record
Attribute 1
Attribute 2

Middleware

Connected Info
Salesforce Record ID
Connected System Record ID

System 1
System 2
System 3
System *n*

1. Invocation of data update from Salesforce
2. Middleware queries for system identifiers associated with Salesforce record from internal database
3. Data updates made to systems associated with Salesforce record

Figure 14.6 – Middleware holding the golden record associations

The following can be used as an aid for the topic of MDM, where we explored an MDM scenario with an external system/registry as the keeper for golden record associations:

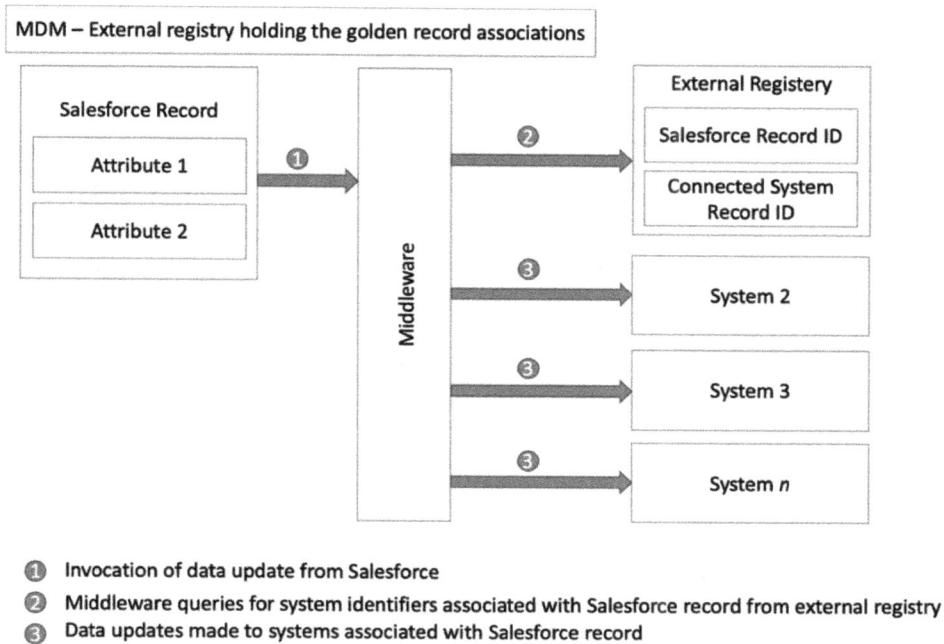

① Invocation of data update from Salesforce
② Middleware queries for system identifiers associated with Salesforce record from external registry
③ Data updates made to systems associated with Salesforce record

Figure 14.7 – External registry holding the golden record associations

Let's continue with Salesforce data management.

Salesforce data management

Let's now look at Salesforce data management revision aids.

Introduced earlier in this book in *Chapter 4, Salesforce Data Management*, let's recap the licensing for Experience Cloud so that you can be best equipped when answering questions on Experience Cloud and licensing options:

Salesforce Experience Cloud Licensing

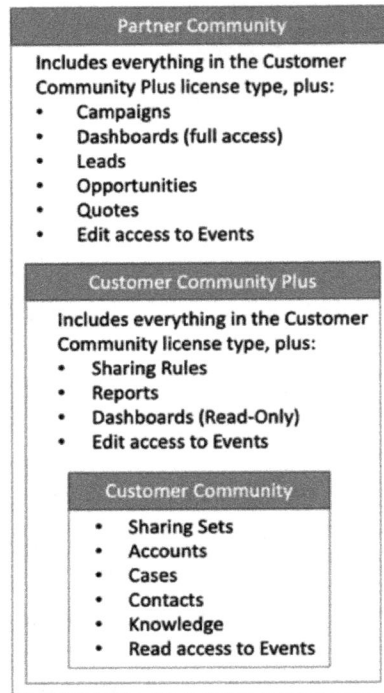

Partner Community

Includes everything in the Customer Community Plus license type, plus:
- Campaigns
- Dashboards (full access)
- Leads
- Opportunities
- Quotes
- Edit access to Events

Customer Community Plus

Includes everything in the Customer Community license type, plus:
- Sharing Rules
- Reports
- Dashboards (Read-Only)
- Edit access to Events

Customer Community

- Sharing Sets
- Accounts
- Cases
- Contacts
- Knowledge
- Read access to Events

Figure 14.8 – Salesforce Experience Cloud licensing

Let's now move on to data governance.

Data governance

In *Chapter 5*, *Data Governance*, we introduced the concept of an enterprise data governance strategy.

Let's recap the enterprise data governance strategy:

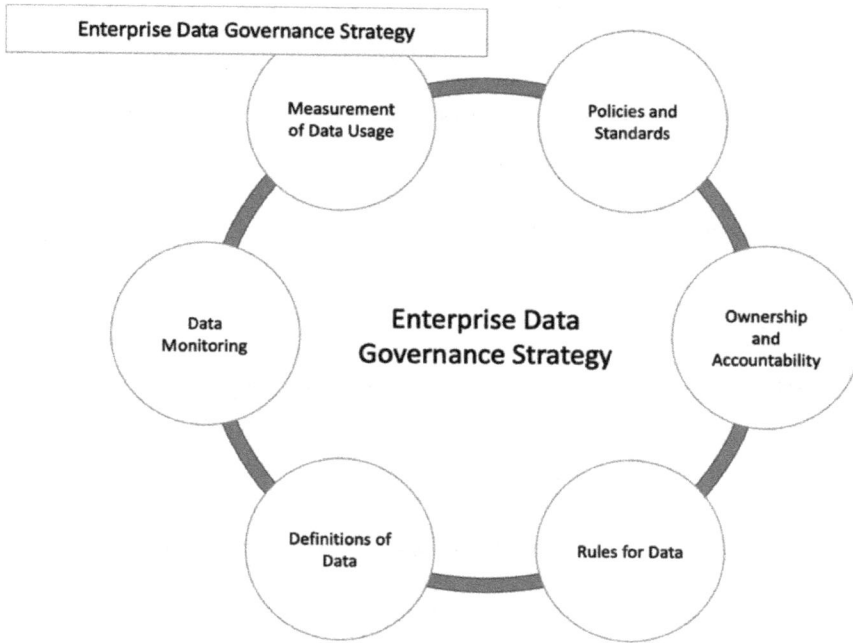

Figure 14.9 – Enterprise data governance strategy

Next up, let's move on to large data volumes.

Large data volumes

Chapter 6, Understanding Large Data Volumes, saw us go in depth into **Large Data Volumes (LDVs)** in Salesforce, including techniques for mitigation.

We touched upon indexing when exploring LDV, so let's recap that here:

Salesforce Query Optimizer – Standard Indexes

30% of up to 1 Million Records + 15% of Additional Records over 1 Million, up to a total of 1 Million Records

Examples:
2 million records -- 300,000 + 150,000 = 450,000 records
6 million records -- 300,000 + 700,000 = 1 Million records

Salesforce Query Optimizer – Custom Indexes

10% of up to 1 Million Records + 5% of Additional Records over 1 Million, up to a total of 333,333 records

Examples:
2 million records – 100,000 + 50,000 = 150,000 records
6 million records – 100,000 + 233,333 = 333,333 Million records

Figure 14.10 – Salesforce Query Optimizer index thresholds

Data migration is next up, so let's investigate that further.

Data migration

Next up in our journey through the revision aids is data migration.

We covered the stages involved with a typical data migration, so let's refresh our knowledge here:

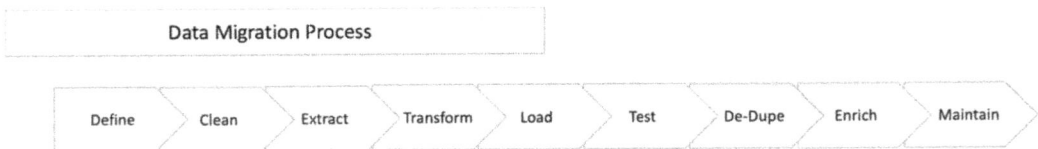

Data Migration Process

Define	Clean	Extract	Transform	Load	Test	De-Dupe	Enrich	Maintain

Figure 14.11 – Data migration process

Now, let's move on to accounts and contacts.

Accounts and contacts

In *Chapter 8, Accounts and Contacts*, we explored the relationships and various join objects for these two core objects on the Salesforce platform.

Let's review our account and contact diagrams to refresh our memories on this topic, beginning with the Person Account and Contact Role data models:

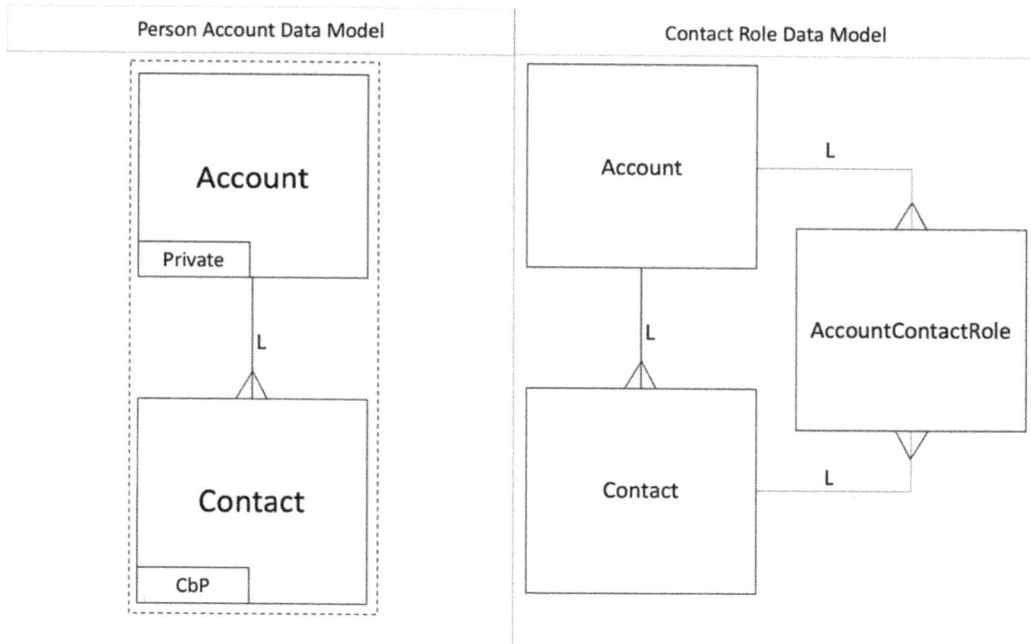

Figure 14.12 – Person Account and Contact Role data models

Next, let's revisit the Account Team and Account/Contact Relation data models:

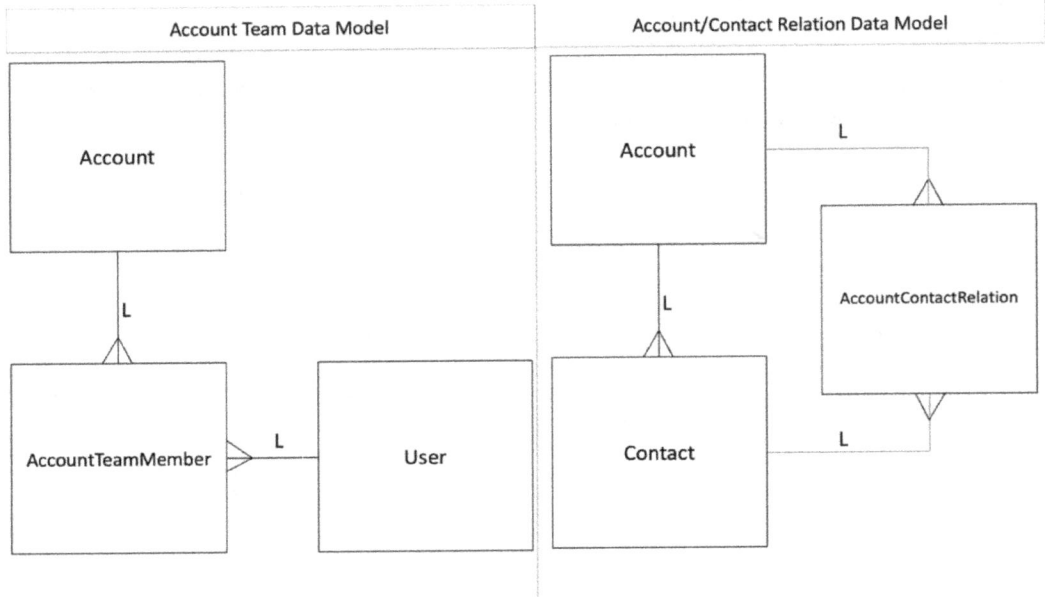

Figure 14.13 – Account Team and Account/Contact Relation data models

With accounts and contacts covered, let's summarize what we've covered in this chapter.

Summary

In this chapter, we've introduced several cheat sheets or revision aids that you can use to jog your memory and understanding of several topic areas.

In *Chapter 15, Further Resources*, we'll highlight links to further resources that you can explore to bolster your understanding of a given topic area that we've covered in this book.

15

Further Resources

During our learning journey, we have covered many different topics. However, there is still more you can learn to enhance your understanding of specific topics. In this chapter, additional resources and Salesforce official documentation (where available) will be highlighted.

Let's start with *Data modeling and database design*.

Data modeling and database design

The following resources can be used to further explore topics we highlighted when we covered data modeling and database design:

- *Data access in Salesforce*: `https://developer.salesforce.com/docs/atlas.en-us.dat.meta/dat/dat_components.htm`

- *Salesforce standard objects*: `https://developer.salesforce.com/docs/atlas.en-us.api.meta/api/sforce_api_objects_list.htm`

- *Salesforce data model diagrams*: `https://developer.salesforce.com/docs/atlas.en-us.api.meta/api/data_model.htm`

- *Salesforce object relationships overview*: `https://help.salesforce.com/articleView?id=overview_of_custom_object_relationships.htm&type=0`

- *Restriction rules*: `https://help.salesforce.com/s/articleView?id=release-notes.rn_forcecom_sharing_restriction_rules.htm&type=5&release=234`

- *Data Modeling (Trailhead)*: `https://trailhead.salesforce.com/content/learn/modules/data_modeling`

- *Salesforce Data Modeling 101*: `https://www.youtube.com/watch?v=2VGWIM4yMAs`

Now, let's move on to master data management.

Master data management

For further information on master data management, please refer to the following resources:

- *Beginners Guide to MDM*: `https://www.dataqualitypro.com/blog/beginners-guide-to-mdm-master-data-management`
- *What is Master Data Management (MDM)?*: `https://www.mulesoft.com/resources/esb/what-is-master-data-management-mdm`
- *Salesforce Connect*: `https://developer.salesforce.com/docs/atlas.en-us.234.0.apexcode.meta/apexcode/platform_connect_about.htm`
- *Ask an Architect: 5 Steps to an Effective Salesforce Data Management Strategy (Part 1)*: `https://www.salesforce.org/blog/ask-architect-5-steps-effective-salesforce-data-management-strategy/`
- *What is Master Data Management*: `https://www.youtube.com/watch?v=2vhArFG_eCo`
- *Master Data Management (MDM) & plm in context of enterprise product management*: `https://www.slideshare.net/tataconsultancyservices/master-data-management-mdm-plm-in-context-of-enterprise-product-management`

Next, let's move on to Salesforce data management.

Salesforce data management

For greater insights into Salesforce data management, please see the following resources:

- *Salesforce Experience Cloud licensing*: `https://help.salesforce.com/s/articleView?id=users_license_types_communities.htm&type=5&language=en_US`
- *Setting up sharing sets*: `https://help.salesforce.com/s/articleView?id=sf.networks_setting_light_users.htm&type=5`
- *Salesforce data storage allocations*: `https://help.salesforce.com/s/articleView?id=sf.overview_storage.htm&type=5`
- *The Customer Data platform*: `https://www.salesforce.com/ap/solutions/customer-360/`
- *Salesforce to Salesforce*: `https://help.salesforce.com/s/articleView?id=sf.business_network_intro.htm&type=5`
- *Introduction to Bulk API 2.0*: `https://developer.salesforce.com/docs/atlas.en-us.api_asynch.meta/api_asynch/asynch_api_intro.htm`

- *Apex Governor limits*: https://developer.salesforce.com/docs/atlas. en-us.236.0.salesforce_app_limits_cheatsheet.meta/salesforce_ app_limits_cheatsheet/salesforce_app_limits_platform_apexgov.htm
- *Data Management (Trailhead)*: https://trailhead.salesforce.com/content/ learn/modules/lex_implementation_data_management?trailmix_ creator_id=strailhead&trailmix_slug=architect-data-architecture- and-management

Next up is data governance.

Data governance

For more information on data governance, see the following resources:

- *The Individual Object*: https://developer.salesforce.com/docs/atlas. en-us.api.meta/api/sforce_api_objects_individual.htm
- *Salesforce Shield Encryption versus Salesforce Classic Encryption*: https://developer. salesforce.com/docs/atlas.en-us.securityImplGuide.meta/ securityImplGuide/security_pe_vs_classic_encryption.htm
- *Enabling Salesforce Shield event monitoring*: https://help.salesforce.com/s/ articleView?id=000339868&type=1
- *Session security*: https://help.salesforce.com/s/articleView?id=sf. admin_sessions.htm&type=5
- *Field history tracking*: https://help.salesforce.com/s/articleView?id=sf. tracking_field_history.htm&type=5
- *Data Governance, Data Stewardship, Planning & Data Quality*: https://www.youtube. com/watch?v=lA9i190y_0I

Next, let's explore some resources applicable to large data volumes.

Large data volumes

More information on large data volumes can be found by checking out the following resources:

- *Salesforce Trust*: https://trust.salesforce.com
- *Search Architecture*: https://developer.salesforce.com/docs/atlas.en-us. salesforce_large_data_volumes_bp.meta/salesforce_large_data_ volumes_bp/ldv_deployments_concepts_search_architecture.htm

- *Indexes*: https://developer.salesforce.com/docs/atlas.en-us.salesforce_large_data_volumes_bp.meta/salesforce_large_data_volumes_bp/ldv_deployments_infrastructure_indexes.htm

- *Skinny tables*: https://developer.salesforce.com/docs/atlas.en-us.salesforce_large_data_volumes_bp.meta/salesforce_large_data_volumes_bp/ldv_deployments_infrastructure_skinny_tables.htm

- *Salesforce Architects – Large Data Volumes*: https://medium.com/salesforce-architects/tagged/large-data-volumes

- *Big Objects*: https://developer.salesforce.com/docs/atlas.en-us.236.0.bigobjects.meta/bigobjects/big_object.htm

- *Best Practices for Deployments with Large Data Volumes*: https://developer.salesforce.com/docs/atlas.en-us.salesforce_large_data_volumes_bp.meta/salesforce_large_data_volumes_bp/ldv_deployments_introduction.htm

- *Large Data Volume (LDV) Management in Salesforce*: https://www.youtube.com/watch?v=TzrRZs2VQEU

Let's now move on to data migration resources.

Data migration

Additional resources on data migration are listed as follows:

- *Data export options from Salesforce*: https://trailhead.salesforce.com/content/learn/modules/lex_implementation_data_management/lex_implementation_data_export

- *PK chunking in Salesforce*: https://developer.salesforce.com/docs/atlas.en-us.234.0.api_asynch.meta/api_asynch/async_api_headers_enable_pk_chunking.htm

- *Data allocation and storage limits*: https://help.salesforce.com/s/articleView?id=sf.overview_storage.htm&type=5

- *Bulk API query*: https://developer.salesforce.com/docs/atlas.en-us.api_asynch.meta/api_asynch/asynch_api_bulk_query_intro.htm

- *Best practices when you migrate data*: https://help.salesforce.com/s/articleView?id=000326326&type=1

- *Data Import: Best Practices for Importing Data | Salesforce*: https://www.youtube.com/watch?v=GgBtfffWqw0

Accounts and contacts resources are next.

Accounts and contacts

For more information on accounts and contacts, please see these additional resources:

- *The Account object API documentation*: https://developer.salesforce.com/docs/atlas.en-us.object_reference.meta/object_reference/sforce_api_objects_account.htm

- *The Contact object API documentation*: https://developer.salesforce.com/docs/atlas.en-us.object_reference.meta/object_reference/sforce_api_objects_contact.htm

- *Enable person accounts*: https://help.salesforce.com/s/articleView?id=sf.account_person_enable.htm&type=5

- *Enable contacts to multiple accounts*: https://help.salesforce.com/s/articleView?id=sf.shared_contacts_set_up.htm&type=5

- *Comparing contacts to multiple accounts to other options*: https://help.salesforce.com/s/articleView?id=sf.shared_contacts_comparison.htm&type=5

- *AccountContactRelation API documentation*: https://developer.salesforce.com/docs/atlas.en-us.object_reference.meta/object_reference/sforce_api_objects_accountcontactrelation.htm

- *AccountContactRole API documentation*: https://developer.salesforce.com/docs/atlas.en-us.object_reference.meta/object_reference/sforce_api_objects_accountcontactrole.htm

- *AccountTeamMember API documentation*: https://developer.salesforce.com/docs/atlas.en-us.object_reference.meta/object_reference/sforce_api_objects_accountteammember.htm

- *Considerations for accounts and contacts in Sales Cloud*: https://www.youtube.com/watch?v=ZXceWxOTNmQ

Let's now turn to resources for data APIs and Apex.

Data APIs and Apex

Further information relating to data APIs and Apex can be found here:

- *OAuth 2.0 with Salesforce*: https://developer.salesforce.com/docs/atlas.en-us.api_rest.meta/api_rest/intro_oauth_and_connected_apps.htm

- *Batch API*: `https://developer.salesforce.com/docs/atlas.en-us.api_asynch.meta/api_asynch/asynch_api_intro.htm`

- *Bulk API 2.0 – How requests are processed*: `https://developer.salesforce.com/docs/atlas.en-us.api_asynch.meta/api_asynch/how_requests_are_processed.htm`

- *Batch Apex*: `https://developer.salesforce.com/docs/atlas.en-us.222.0.apexcode.meta/apexcode/apex_batch_interface.htm`

- *Executing Batch Apex*: `https://help.salesforce.com/s/articleView?id=000328480&type=1`

- *The Apex Batchable Interface*: `https://developer.salesforce.com/docs/atlas.en-us.apexref.meta/apexref/apex_interface_database_batchable.htm#apex_Database_Batchable_execute`

- *The Apex Schedulable class*: `https://developer.salesforce.com/docs/atlas.en-us.222.0.apexcode.meta/apexcode/apex_scheduler.htm`

- *Future methods in Apex*: `https://developer.salesforce.com/docs/atlas.en-us.222.0.apexcode.meta/apexcode/apex_invoking_future_methods.htm`

- *The Apex Database class*: `https://developer.salesforce.com/docs/atlas.en-us.apexref.meta/apexref/apex_methods_system_database.htm`

- *Fast Parallel Data Loading with the Bulk API*: `https://www.youtube.com/watch?v=OiOHST8SZ7A&t=1962s`

With data APIs and Apex resources now highlighted, let's now move on to tuning performance.

Tuning performance

For further resources on tuning performance, please see the following links:

- *PK chunking*: `https://developer.salesforce.com/docs/atlas.en-us.api_asynch.meta/api_asynch/async_api_headers_enable_pk_chunking.htm`

- *Skinny tables*: `https://developer.salesforce.com/docs/atlas.en-us.salesforce_large_data_volumes_bp.meta/salesforce_large_data_volumes_bp/ldv_deployments_infrastructure_skinny_tables.htm`

- *Techniques for optimizing performance*: `https://developer.salesforce.com/docs/atlas.en-us.salesforce_large_data_volumes_bp.meta/salesforce_large_data_volumes_bp/ldv_deployments_techniques_for_performance.htm`

- *Salesforce Data Architecture Designer Series – Session 6 PERFORMANCE TUNING*: `https://www.youtube.com/watch?v=-QTDZObPOac`

Let's now move on to backup and restore resources.

Backup and restore

Check out the following for more information on backup and restore:

- *Best practices to backup Salesforce data*: `https://help.salesforce.com/s/articleView?id=000334121&type=1`

- *Export data using data loader*: `https://help.salesforce.com/s/articleView?id=sf.exporting_data.htm&type=5`

- *Export data using report exports*: `https://help.salesforce.com/s/articleView?id=sf.reports_export.htm&type=5`

- *Export data using weekly backups*: `https://help.salesforce.com/s/articleView?id=sf.admin_exportdata.htm&type=5`

- *Creating a sandbox environment*: `https://help.salesforce.com/s/articleView?id=sf.data_sandbox_create.htm&type=5`

- *Ant migration tool*: `https://developer.salesforce.com/docs/atlas.en-us.daas.meta/daas/meta_development.htm`

- *SFDX*: `https://developer.salesforce.com/tools/sfdxcli`

- *Salesforce Backup and Restore*: `https://www.youtube.com/watch?v=znfkpQDOpyw`

Next up is territory management.

Territory management

Reference materials for territory management for additional learning can be found here:

- *Territory management implementation guide*: `https://resources.docs.salesforce.com/latest/latest/en-us/sfdc/pdf/salesforce_implementing_territory_mgmt2_guide.pdf`

- *Get Started with Enterprise Territory Management*: `https://trailhead.salesforce.com/content/learn/modules/territory-management-basics/get-started-with-enterprise-territory-management`

- *Automating with Territory Management*: `https://www.youtube.com/watch?v=upFY2uMvCIY`

Let's now summarize what we've covered in this chapter.

Summary

In this chapter, we've introduced many additional resources that you can use to further enhance your understanding of various topic areas.

In the next chapter, we'll look at how to sign up for and take the Salesforce Certified Data Architect exam.

16

How to Take the Exam

When you feel ready to take the exam, you'll need to go through the process of registering for it and then taking the exam either virtually or in person. Read on to find out more about how this process works. By the end of this chapter, you'll know exactly what you need to do in order to take the exam. If you have already used Webassessor to take a Salesforce exam, you can skip this chapter if you wish.

We'll cover the following topics in this chapter:

- Webassessor
- Taking the exam in person
- Taking the exam remotely
- The result

Now, let's dive into how to take the exam, starting by introducing the Webassessor platform.

Webassessor

Kryterion Webassessor is a platform used for scheduling, paying for, and taking exams. Used by Salesforce, **Amazon Web Services (AWS)**, and other organizations to administer credential exams, it provides a secure mechanism from which to book and pay for your exam, and then launch the exam itself. Results are stored forever, which means that all of your test-taking history for a given product suite (such as Salesforce) is kept in one place.

Let's look at how to sign up for a Webassessor account now.

Signing up for a Webassessor account

In order to schedule an exam, you must sign up for a Webassessor account first if you do not already have one for Salesforce exams.

To do this, first, navigate to `https://www.webassessor.com/salesforce` and click the **Create a new Webassessor login now** link:

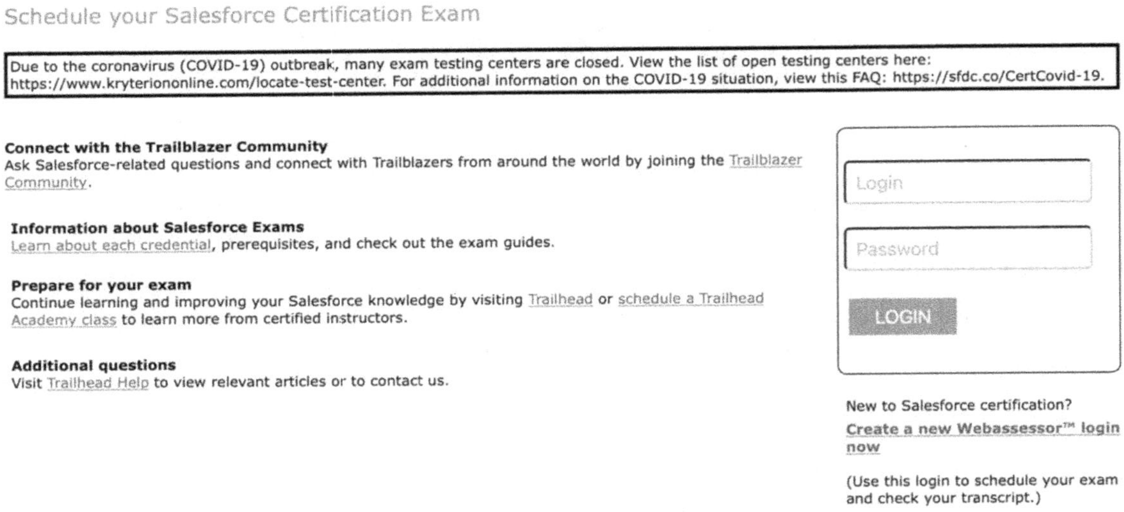

Schedule your Salesforce Certification Exam

Due to the coronavirus (COVID-19) outbreak, many exam testing centers are closed. View the list of open testing centers here: https://www.kryterononline.com/locate-test-center. For additional information on the COVID-19 situation, view this FAQ: https://sfdc.co/CertCovid-19.

Connect with the Trailblazer Community
Ask Salesforce-related questions and connect with Trailblazers from around the world by joining the Trailblazer Community.

Information about Salesforce Exams
Learn about each credential, prerequisites, and check out the exam guides.

Prepare for your exam
Continue learning and improving your Salesforce knowledge by visiting Trailhead or schedule a Trailhead Academy class to learn more from certified instructors.

Additional questions
Visit Trailhead Help to view relevant articles or to contact us.

Login

Password

LOGIN

New to Salesforce certification?
Create a new Webassessor™ login now

(Use this login to schedule your exam and check your transcript.)

Figure 16.1 – The Webassessor login screen

When filling out the form details, be sure to use the same email account that you use for your **Trailhead** account. When all fields are filled out, click the **Save** button:

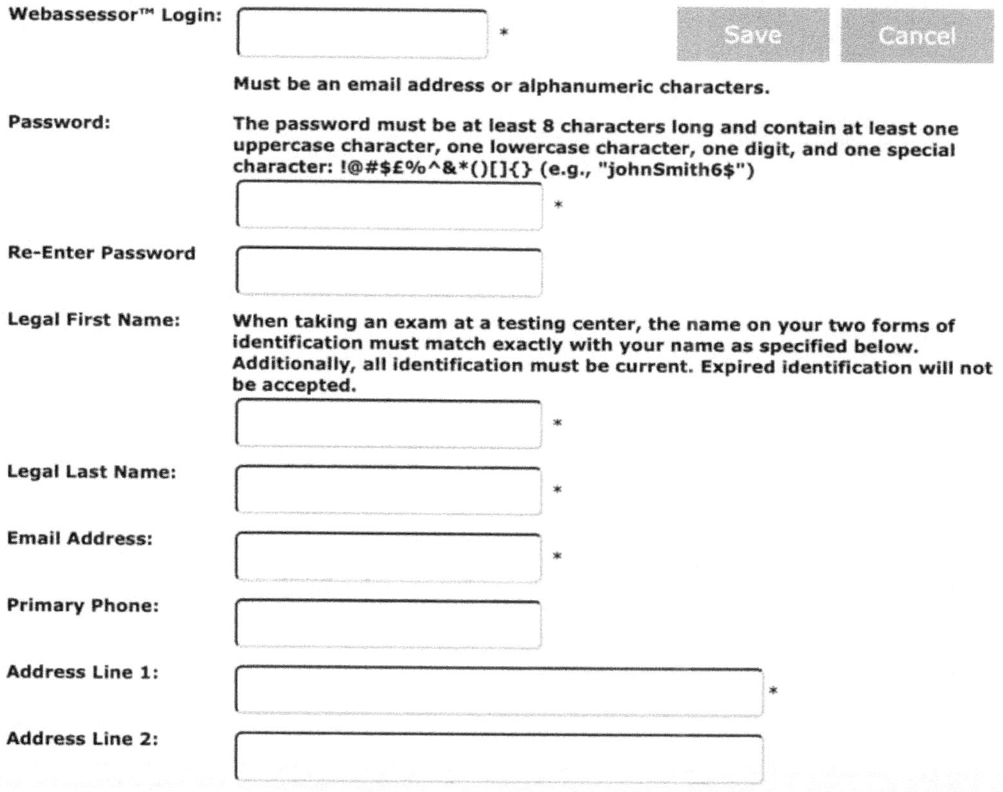

Webassessor™ Login: [   ] *   Save   Cancel

Must be an email address or alphanumeric characters.

Password: The password must be at least 8 characters long and contain at least one
uppercase character, one lowercase character, one digit, and one special
character: !@#$£%^&*()[]{} (e.g., "johnSmith6$")

[   ] *

Re-Enter Password [   ]

Legal First Name: When taking an exam at a testing center, the name on your two forms of
identification must match exactly with your name as specified below.
Additionally, all identification must be current. Expired identification will not
be accepted.

[   ] *

Legal Last Name: [   ] *

Email Address: [   ] *

Primary Phone: [   ]

Address Line 1: [   ] *

Address Line 2: [   ]

Figure 16.2 – The Webassessor new account sign-up screen

Complete any email verification that may be required and your account is ready for use.

Let's now look at what's required to take the exam in person.

Taking the exam in person

In order to take an exam, we must register for it first:

1. To do this, log in to Webassessor using your credentials (if you are not already logged in), and
    click on the **Register For An Exam** tab:

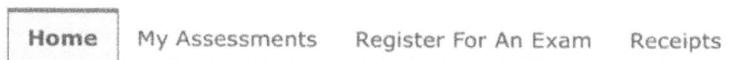

Home   My Assessments   Register For An Exam   Receipts

Figure 16.3 – The Webassessor tabs

2. Next, expand the **Architect Exams** section to access the exams that are part of the Salesforce architect exam curriculum:

Figure 16.4 – The exam sections

3. Expand the **Salesforce Certified Data Architect** section and click **Register** next to **Onsite Proctored**. You'll then be presented with a list of test centers and options for filtering. Check the checkbox next to an appropriate test center and click **Select**:

Choose options below to narrow down the list of testing centers displayed.

Select the Testing Center where you wish to take the test.

Available Testing Centers

	Testing Location Name	Address	City	Province/State	Country	Map	Important Location Information
☐	Spark Exam Centre	30-31 Friars Street, Nando's Building, OFF MERCHANTS PLACE	Reading	Berkshire	United Kingdom	Map	
☐	Pitman Training Centre_Cambridge	2nd Floor, St Andrews House, 59 St Andrews Street	Cambridge	Cambridgeshire	United Kingdom	Map	
☐	Exams Ltd	Sefton House, Adam Court, Newark Road	Peterborough	Cambridgeshire	United Kingdom	Map	
☐	Pitman Training_Enfield	2nd Floor Nicon House, 45 Silver Street	Enfield	Enfield	United Kingdom	Map	
☐	Oriac Information Systems	Oriac House, 10 The Glenmore Centre, Pent Road	Folkestone	Kent	United Kingdom	Map	
☐	SMARTTHINK LIMITED_Maidstone-Kent	F10 & F14 First Floor Kestrel House,, Knightrider Street	Maidstone	Kent	United Kingdom	Map	

Figure 16.5 – Choosing a testing center

4. Next, choose a date and time. Check the checkbox to acknowledge that you've read the text in the textbox and click **Select**:

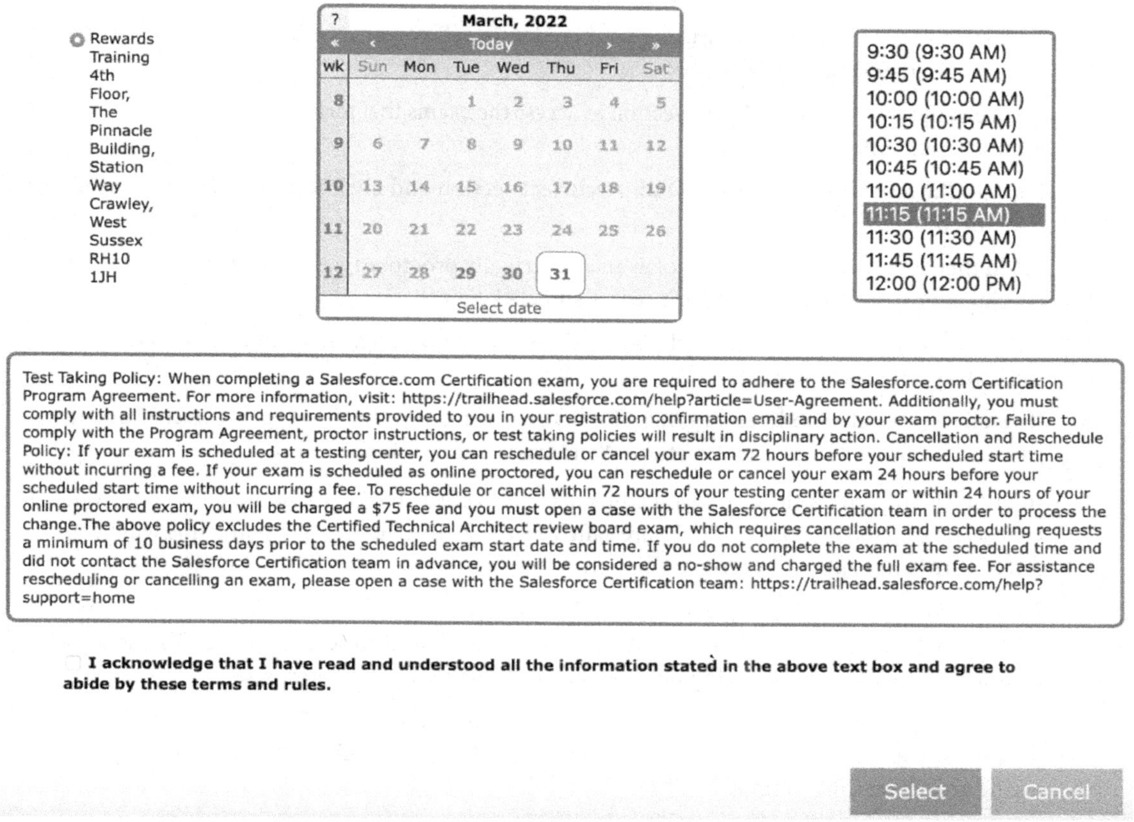

○ Rewards
Training
4th
Floor,
The
Pinnacle
Building,
Station
Way
Crawley,
West
Sussex
RH10
1JH

?		March, 2022					
«	‹		Today			›	»
wk	Sun	Mon	Tue	Wed	Thu	Fri	Sat
8			1	2	3	4	5
9	6	7	8	9	10	11	12
10	13	14	15	16	17	18	19
11	20	21	22	23	24	25	26
12	27	28	29	30	31		
			Select date				

9:30 (9:30 AM)
9:45 (9:45 AM)
10:00 (10:00 AM)
10:15 (10:15 AM)
10:30 (10:30 AM)
10:45 (10:45 AM)
11:00 (11:00 AM)
11:15 (11:15 AM)
11:30 (11:30 AM)
11:45 (11:45 AM)
12:00 (12:00 PM)

Test Taking Policy: When completing a Salesforce.com Certification exam, you are required to adhere to the Salesforce.com Certification Program Agreement. For more information, visit: https://trailhead.salesforce.com/help?article=User-Agreement. Additionally, you must comply with all instructions and requirements provided to you in your registration confirmation email and by your exam proctor. Failure to comply with the Program Agreement, proctor instructions, or test taking policies will result in disciplinary action. Cancellation and Reschedule Policy: If your exam is scheduled at a testing center, you can reschedule or cancel your exam 72 hours before your scheduled start time without incurring a fee. If your exam is scheduled as online proctored, you can reschedule or cancel your exam 24 hours before your scheduled start time without incurring a fee. To reschedule or cancel within 72 hours of your testing center exam or within 24 hours of your online proctored exam, you will be charged a $75 fee and you must open a case with the Salesforce Certification team in order to process the change. The above policy excludes the Certified Technical Architect review board exam, which requires cancellation and rescheduling requests a minimum of 10 business days prior to the scheduled exam start date and time. If you do not complete the exam at the scheduled time and did not contact the Salesforce Certification team in advance, you will be considered a no-show and charged the full exam fee. For assistance rescheduling or cancelling an exam, please open a case with the Salesforce Certification team: https://trailhead.salesforce.com/help?support=home

☐ **I acknowledge that I have read and understood all the information stated in the above text box and agree to abide by these terms and rules.**

Select   Cancel

Figure 16.6 – Picking a date and time to take the exam

5. If you have a voucher code, enter it into the payment screen – otherwise, go to **Check Out** and pay using an accepted payment method. Your exam is now booked.

The next step is to attend the test center in person at your scheduled time and take the exam. You'll be required to show identification to prove who you are. The nature of each test center means that you may be solo or sharing a room with other test takers, but suffice to say, the exam will be delivered by you sitting at a computer and using your computer mouse.

Now that we understand how the exam works when taking it in person, let's explore what it means to take the exam virtually.

Taking the exam virtually

As with taking the exam in person, we must register for it first:

1. To do this, log in to Webassessor using your credentials (if you are not already logged in), and click the **Register for an exam** tab.

2. Next, expand the **Architect Exams** section to access the exams that form the Salesforce architect exam curriculum.

3. Expand the **Salesforce Certified Data Architect** section and click **Register** next to **Online Proctored**.

4. You'll then be presented with a list of available virtually proctored dates and times. Check the checkbox next to an appropriate test center and click **Select**.

5. Next, choose a date and time. Check the checkbox to acknowledge that you've read the text in the textbox and click **Select**.

6. If you have a voucher code, enter it into the payment screen – otherwise, go to **Check Out** and pay using an accepted payment method. Your exam is now booked.

   In order to prepare for the exam, you'll be required to create biometric identification on your laptop and download a piece of software called **Sentinel**. Instructions for doing this will be in the confirmation email you receive when the exam is booked.

   When it comes to exam time, be sure to find a room that you will not be disturbed in, is free from noise, and doesn't contain any notes or similar that could indicate cheating. The exam is of a closed book format, meaning no notes or materials are to be referenced.

   When taking the exam, you will be asked to temporarily remove and show your glasses to the proctor (if you wear glasses, of course), and you may be asked to show the proctor your test-taking area from time to time.

Now that we've covered taking the exam virtually, let's turn our attention to the result of the exam.

The result

Irrespective of the format of the exam (whether in person or virtual), when you finish your exam, you are immediately presented with the result and a breakdown of your scoring in each area of the exam (represented as a percentage). If you pass, congratulations! If you didn't pass, then use the score breakdown in order to determine where to revisit and revise. Book a retake using the same process as booking for the exam. The retake will incur a fee, although this is cheaper than the initial exam fee. Don't see a failure to pass as a bad thing. You're given feedback so that you can score better and pass next time, as your revision can be more targeted the second time around.

Now that we have seen what format the results take, let's now summarize what we've covered.

Summary

In this chapter, we covered how to take the Salesforce Certified Data Architect exam in both an in-person and virtual format. We introduced ourselves to Webassessor and learned how to sign up for the exam.

If you attempted the practice questions from *Chapter 13, Practice Exam Questions*, then you can check your answers in *Chapter 17, Answers to Practice Questions*.

Answers to Practice Questions

For the sets of practice questions introduced in this part of the book, candidates are provided with the answers with the answers in this chapter.

Answers for question set 1-20

1. b
2. b
3. c
4. d
5. a
6. d
7. a
8. c
9. d
10. a
11. a
12. b and d
13. a, c, and d
14. d
15. b
16. a and b
17. a
18. b and d

19. b

20. d

Answers for question set 21-40

1.   a

2.   a

3.   a and b

4.   a

5.   a

6.   a

7.   a

8.   c

9.   b

10. d

11. b

12. a

13. b

14. a

15. c

16. a

17. a, b, and d

18. b and d

19. a

20. a

Answers for question set 41-60

1.   a and b

2.   c

3.   a and d

4.   a and c

5.   b

6. d

7. a and b

8. c

9. a

10. a

11. b and d

12. a

13. c

14. d

15. a

16. c and e

17. a and d

18. b and c

19. a and c

20. b

Answers for question set 61-80

1. a

2. b

3. c

4. b

5. b and c

6. a, b, and d

7. a

8. b, c, and d

9. a

10. b, c, and d

11. a and b

12. b

13. a

14. d

15. a

16. d

17. a

18. a and d

19. a

20. a

Answers for question set 81-100

1. b

2. c

3. c

4. a

5. b and c

6. c

7. a, c, and e

8. a and c

9. b

10. a, b, and c

11. b

12. a and c

13. a

14. b

15. a and b

16. a, c, and d

17. a, b, and c

18. a and b

19. b, c, and d

20. a, b, and c

Index

‹packt›

Packt.com

Subscribe to our online digital library for full access to over 7,000 books and videos, as well as industry leading tools to help you plan your personal development and advance your career. For more information, please visit our website.

Why subscribe?

- Spend less time learning and more time coding with practical eBooks and Videos from over 4,000 industry professionals
- Improve your learning with Skill Plans built especially for you
- Get a free eBook or video every month
- Fully searchable for easy access to vital information
- Copy and paste, print, and bookmark content

Did you know that Packt offers eBook versions of every book published, with PDF and ePub files available? You can upgrade to the eBook version at packt.com and as a print book customer, you are entitled to a discount on the eBook copy. Get in touch with us at customercare@packtpub.com for more details.

At www.packt.com, you can also read a collection of free technical articles, sign up for a range of free newsletters, and receive exclusive discounts and offers on Packt books and eBooks.

Other Books You May Enjoy

If you enjoyed this book, you may be interested in these other books by Packt:

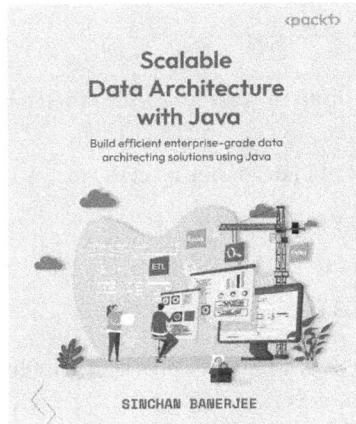

Scalable Data Architecture with Java

Sinchan Banerjee

ISBN: 978-1-80107-308-0

- Learn how to clean your data and ready it for analysis
- Analyze and use the best data architecture patterns for problems
- Understand when and how to choose Java tools for a data architecture
- Build batch and real-time data engineering solutions using Java
- Discover how to apply security and governance to a solution
- Measure performance, publish benchmarks, and optimize solutions
- Evaluate, choose, and present the best architectural alternatives
- Understand how to publish Data as a Service using GraphQL and a REST API

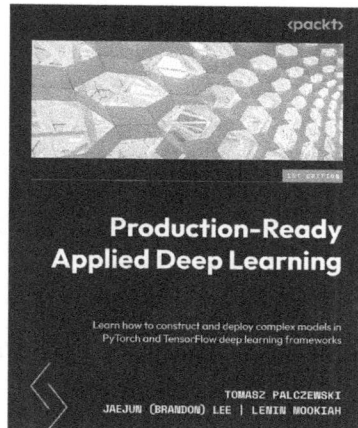

Production-Ready Applied Deep Learning

Tomasz Palczewski , Jaejun (Brandon) Lee , Lenin Mookiah

ISBN: 978-1-80324-366-5

- Understand how to develop a deep learning model using PyTorch and TensorFlow
- Convert a proof-of-concept model into a production-ready application
- Discover how to set up a deep learning pipeline in an efficient way using AWS
- Explore different ways to compress a model for various deployment requirements
- Develop Android and iOS applications that run deep learning on mobile devices
- Monitor a system with a deep learning model in production
- Choose the right system architecture for developing and deploying a model

Packt is searching for authors like you

If you're interested in becoming an author for Packt, please visit `authors.packtpub.com` and apply today. We have worked with thousands of developers and tech professionals, just like you, to help them share their insight with the global tech community. You can make a general application, apply for a specific hot topic that we are recruiting an author for, or submit your own idea.

Share your thoughts

Now you've finished *Salesforce Data Architect Certification Guide*, we'd love to hear your thoughts! Scan the QR code below to go straight to the Amazon review page for this book and share your feedback or leave a review on the site that you purchased it from.

`https://packt.link/r/1-801-81355-8`

Your review is important to us and the tech community and will help us make sure we're delivering excellent quality content.

Download a free PDF copy of this book

Thanks for purchasing this book!

Do you like to read on the go but are unable to carry your print books everywhere?

Is your eBook purchase not compatible with the device of your choice?

Don't worry, now with every Packt book you get a DRM-free PDF version of that book at no cost.

Read anywhere, any place, on any device. Search, copy, and paste code from your favorite technical books directly into your application.

The perks don't stop there, you can get exclusive access to discounts, newsletters, and great free content in your inbox daily

Follow these simple steps to get the benefits:

1. Scan the QR code or visit the link below

https://packt.link/free-ebook/9781801813556

2. Submit your proof of purchase
3. That's it! We'll send your free PDF and other benefits to your email directly

www.ingramcontent.com/pod-product-compliance
Lightning Source LLC
Chambersburg PA
CBHW061403210326
41598CB00035B/6078